Politics at Work

Politics at Work

*How Companies Turn Their Workers
into Lobbyists*

ALEXANDER HERTEL-FERNANDEZ

OXFORD
UNIVERSITY PRESS

OXFORD

UNIVERSITY PRESS

Oxford University Press is a department of the University of Oxford. It furthers
the University's objective of excellence in research, scholarship, and education
by publishing worldwide. Oxford is a registered trade mark of Oxford University
Press in the UK and certain other countries.

Published in the United States of America by Oxford University Press
198 Madison Avenue, New York, NY 10016, United States of America.

CIP data is on file at the Library of Congress
ISBN 978–0–19–062989–2

1 3 5 7 9 8 6 4 2

Printed by Sheridan Books, Inc., United States of America

For my parents:
Thank you for mobilizing my curiosity.

CONTENTS

8. Employer Mobilization and Elections

9. What Employer Mobilization Means for the Study
   of American Politics

Conclusion: Employer Mobilization and American Democracy

PREFACE: ORGANIZING FOR
CORPORATE AMERICA

Spirits were running high at the RightOnline conference in July 2010, where hundreds of conservative activists had assembled in the Venetian Hotel in Las Vegas for the annual meeting of right-wing bloggers, pundits, and politicians.[1] Over two jam-packed days, participants attended panels celebrating the rise of the conservative Tea Party movement and strategized about how to translate grassroots energy into electoral wins in November. In one session an eclectic group took to the stage to announce an initiative billed as "Prosperity 101." Led by GOP presidential contender Herman Cain, a candidate best known for his flat-tax plan, the speakers bemoaned the fact that so many employees these days were casting ballots against their economic interests. As Linda Hansen, one of the speakers and the founder of the group selling Prosperity 101, had described elsewhere, American workers "may be voting to end their job—and they don't even realize it." Cain put the point more bluntly: "There are a lot of uninformed people [in the workplace]. . . . They just have not been given access to easy-to-understand information about some of the garbage that they are hearing about these various pieces of legislation. So, it's this uninformed group that is the target for Prosperity 101."

What could be done? As a short promotional video explained to the crowd, employers could host reading groups, lectures, and even short courses for their employees to educate them on free-market economics using a new curriculum developed by Prosperity 101. Suggested readings included excerpts from conservative *Wall Street Journal* columnist Stephen Moore, one of the spokesmen for the curriculum, and other right-wing writers decrying the role of government and extolling the virtues of an unfettered free-enterprise system. Policies such as the minimum wage, corporate regulations, and climate change legislation all threatened prosperity—and thus workers' job security. In one version of the curriculum, workers were told that tax rates on business represent "an attack on American job security and our future securities as leader in the free market and free world" and reminded workers that the "rich pay more than their fair share" to government.[2] "Taxation, regulation, and legislation can all . . . make it more difficult for a business to make a profit [and] will, in the end, negatively affect you and me. They make profits smaller, and smaller profits mean fewer jobs and less tax revenue collected by the government," explained the course materials.[3] "Job security only comes through business prosperity. . . . Business prosperity can only be achieved through free market, free enterprise policies," the guide summed up.[4]

The possibilities of an employee economics curriculum were powerful, the speakers noted. "When we can educate them," Hansen has boasted about the efforts, "we can begin to make a difference. It's not the only way to take back our country, but it is one answer."[5] Cain was even more enthusiastic. "It's conservatives' answer to ACORN," he likes to exclaim about these efforts, referring to the now-defunct progressive community group that had become a bugaboo for the Right.[6] Prosperity 101 not only could help companies to lobby for lower taxes and regulations; it could also secure votes for politicians who would protect America's free-market system.

What happens when employers, like the ones organized by Cain, Hansen, and Moore, attempt to recruit their workers into politics? What does it mean for American democracy that employers are trying to become community organizers? And have we ever seen this kind of corporate grassroots organizing before?

This book answers these questions. It documents, for the first time, how many companies are sending political messages to their workers, showing that around 25 percent of American employees have received a political message from a boss, and nearly 50 percent of all managers in recent surveys report sending political messages to their workers. It explains why businesses are increasingly turning to their workers as a political resource to change elections and policy, arguing that changes in the balance of economic power between workers and managers, shifts in election and labor law, new workplace technologies, and entrepreneurial business group leaders have made it easier for employers to recruit their workers into politics. It documents the concrete ways that employer-led mobilization of workers can be a very effective tool for electing friendly politicians and ensuring favorable public policies. And it explores the consequences—both beneficial and worrisome—of this corporate mobilization for American politics.

The book shows that while employer mobilization helps to close some gaps in civic participation, there are serious issues raised by the employer political recruitment process. Workers fearful of losing their jobs are much more likely to report responding to their employers' political requests, raising the concern of economic coercion of workers by their managers. Indeed nearly 30 percent of workers report being concerned about the potential for employer political retaliation—and 16 percent of employees have actually seen such retaliation at their jobs. Troublingly, lower income employees were substantially more likely than higher income employees to report either fear of political coercion or actual accounts of political retaliation from their bosses. Moreover employer mobilization disproportionately favors a narrow set of policy interests and political goals, exacerbating already existing imbalances of political power and voice. Above all, the book emphasizes that scholars, politicians, and citizens need to think of the workplace as a deeply political arena—and one that may well become an intimidating battleground without new protections for private-sector workers.

ACKNOWLEDGMENTS

This book came as a surprise in several ways. Until five years ago I had no idea about the latitude employers possessed for recruiting their workers into politics. Even after learning about the extent to which employers were mobilizing employees into politics, I had no expectation that I would write a book about it. (Indeed I was supposed to be writing another book—my dissertation—at the time!) But encouragement from Theda Skocpol, my dissertation chair, helped me to see the possibilities for piecing together the employer surveys I was doing into a bigger project. Aside from that early and continued advice, Theda was instrumental in helping me to secure the funds to field the 2015 telephone survey of workers. It is no exaggeration to say that the book would not exist without her generous support and constructive feedback and, perhaps most important, the model she has provided of rigorous, civically engaged scholarship on politics and policy.

The book additionally benefited from the early support of Richard Freeman, who offered helpful advice on my initial surveys and, later, the opportunity to get feedback from the participants in the 2015 Political Economy of Labor Regulation workshop at Columbia Law School. (Comments from Mark Barenberg, Craig Becker, Joseph McCartin, Damon Silvers, and Dorian Warren were especially helpful.) A second workshop held at the New America Foundation was also very useful in developing my thinking on the project, and Mark Schmitt and Lee Drutman deserve special thanks for helping to organize the workshop and providing detailed comments on the related policy paper. Back at Harvard I was fortunate to have a wonderful writing group in the last stretch of graduate school—Volha Charnysh, James Conran, Leslie Finger, and Noam Gidron—who endured multiple drafts of each chapter and provided supportive feedback each time. Many others offered detailed and helpful advice as well, including (but by no means limited to) Steve Ansolabehere, Charlotte Cavaille, Greg Elinson, James Feigenbaum, Paul Frymer, Peter Hall, Chase

Harrison, Torben Iversen, Sandy Jencks, Carly Knight, John Marshall, Cathie Jo Martin, Rob Mickey, Mike Miller, Melissa Sands, Kathy Thelen, Kris-Stella Trump, Peter Volberding, as well as participants at the 2015 Midwest Political Science Association and 2015 American Political Science Association meetings and workshops at Harvard, Columbia, Barnard, UCLA, and Tufts. Vanessa Williamson deserves a big thanks for giving detailed comments on the first draft of the book even as she was completing her own manuscript.

After I arrived at the School of International and Public Affairs at Columbia, Ester Fuchs helped me to arrange a workshop for the manuscript, where I was incredibly lucky to get together a terrific group of scholars to comment on the book, including Frank Baumgartner, Cynthia Estlund, Jacob Hacker, Hahrie Han, Greg Huber, Adam Levine, Matto Mildenberger, Suresh Naidu, Kay Schlozman, Paul Secunda, Bob Shapiro, Leah Stokes, and Ed Walker. I am very grateful for their generosity. As will be apparent to the reader of chapter 7 and the conclusion, joint work with three of those workshop participants—Paul Secunda, Matto Mildenberger, and Leah Stokes—has deeply informed the analysis and arguments in this book.

Will Jordan (at Columbia) and Geoff Henderson (at the University of California, Santa Barbara) were invaluable research assistants on this project. Will read and cite-checked the entire manuscript and offered helpful feedback along the way. Geoff helped Matto, Leah, and me to field the legislative staffer survey, and now knows more than he probably ever wanted to know about the current chiefs of staff and legislative directors in Congress.

I am very grateful for the enthusiasm and patience of Dave McBride at Oxford University Press, as well as the anonymous reviewers for the manuscript. Their probing comments and feedback were incredibly helpful in strengthening the book.

Ideas alone are not enough to finish research projects, and I benefited from generous financial support from a variety of sources. The Harvard Multidisciplinary Program in Inequality and Social Policy (with the help of Pam Metz in particular) helped me (along with Vanessa Williamson) to fund a pilot worker survey, as well as supporting my work through its graduate fellowship. Through the research project on the Shifting U.S. Political Terrain, Bob Bowditch supported the telephone worker survey; the Ash Center at the Harvard Kennedy School supported the employer survey; the Dirksen Congressional Center supported the legislative staffer survey; and the School of International and Public Affairs at Columbia University supported the survey experiments of workers and managers through its faculty research funding.

I am very appreciative of the corporate and trade association managers who participated in the interviews I report in this book. Their perspectives were invaluable to the analysis. In addition I owe a big thanks to the staff at BIPAC who participated in interviews and provided the 2014 electoral data reported in chapter 8. Ilona Babenko, Viktar Fedaseyeu, and Song Zhang also generously shared data reported in that chapter from their unpublished working paper, "Do CEOs Affect Employee Political Choices?"

Last, but by no means least, I am grateful for the emotional support of my family. I could not have done any of this without Nate, who knew just when to offer the enthusiasm I needed to keep going—but also when to break out the red wine and Goldfish. My parents, Adriela and Tom, have stood beside me in everything I have done. They have been incredible role models, and my hope is that this work reflects what they have both tried to teach me about the power of using social science to tackle big questions. This book is dedicated to them.

Alexander Hertel-Fernandez
New York, New York

ABBREVIATIONS

ACA	Affordable Care Act
ACORN	Association of Community Organizations for Reform Now
AFL-CIO	American Federation of Labor and Congress of Industrial Organizations
AGC	Associated General Contractors of America
BIPAC	Business-Industry Political Action Committee
CCES	Cooperative Congressional Election Study
CEO	chief executive officer
CFO	chief financial officer
CIO	chief information officer
COO	chief operating officer
COPE	Committee on Political Education
CTO	chief technology officer
E2E	Employer to Employee Political Communication
EPA	Environmental Protection Agency
FCC	Federal Communications Commission
FEC	Federal Election Commission
GE	General Electric
GMO	genetically modified organism
GOTV	Get Out the Vote
LGBT	lesbian, gay, bisexual, and/or transgender
NAM	National Association of Manufacturers
P2	BIPAC Prosperity Project
PAC	political action committee
SHRM	Society for Human Resource Management

Politics at Work

Introduction: The New Office Politics

Imagine that you and your coworkers begin receiving letters from your employer's CEO endorsing candidates for an upcoming election. Those messages not only list the politicians that your CEO prefers but also contain the threat that your business might need to lay off workers if those candidates are not elected. As Election Day approaches, your managers ask you to volunteer for the campaigns of the political candidates that your CEO has endorsed. When some of your coworkers demur, the managers tell you that political volunteering is a requirement of your job and that any worker who refuses could be fired. Can your employer get away with such a practice? Remarkably, the answer is often yes for private-sector workers.

Thanks to changes in American election law associated with the 2010 *Citizens United* Supreme Court decision, as well as long-term shifts in the economic and technological context of the workplace, employers now have sweeping legal rights as well as the technical means to campaign for political candidates in the workplace. Employers can even require that their workers participate in politics as a condition of employment. Just as a private employer can discipline or fire workers for failing to perform their regular duties, so too can managers generally discipline or fire workers for not participating in political activities that the company deems part of a worker's job.

The latitude employers have for political campaigning can also encompass other, less extreme examples. An employer could simply choose to remind workers to register to vote or to turn out to vote for elections, sending emails to workers with links to a website that helps them download registration forms and find their polling places. Or employers could inform workers about the implications of pending legislation in Congress or state legislatures, asking employees to contact their elected officials to support bills that would benefit the company's bottom line. And some contact might fall in between these categories, such as when managers refrain from explicitly endorsing candidates for elected office but distribute "voter guides" to workers rating the policy stands of political candidates. The similarity underlying all of these activities is that managers are using the relationship they have with their workers to promote particular political stances and behaviors. That is the subject of this book.

Employers' abilities to engage in these practices are not merely hypothetical. Consider the following examples from the past few years:

- An Ohio coal-mining business invited Republican presidential candidate Mitt Romney to a rally at their plant.[1] Miners were told that they would be required to attend the rally and that they would not be paid for their participation. Although managers later explained that no one was actually required to attend the event, miners still reported showing up out of fear they would be disciplined or even dismissed. One radio host summed up the incident in the following way: "What I gathered was employees feel they were forced to go. They had to take the day off without pay. That they took a roll call, and they had a list of who was there and who wasn't and felt they wouldn't have a job if they did not attend."[2]

- Executives at Cintas, a provider of uniforms and other workplace supplies, and Georgia Pacific, a major paper product manufacturer, sent letters to their respective workforces expressing clear partisan stances during the 2012 election.[3] In the case of Georgia Pacific, executives distributed a flyer that indicated all of the candidates that the business had endorsed, from the presidency down to state legislatures. These flyers also included warnings that workers "may suffer the consequences" if the company's favored candidates were not elected.[4] One such flyer is reproduced in Figure I.1.

- A renewable energy company I interviewed encouraged its workers to contact their members of Congress in an effort to reauthorize a federal tax credit for wind energy, warning its workers of the decline in sales of their products if the credit were to expire.

- In the wake of a number of highly publicized episodes of racial violence, Starbucks executives launched a campaign for their baristas to start conversations with their patrons about race relations in America.[5] Baristas were asked to write the words "Race Together" on customers' coffee cups. Staff were also encouraged to visit a company website with essays and videos about race relations.

- In the run-up to the 2012 presidential election, the CEO of a major timeshare company sent an email to all of his employees, warning them that their jobs would be threatened by "another 4 years of the same Presidential administration." If Obama were reelected, the CEO went on to say, he "[would] have no choice but to reduce the size of the company."[6]

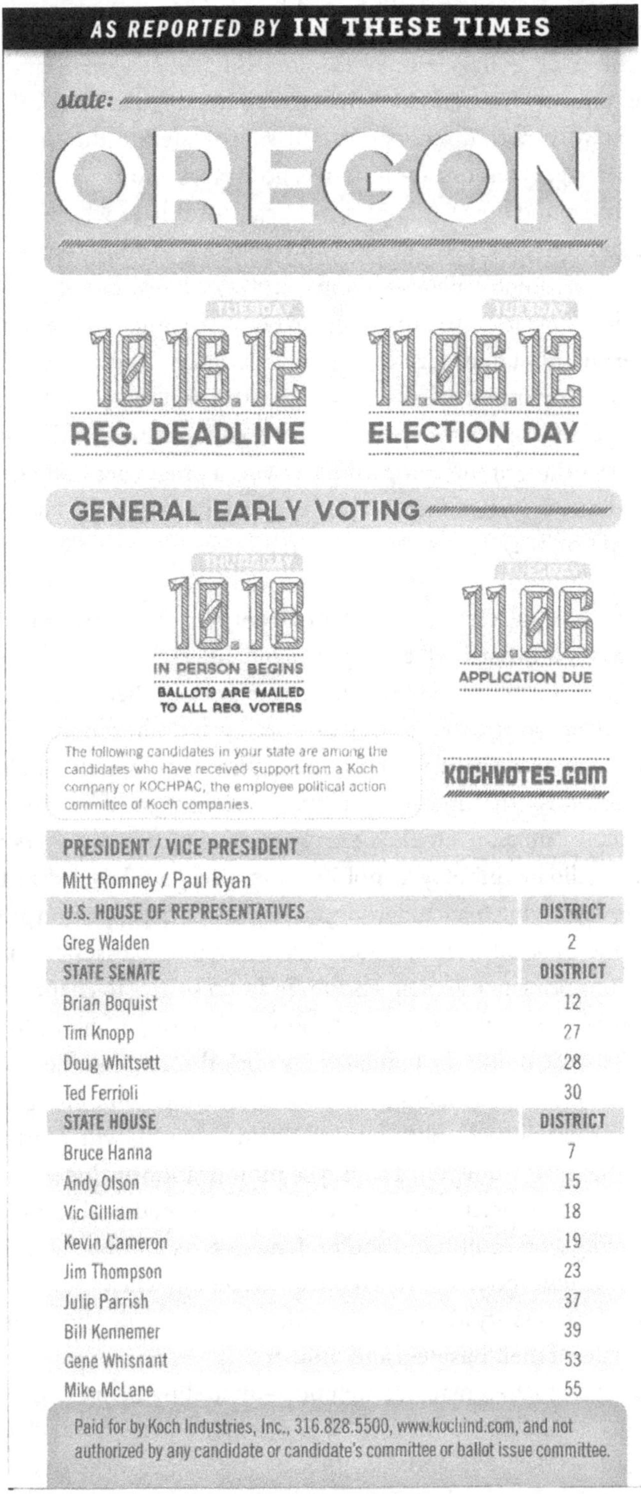

Figure I.1 Georgia Pacific mailer to Oregon employees. Reproduced from Elk 2012b.

- At franchises of College Hunks Hauling Junk, a cleverly branded garbage removal and moving company, managers have regular "roll call" meetings with their workers to discuss political issues related to the "free enterprise" system. Managers discuss, for instance, how taxes and regulation affect companies' profits and how to support political candidates who would maintain and expand free enterprise in the United States.[7] At one session a manager explained to a roomful of movers that Gandhi's protest campaigns were about fighting unfair taxation and that such levies were similar to the American federal government's unjust taxation of job creators.
- During tight congressional elections in 2010, a regional president at Harrah's casinos and resorts sent a spreadsheet to supervisors with a row for each employee working at the company's Las Vegas properties.[8] Supervisors were instructed to ask each of their employees whether he or she had voted in the race, and if not, why.

All of these examples are legal under current federal election and labor laws. And all are cases of what I call *employer mobilization of workers*—when the top managers of a company attempt to change the political behaviors and attitudes of their employees as a matter of company policy. By "top managers," I am referring to those senior executives who make, rather than merely implement, key company decisions. That means employer mobilization does not encompass cases of a single company employee trying to persuade coworkers to support an issue or candidate. Employer mobilization also goes beyond instances of a single supervisor trying to channel support for a political position among his or her supervisees. Instead employer mobilization refers to cases of top corporate executives attempting to use their workforce as a resource to change politics and policy, whether to encourage greater turnout (as with Harrah's), to encourage support for specific political candidates (as with the coal-mining company), to build support for particular legislation (as with the renewable energy firm), or to change the way employees think about political issues (as with Starbucks or the junk-hauling college students). Employer mobilization includes both recruitment of workers into specific political activities and broader education initiatives aimed at moving worker attitudes and preferences. As one manager explained to me, employer mobilization efforts are most successful when they get employees "activated in their identity as workers" so they start thinking about their political interest in terms of their business and industry.

Given the fact that so many companies—including many large and prominent businesses—are now turning to their workers as a means of changing public policy, shifting elections, and even determining how workers construct their political identities, you might think that there would be a slew of surveys and studies tracking the prevalence of employer mobilization and its implications for workers, companies, and American politics. Yet, remarkably, you would be wrong. Beyond a smattering of investigative pieces from journalists, there is virtually no systematic work that could help us to understand how common mobilization is across companies and employees, let alone what its effects might be on workers' political attitudes and behaviors, public policy, and elections. This book represents one early step at answering those questions and in the process unpacking what employer mobilization means for American democracy. I make three main arguments:

- *Employer mobilization is prevalent.* Broad swaths of the business community describe mobilizing their workers into politics, and many workers report that they have received political messages from their employers. According to surveys I describe in subsequent chapters, I estimate that nearly 50 percent of American managers report mobilizing their workers in some way, and around 25 percent of employees reported in 2015 that their bosses have ever attempted some kind of mobilization. That share increased to about 30 to 40 percent of employees around the 2016 election. Employer mobilization, in short, has become a way many Americans hear about political issues and are recruited into politics.
- *Employer mobilization shapes worker political participation, public policy, and elections and is now an important source of corporate influence in politics.* Corporate managers report that mobilization of their workers is one of the most important ways their businesses engage in politics. In surveys I describe throughout the rest of the book, I show that managers rank mobilization of their workers as being just as effective at shaping public policy as hiring a professional lobbyist, and even more effective than making PAC contributions to political campaigns and participating in major business associations. Beyond managers' own perceptions, I provide a range of evidence to show how employer messages deeply shape how workers think about politics, how Congress and state governments make policy, and which politicians are elected to office. To understand how businesses influence politics, we need to focus on employer mobilization.
- *Employer mobilization pulls workers into politics—yet raises serious concerns.* I document that employer mobilization is effective at recruiting workers into politics, including spurring workers to register to vote, turn out to vote, and contact their elected officials. Yet I also find that not all workers are equally likely to respond to their employers' messages. Workers who are especially fearful about their economic security, those who are worried about retaliation from their bosses, and those who lack political privacy at work are most likely to respond to their employers, raising concerns about economic coercion of workers by their managers. If workers are responding to their

managers not because they are genuinely persuaded by corporate political messages but because they are fearful of losing their jobs, we ought to worry that some workers are being pressured into giving up their political voice to their employers.

The nine chapters of the book make the case for each of these arguments, drawing on a range of evidence—surveys of workers, managers, and senior legislative aides, interviews, experiments, and archival materials—which I document in more detail in chapter 2. At this point I turn to answering the question of why a close study of employer mobilization matters now more than ever.

Why Does Employer Mobilization Matter—Especially Now?

Why study employer mobilization when few others have? I believe there are good academic and practical reasons why employer mobilization warrants rigorous, scholarly treatment. To the extent that we want to understand how Americans participate in politics, we ought to care about employer mobilization as a new way that citizens are being recruited into politics. If we focus only on the usual suspects for civic engagement—such as political contacts from the parties, unions, churches, social clubs, and interest groups—we will miss a growing part of political life in the United States. As I show using new national survey data, employer recruitment efforts may be about as effective at spurring worker political participation as outreach by the political parties and unions.

Aside from widening the picture of American civic engagement, employer mobilization also has an important bearing on our understanding of corporate political behavior. As I discuss in the coming chapters, managers themselves report that mobilization is one of their most effective means of changing public policy. But we do not need to take managers' word for it. Looking across a number of case studies, I document concrete changes in politics, elections, and policy as a result of employer mobilization efforts. To ignore mobilization would be to neglect an important mechanism of corporate influence in the policymaking process.

Last, mobilization raises thorny ethical questions about the role employers should play in the political lives of their workers. What kinds of communications between managers and workers are acceptable, and what kinds of messages should be banned? Do employer messages—especially those that rely on the threat of changes in employment or wages—infringe on the rights of workers to arrive at their political choices free from outside interference? These questions touch upon broader issues of economic power, corporate free speech, and worker political freedom, and merit a serious discussion among the public, corporate executives, and policymakers.

Apart from concerns about the agency of individual workers, many forms of employer mobilization may pose a challenge to our democratic institutions by granting outsized political influence to businesses. Even before the controversial *Citizens United* case, which lifted restrictions on corporate electoral giving, many citizens and politicians from the Left and the Right were worried about the disproportionate power that corporations possessed in the electoral and policymaking process. For instance, nearly half of all Democrats and well over half of all Republicans reported in 2009 that big business had "too much influence" over the decisions made by government.[9] And poll after poll finds that most Americans believe government is more responsive to special interests than to ordinary citizens.

A growing body of academic research backs up these opinions. Regardless of the measure one chooses—the number of groups, the breadth of political activity, or the depth of financial resources—organizations representing business interests do indeed vastly outnumber groups representing labor or the general public in Washington, DC. Figure I.2 shows just how much better companies are represented in America's capital than are labor unions, for instance, looking at disclosed dollars spent on federal lobbying.[10] Between 1998 and 2015 businesses spent an enormous 50 to 60 times more on lobbying than did labor unions, according to the Center for Responsive Politics—and the trend is upward over this period. Ordinary workers are outmatched compared to business, and that political gap is only growing.

As Kay Schlozman, Sidney Verba, and Henry Brady sum up in their exhaustive survey of Washington interest groups, "Although the weight of advocacy by organizations representing business interests varies across domains of organized interest activity, in no case is it outweighed by the activity of either organizations representing the less privileged or public interest groups."[11] Corporations also possess outsized advantages in lobbying the states, especially states with only weakly professionalized, part-time legislatures that are highly dependent on business lobbies for ideas, research, and other resources.[12] The product of these disparities in representation is captured in compelling research by Martin Gilens and Benjamin Page, who find that organized business interests are substantially better represented in national policy decisions than either mass-based interest groups or average citizens.[13] The authors conclude that "business groups are far more numerous and active [in national politics]; they spend much more money; and they tend to get their way."[14]

Employer mobilization therefore provides an additional opportunity for already politically powerful businesses to further influence legislation, regulation, and elections at the federal and state levels. Importantly, the priorities

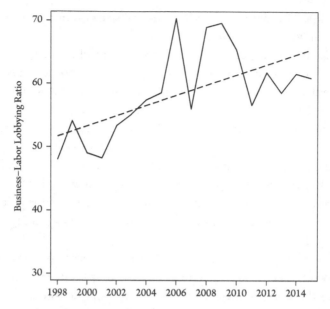

Figure I.2 Business lobbying vastly outweighs labor lobbying in Washington, DC. Figure shows the ratio of total federally disclosed lobbying spending by business relative to labor unions using data from the Center for Responsive Politics. Dashed line indicates trend line.

that businesses pursue through mobilization are not a random cross section of policies. Companies are, by and large, seeking to lower their taxes and reduce regulations. And when managers educate their workers about politics, corporate messages often involve material that cheerleads the free market and attacks government action.

The fact that employer mobilization overwhelmingly benefits one narrow set of corporate and pro-market priorities over all others might be concerning at any historical juncture. But it is especially worrisome today. We are living in an era when powerful segments of the business community and the conservative movement have succeeded in demonizing the role that government plays in sustaining a prosperous economy.[15] Employer mobilization threatens to tilt the political playing field even more sharply against government regulations and the investments that are necessary for a safe, productive, and relatively egalitarian society. It also threatens to enable greater capture of government by private interests. That is a consequence that ought to worry libertarians as much as liberals who are concerned about businesses using public policy to disadvantage their competitors. As we will see, employers often use mobilization as a tactic to secure narrow provisions that disadvantage their competitors or customers—a form of regressive, upwardly slanted redistribution.[16]

The rise in employer mobilization also comes at a time when we have seen skyrocketing levels of economic inequality, summarized in Figure 1.3. The top 1 percent is on pace to capture almost a fifth of all income in the United States—and the even more rarefied group of the top 0.1 percent is nearly set to take home a full tenth of all income. This concentration means that the wealthy managers and business owners who control major companies in the United States will have even more resources to invest in politics.

Employer mobilization, then, not only adds to the power of business and wealthy individuals; it does so at a time when imbalances of economic and political power are already large and continuing to grow quite rapidly. Even if we were not concerned about the potential for coercion in the workplace when employers communicate with their workers about politics, there are thus good reasons to be worried about the fact that organized business interests now have access to a new means of shaping elections and policy debates—especially since this is a means of engaging citizens in politics that other actors do not possess.

This imbalance is particularly troubling because the mobilization of citizens through the workplace is being done in an increasingly unbalanced environment, where labor unions struggle to maintain a presence throughout the private sector. A deep irony is that employer mobilization was inspired by labor unions' recruitment efforts in the workplace (as I explain in chapter 5), yet employer mobilization is currently unfolding in a context wherein the vast majority of

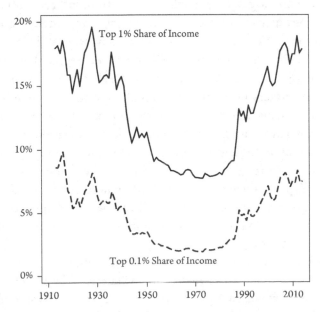

Figure I.3 Rising economic inequality in the United States. Data from the World Wealth and Income Database.

private-sector workers will never interact with a labor union. Just 6 percent of the private-sector workforce was covered by a union in 2016, down from 24 percent in 1973. The political voices workers hear at work are thus more often than not from managers, meaning that employees get only one side of the political story. It is not a coincidence that employer mobilization is flourishing in the contemporary economy. We will see that the diminished voice that employees possess at work has played an important role in fostering an environment in which the costs faced by employers for recruiting workers into politics are considerably lower than they were in previous decades. In sum, employer mobilization is a trend that merits attention now more than ever—and that is what I intend to do in this book.

Plan of the Book

The rest of the book proceeds as follows. In chapter 1, I lay out a guide for thinking about employer mobilization both as a means of corporate involvement in politics and as a source of political recruitment for individual workers. The chapter describes why profit-seeking private-sector companies decide to become political recruiters—and in particular, the value that employer mobilization can offer to managers and the investors they serve. It also describes why workers might think about employer messages and requests as being distinct from messages they might receive from other political recruiters, like unions, parties, or political campaigns. The underlying message in this chapter is that employers, unlike nearly any other political actor, have direct control over the economic livelihood of the people they are trying to recruit. Employers also have the means of closely monitoring the participation of their workers in politics, potentially rewarding complying workers and punishing defiers. That means we should expect that workers who are especially worried about the prospect of job loss or drops in their wages will be more responsive to their bosses' political requests compared to workers who feel more secure in their jobs. The fact that economic security dictates employees' responses to employer political requests represents an important contribution to our understanding of political behavior and participation. It also introduces a serious concern with employer mobilization that I explore throughout the book.

In chapter 2 I summarize the data sources and methodological strategy I use to study employer mobilization in the United States. Unlike other types of political recruitment, major surveys of American workers and voters do not ask about political contact with employers. I therefore had to design a series of new surveys of workers and managers to capture how often employer mobilization has occurred throughout the American labor force and the effects it has had on politics and policy. I also describe how I triangulate among a range of different sources, including surveys of workers, managers, and top legislative staffers, in-depth interviews with top corporate executives, and media accounts to understand why employer mobilization happens, where it is most effective, and the specific outcomes in legislative debates and elections that we can trace back to employer mobilization drives. Readers who are less interested in the methodological guts of this project can skip this chapter without losing much context and proceed directly to chapter 3, which begins presenting the substantive conclusions from my research.

Given that so little research has focused on employer mobilization, part I aims to provide a comprehensive guide of what employer political recruitment efforts look like now—and how contemporary employer strategies compare to the past. Chapters 3 and 4 describe the landscape of employer mobilization in the United States as it stands today.

Chapter 3 provides a picture of employer mobilization from the perspective of managers, including how many businesses report mobilizing their workers, the messages and requests mobilization encompasses, and how managers rank mobilization as a political strategy. This chapter further explores when companies are most likely to make employee political recruitment part of their "core strategy" for changing policy, as one of my interviewees put it. Businesses were more likely to engage their workers in politics and to rate employee mobilization as being more effective when they already engaged in other political activities that complemented mobilization, when businesses faced specific regulatory threats from government, and when businesses monitored their employees' political attitudes and behaviors more closely. The potential for worker backlash also weighed heavily on managers' minds. When managers fear backlash, they are less likely to opt for mobilizing their rank-and-file workers and more likely to switch to more traditional tactics, like giving electoral contributions or buying political ads.

Chapter 4 flips the perspective from managers to workers and documents how many workers report receiving employer requests, what those requests and messages contain, what workers think about employer messages, and how messages have shaped workers' behaviors and attitudes. This chapter shows that most employer messages focus on specific policy issues facing companies, especially health care, education and training, taxes, and regulation. Messages related to voting—including reminding workers to register to vote or to turn out to vote on Election Day—were also quite common. By all accounts, workers consider employer messages to be relatively persuasive: large proportions of surveyed workers report changing their political thinking and actions in some way as a result of employer mobilization.

A significant minority of workers also report that their employers made explicit threats to them about job loss, wage cuts, or business closings linked to political outcomes. Workers tended to take these threats seriously. I follow up on the question of managerial threats by presenting data on the number of workers who either are concerned about the potential for employer coercion or have actually seen such political retaliation at their jobs. These data present a picture of a small but nontrivial swath of workplaces where employees, especially low-income workers, experience considerable pressure to toe the company line or face retribution.

I next contrast employer mobilization with political recruitment by labor unions, discussing how the prevalence and character of union messages differ from messages from managers and supervisors. In a final section of the chapter, I consider how employer mobilization shapes inequalities in civic participation, looking at the ways employer recruitment both mitigates and exacerbates class differences in political action. Even as employer mobilization closed some gaps in political participation, it exacerbated others. I also find that it was disproportionately lower income workers who reported changing their beliefs and attitudes in response to employer messages, switching from more liberal positions and preferences to more conservative stands.

While chapters 3 and 4 focus on the contemporary picture of employer messages, chapter 5 takes a longer historical perspective to map out exactly how mobilization has evolved over time. I describe how a specific constellation of economic, legal, and technological changes spurred the return of employer mobilization to American politics since its heyday in the nineteenth and early twentieth centuries. These shifts were insufficient, however, to make political recruitment into a viable political strategy. Business associations were critical in teaching managers that mobilization was well within their legal rights. Associations also played an important role in selling managers the technical capacity necessary to mobilize workers.

Part II switches from describing what employer mobilization looks like to tracing the effects of employer messages on political participation, public policy, and elections. Chapter 6 explores how employer messages fit into our understanding of individual political participation. I first use a survey experiment of workers to show that messages workers think come from an employer shift employee attitudes toward policy and employees' likelihood of engaging in the policy process. These experiments also provide evidence supporting the prediction I offered in chapter 1: that workers most concerned about losing their jobs would be more likely to respond to their employers' messages. The chapter next reviews surveys of workers who have received actual employer messages to show that employer contacts shift these workers' political attitudes and behaviors—though not their basic knowledge about politics. Just as in the survey experiments, I also find that employees who were more concerned about losing their jobs were more likely to respond to employer messages. Apart from these differences in economic security, I show that employee perceptions of employer monitoring also mattered, consistent with the employer-level findings from chapter 3. Employer political requests had the strongest effect on employees who perceived that their managers were tracking employee political behaviors and attitudes.

Workers reported that they were responding to employer messages, but can we actually observe changes in policy as a result of employer mobilization? Chapter 7 marshals a range of data to show that employer mobilization has significant consequences for policymaking in Congress and the states. I first present results from a survey of top legislative staffers working on Capitol Hill to show that Congress pays especially close attention to the messages employers have their workers send to U.S. senators and representatives. I also report results from an experiment embedded in that survey that shows employee messages can deeply affect staffers' perceptions about their constituents' opinions, especially when congressional offices are more attuned to the threat of joblessness in their districts and states. I provide a case study involving a ballot initiative in Alaska to document the effect employer messages can have on state policy outcomes, presenting evidence that mobilization of workers helped to lower taxes on oil producers even in the face of public support for tax hikes on the oil and gas sector. In another example, I show that employer messages to workers opposing the Affordable Care Act were an important source of durable public opposition and skepticism to national health reform.

Chapter 8 moves from the realm of policy battles to elections and focuses on the 2014 races to show how employer messages coordinated by a conservative business organization worsened the electoral fates of Democratic candidates in the 2014 election cycle. Employees subjected to more intensive recruitment drives were less likely to vote for Democratic gubernatorial candidates. Beyond convincing employees to cast ballots for Republican candidates, employers can powerfully shape workers' electoral giving. Candidates endorsed by the top management of companies ended up receiving substantially more contributions from employees at those companies compared to candidates who were not favored by managers.

In the two concluding chapters, I reflect on the implications of my findings for the study of American politics, as well as for judging the quality of American democracy at the ballot box and in the workplace. I summarize the positive and negative aspects of employer recruitment efforts, and then focus especially closely on the concerns created by coercive employer messages. I end by proposing a variety of reforms for addressing political intimidation at work and discuss the political coalitions that might support such efforts. Polling data suggest that large majorities of Americans—including majorities of both Republicans and

Democrats alike—favor strict limits on employer abilities to recruit workers into politics. As I will argue, now is the moment to curb coercive employer mobilization practices, before they spread further into the American labor force. To delay action will only increase the risk of inciting a political war at work between managers and employees.

PART I

WHAT IS EMPLOYER MOBILIZATION AND FROM WHERE DID IT COME?

1

How Should We Think about
Employer Mobilization?

"Why on earth would employers want to do this—and why would employees ever respond assuming that employers did contact them?" Those were some of the first questions I received from a fellow political scientist at an early academic talk on my research on employer mobilization. The political scientist, one of my department colleagues, was puzzled as to why employers would ever want to wade into the potentially controversial area of workplace political recruitment, especially since workers could easily ignore the messages they received from their bosses. Americans are bombarded with political messages and requests every day that do not make much of a difference one way or another. What, then, could possibly be the upside for managers to workplace political mobilization?

This chapter answers my colleague's questions, showing why businesses would want to deploy their workers as a political resource to shift elections and change public policy. I also explain why workers might take their managers' messages quite seriously, especially when workers are fearful of losing their jobs and wages. This chapter provides a guide for thinking about employer political recruitment from the perspectives of both managers and workers.

The Value to Business of Employer Mobilization

Why would profit-seeking private-sector companies decide to become political recruiters? Top managers sometimes engage in political recruitment, especially efforts to encourage greater voter registration and turnout, as part of corporate social responsibility campaigns. Starbucks launched such a nonpartisan effort in the run-up to the 2016 presidential election, partnering with a tech start-up that helps with voter registration. In announcing the decision, Starbucks's CEO explained that the company had asked, "What is our role and responsibility as a for-profit company, and as citizens in a wider world?"[1] One answer that stood out to him was helping to address the problem of chronically low voter registration and turnout. (TurboVote, the platform Starbucks used, aims to replicate the same approach across other major companies, like Lyft, Airbnb, Google, Univision, and Target.[2]) Corporate executives sometimes also mobilize their employees simply to advance their own personal beliefs, using all of the resources available at their company to elect favored politicians, as in the case of the Florida timeshare mogul I mentioned in the introduction. But in general most companies are not like Starbucks or the timeshare enterprise. Companies tend to invest in mobilization because of its value to corporate bottom lines.[3] Throughout the subsequent chapters, I will point to a number of cases where businesses used mobilization to secure valuable gains through public policy, such as stymieing the passage or implementation of onerous regulations or securing tax cuts. These examples help us to understand why managers rank employee mobilization as one of the most effective tools in their political arsenal.[4]

There are at least four different strategies employers can use to influence politics and policy by mobilizing their workforce. Though I present these strategies as being distinct, in practice companies often combine them. The first is through elections: if businesses prefer a policy change that is likely to come about under a particular legislator or party, mobilization of workers could provide the votes necessary to elect those favorable candidates, especially in tight or low-turnout races. For instance, if a company is seeking to reduce its tax burden, then electing antitax Republican lawmakers would be one way to increase the probability that a state legislature or Congress would consider enacting tax cuts. This strategy involves sending material to workers that encourages them to support or oppose particular political candidates, reminding workers about elections, and then ensuring that workers turn out on Election Day.

Wynn Resorts employed such an approach when the company mailed a voter guide to their resort and casino workers in Nevada, which pushed them to register and turn out to vote for the company's preferred candidates. Those were politicians who "support policies that help promote a friendly business and living environment to Wynn Resorts, our . . . employees, and the gaming industry as a whole."[5] In an interview with the *Huffington Post*, CEO Steve Wynn explained that his company was engaged in electoral outreach because "it would be a complete disaster if Obama wins, which is why I'm urging my employees to vote for Romney."[6]

Employers often point out that sending messages to their workers about elections can have ripple effects that extend well beyond their workforce. As one business representative put it in a pitch to other companies, "If you have a thousand employees, and you educate those thousand employees, each one of them touches 20, 30, 50 people in their family, in their community. And if they're educated about their own livelihood, they'll make the right decision, and the right decision is to keep the free enterprise system strong."[7]

Closely related to the first strategy, mobilization can serve as a mechanism for employers to demonstrate a commitment to a lawmaker (or aspiring lawmaker), building relationships the company can leverage for access to the policymaking process at a later time. In this manner, employer mobilization could be seen as achieving one of the same goals as campaign contributions: supporting political allies so as to "buy time and effort" from them in the future by building a reputation as an organized force that can effectively mobilize voters.[8]

As with the first strategy, this one requires employers to send material to workers supporting or opposing candidates for elected office. But in addition to that, employers must also signal to politicians that managers have mobilized workers in ways relevant to a candidate's campaign. The National Association of Manufacturers (NAM) recommends that its member companies use just such an approach to build ties with important lawmakers, especially by arranging for elected or aspiring officials to visit factories. "Manufacturing plant visits offer an opportunity to build lasting relationships with members of Congress and their staff," explained NAM's vice president of public affairs, Tiffany Adams. "They provide opportunities for lawmakers to meet with their constituents, hear the success stories and the struggles that manufacturers face, and witness how their policies work in real life."[9] A critical part of the tour, of course, is interacting with plant workers and offering politicians an opportunity to "speak candidly" with potential supporters.

A household goods manufacturer (and NAM member) reiterated the importance of building these ties to members of Congress in an interview with me. That manufacturer mentioned that they relied on the relationships they had previously developed by bringing politicians into their plants to "give them rallies and that kind of support" during a recent legislative debate over reauthorization of the president's trade promotion authority, a measure the company strongly supported. This strategy can also function as a warning for politicians: employers can threaten to encourage their workers to vote against a candidate in a subsequent election if candidates do not follow the policy positions favored by the company. That same household goods manufacturer told me that they might do this as well if they were "concerned about members of Congress's votes" on the trade promotion authority bill. In a similar vein, the head of grassroots mobilization at a major business association said that employee messages could help put pressure on a wayward member of Congress, especially if they reminded the member that their businesses had defeated similarly wayward legislators in other primaries. Above all, that business association executive said that his goal with employee political recruitment was to remind potentially unruly legislators that "they [businesses and the association] just threw a body in the street in the last election in the district next to mine."

Employer mobilization need not be confined to generating support for political candidates during elections. It can also be a tool for directly generating grassroots support for—or against—policy changes, what political scientist Ken Kollman has described as "outside lobbying."[10] An employer could, for example, encourage workers to contact elected officials to express the company's preferred position on a particular bill under consideration by a state legislature or Congress, or even a proposed regulation. This sort of legislative contacting can provide an important signal to lawmakers about the public attitudes of a mobilized group of citizens in their district. As Kollman has put it, outside lobbying has "the common purpose of trying to show policymakers that the people [an interest group] claims to represent really do care about some relevant policy issue. These tactics say, in effect, 'See, we told you constituents were angry about policy X, and now you can hear it from them.'"[11] I will present evidence from an in-depth survey of top congressional staffers that this sort of contact can be quite effective, deeply shaping the ways that policymakers think about proposed policy changes.

DuPont, the chemicals manufacturer, provided a good explanation of why it mobilizes its employees to change public policy in a company-wide manual containing frequently asked questions. The document explained:

> Grassroots communications from constituents is one of the most powerful ways to influence the decisions legislators make. While the DuPont Government Affairs staff members are experts in the legislative process and are highly successful in affecting positive public policy, what constituents say matters a great deal to elected officials. Lawmakers listen when informed citizens speak up on issues that affect them, their families and their communities. . . . Regardless of the means of communication, the fact that you have taken time to convey your views puts a human face on the issues and lets them know that the choices they make affect your company and the lives of real people back home. The facts, ideas, and opinions you and other members of DuPont Employee Voice share with lawmakers will help them make better-informed decisions so they can better represent you and DuPont.[12]

There is also a strong parallel between this sort of workplace mobilization and the corporate political strategies described by sociologist Edward Walker, in which companies buy the services of public affairs consultants who can generate the appearance of grassroots support for corporate policy goals.[13] We will see that this is one of the most common uses of mobilization reported by business.

As one employer mobilization consultant stressed in a best practices guide to corporate executives, "Corporations don't vote. Environmentalists vote. Union members vote. Senior citizens vote—big time. But many legislators look upon corporations as piles of bricks that don't vote and thus pose no political perils. Grassroots action by corporate stakeholders lends living, breathing, *voting* faces to your otherwise faceless corporation. With effective grassroots action, your corporation (and thus you) quickly becomes a player to be reckoned with instead of a punching bag."[14]

The last pathway to influence is more indirect and involves changing the political preferences of workers over the long run. In this strategy an employer might not encourage workers to become involved in any one election but instead develop communications that change the ways workers construe their economic and political preferences. Managers I interviewed described this process as "employee education" or, alternatively, turning workers into "employee voters" who take their companies' perspectives into account when thinking about politics. Menards, a large home improvement chain in the Midwest, provides a good example of this practice. In January 2012 the store began encouraging its 40,000 employees to take an online civics course at home, inspired by the Prosperity 101 curriculum I mentioned in the preface.[15] Though the course was optional, it was clear that managers would be tracking who did and did not pay attention to the material. Workers who passed the course were singled out for recognition in company publications. The course was a recitation of conservative policy talking points, emphasizing that "limited government and individual liberties are the foundation of American economic dominance" and that "taxes always limit freedom." Using the language of "takers and makers," the course argued that the rich and business already pay too much in taxes and that workers ought to support candidates who promise to lower taxes on job creators. Figure 1.1 shows an excerpt from the curriculum on tax policy.

It is worth dwelling on the differences between mobilization that companies engage in to advance specific policy objectives (like lobbying Congress to preserve tax credits or to prevent onerous regulation) and more general employee education initiatives, like the Menards textbook. On their face it may seem like these strategies are opposed to one another: the first one is about obtaining company-specific benefits from government, while the second one is about promoting a broader ideology or worldview among employees, which does not yield narrow benefits for a specific company but would instead advance more general conservative political goals. Yet a close examination of employer messages and interviews with corporate managers reveals that these two types of mobilization are more closely linked than they appear at first glance. Companies will often engage in broader employee education to develop an initial political

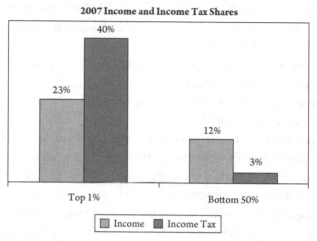

Figure 1.1 Excerpt from Menards employee textbook on economic security.
Reproduced from Nolan 2016.

relationship with workers that lays the foundation for later and more specific
requests.

The government affairs officer at a large extractive resource manufacturing
company explained to me that the first thing a company does when it wants to
mobilize its workers is not to ask them to contact a member of Congress or to
support a particular candidate; instead it wants to "build a relationship with
employees . . . [to] educate and inform them." That involves talking about bigger political issues and how politics and policy—not necessarily an individual
bill or election—shape the company. "Once [employees] feel the passion and
involvement in the political process, everyone [at the company] will start talking
about politics, so it is natural. Hell, that's how we started as a country, just bitch-
ing about politics," he concluded colorfully. Thus employee education may start
off focusing on a more general ideological or political orientation and switch to
business-specific issues as those proposals arise in the political process and a
company has developed a relationship with its employees.

Despite these potential benefits, mobilization is not without pitfalls for
employers. The most obvious concern managers expressed in interviews is
that workers might ignore company requests, resulting in wasted resources.
Worse, workers might disagree with the mobilization requests and protest the
messages—or even do the opposite of what companies request. If workers
are incensed enough by employer requests, they can even leave the company
altogether. Political scientists Kay Schlozman, Sidney Verba, and Henry Brady
have underscored a closely related risk in their review of interest group political

activity, noting the danger that "once a grassroots campaign has been initiated, it may be difficult to control, and the organization may lose control of both the membership and the message."[16] Even if mobilization works initially, it may not continue to inspire large-scale participation from workers over time, and another major issue that managers brought up was worker fatigue. Many executives mentioned that they tried to be strategic about the frequency with which they contacted workers, so that workers did not tire of receiving requests from their managers. Some managers also said they wished they had begun tracking the effectiveness of their efforts earlier so they could figure out which messages were most likely to elicit positive responses.

The opposite of fatigue was sometimes a concern as well. When companies succeeded in mobilizing workers to contact lawmakers, executives fretted about flooding legislative offices with a mountain of carbon-copy letters. Although a handful of corporate representatives told me they were fine with volume over quality, most managers said they strongly encouraged workers to tweak company talking points so that legislative aides would take the letters more seriously.

A third set of potential challenges is that messages managers communicate to their workers have to be detailed enough to motivate participation, but not too detailed as to turn workers off. As one executive put it, you have to "keep the melody simple if you want your constituents to sing your song."[17] He went on to explain that the "toughest challenge in mounting any grassroots campaign is to frame the issue in such a way that your constituents get the information they need to respond without feeling intimidated. If they don't understand the issue, they won't act."[18] This tends to be an issue with grassroots mobilization in general, as political scientist Frank Baumgartner and his collaborators discovered in their comprehensive study of lobbying strategies.[19] Those researchers even identified a big downside risk for groups that tried to mobilize but failed to motivate participation: "Even with a large membership, mobilizing the grassroots is not that easy. And if an organization announces a plan to mobilize its membership but few respond to the call, this is a clear signal that the issue is not a major concern, a point that rivals will be sure to exploit."[20] For instance, if a business attempted to mobilize its workers to oppose new regulation and failed, proponents of that regulation could point to the failed mobilization drive as evidence of broad public support for the measure.

Fourth, managers have reported that mobilization is rarely effective entirely on its own, and so another reason mobilization might flop is if managers neglect to provide "air cover" for their grassroots campaigns through PAC contributions to political candidates or lobbyists whom companies hire to meet with lawmakers and their staffs.[21] Mobilization of employees, in short, often requires additional political efforts to be successful. Accordingly, whether it is aimed at electing favorable politicians, defeating a bill, or rewriting regulations, there is strong evidence that employer mobilization works best when companies are already investing in complementary political activities.[22]

Fifth, employers, particularly consumer-facing firms, are sensitive to the negative publicity that mobilization—like any political activity—might generate.[23] Especially given the backlash against some politically active companies in recent years, managers are wary of taking political stands that large groups of consumers might protest. Explained one government affairs officer I spoke with, many companies looked at those missteps—such as when Target and Chick-fil-A backed groups opposed to LGBT rights—and said, "Holy cow, we never want to be those people." That typically means companies stick to economic issues that directly affect their business. Employer mobilization thus generally focuses on issues related to taxes, regulation, the environment, trade, and spending, and not so much stands related to abortion, LGBT issues, or civil rights.

Employers as Distinctive Political Recruiters

One way of understanding employer mobilization is to focus on how managers perceive the potential costs and benefits to activating their workers in politics. But another way of thinking about mobilization is from the perspective of individual workers. By doing so, we can see how employer mobilization is both similar to and different from other forms of political recruitment that citizens might experience. We can also see why employees might pay just as much, if not more, attention to messages from employers compared to messages from other political actors—including others in the workplace.

Political scientists studying civic engagement have shown that one of the best predictors of participation is direct individual contact and that the workplace is an important site for that recruitment even apart from managers.[24] Political communications scholars Diana Mutz and Jeffery Mondak have argued that workplaces facilitate political discussions between individuals with very different ideologies, forcing coworkers to become exposed to, and perhaps more tolerant of, opposing political perspectives.[25] Echoing the importance of the workplace, political economists Samuel Abrams, Torben Iversen, and David Soskice illustrate how social pressure from colleagues can encourage individuals to follow and participate in politics themselves: if your coworkers are following politics but you are not, you run the risk of being excluded from daily conversations at the company water cooler.[26]

Aside from coworkers, scholars of political participation have also examined the importance of labor unions. Though the formal function of unions is to bargain on behalf of their members with corporate management, unions have long played a social and political role as well.[27] Unions educate their workers about political issues, help workers register to vote, and promote particular candidates and parties. Political scientists have focused most of their attention on the role of unions in encouraging greater voter turnout, especially among low-income and low-education citizens.[28] But there is increasing evidence that unions can also shift the preferences of their members over time and can even change the way their members think about the political process.[29]

Employer mobilization is related to both of these types of political recruitment—through colleagues and labor unions—in that it also focuses on the workplace as a setting where individuals receive political messages, develop political preferences, and decide to engage in political activities. At the same time, political recruitment by employers is fundamentally different from recruitment by coworkers and unions because it implies a relationship between economic unequals.

Power and Politics in the Workplace

A key insight that underpins many of the conclusions in this book is that political mobilization of workers by managers is heavily structured by the imbalance of economic power between them. The relationship between workers and their managers is wholly different from the relationship between coworkers, or between unions and their members, because managers have ultimate control over the employment situation of their workers. Unless private-sector workers or their union representatives have negotiated a written contract with an employer, workers are usually considered to be employed "at will" and can be terminated without cause. Moreover, in the absence of a contract or union representation, managers can change workers' schedules, pay, and work routines without any notice or justification. As labor lawyers often quip, in the United States employers can hire and fire workers for a good reason, a bad reason, or no reason at all.

As a result of American labor law, then, political messages and mobilization efforts from top managers to workers carry a potential threat of retaliation—whether managers articulate that threat directly or not. This in turn puts pressure on workers to comply with managerial messages, even if workers may not agree with a company's political position. To put it differently, employers have the ability to make credible threats about workers' employment and wages and to condition those threats on workers' political participation. This sets employer recruitment apart from, say, the grassroots mobilization of citizens by other interest groups or even efforts by companies or trade associations to mobilize nonemployees (like shareholders or consumers) into politics. Employers also have many more opportunities to monitor employees' political activities and attitudes than other groups given the amount of time that workers spend on the job every day. Employers might have even more information about workers' political activities if the companies monitor workers' email, social media, and other online activities, tracking if employees follow through on managers' political requests.

We can generalize the characteristics of employers that make them distinctive political recruiters in the following way: employers have the means to *monitor* workers' political behaviors given the close interaction of workers within companies on a daily basis; employers have the means to *discipline or reward* workers for their political attitudes and participation given the broad discretion possessed by managers in private, at-will employment; and *political warnings about wage loss and layoffs are especially credible* when they come from companies, given it is managers who ultimately control the employment and wages of workers.

While other political actors, such as churches and unions, might individually possess one or two of these characteristics, collectively no other actor aside from employers possesses all three. For instance, members of a church or another civic association might have the ability to monitor the political leanings of participants through informal conversations. They might also have the ability to socially sanction members who do not follow the group's political positions or recommended activities. But these groups do not possess the same degree of economic control over individuals as do employers. To be sure, this has not always been the case, and in the past unions in particular might have had greater economic control over citizens—for instance, when unions had more discretion over the hiring and firing of workers. But at least in the contemporary era, labor unions, by and large, are not directly responsible for the economic fate of citizens in the same way as are managers and supervisors.

Although employers possess distinctive characteristics as political recruiters, this does not mean employers will necessarily always be more effective at spurring participation compared to other political actors. A relevant distinction to make here is between political recruitment that involves *organizing* and recruitment that simply *mobilizes*. As civic participation scholar Hahrie Han explains, organizers "do not simply aggregate individuals but also create new relationships between them that generate new commitments and resources."[30] Organizers, in short, seek to cultivate future activists and leaders. In contrast, mobilizing is much more transactional, building a base of participants that can be activated for a specific purpose. The implication of this difference is that individuals recruited into politics by organizers will likely continue to engage in political activities well after the initial contact from the organizer has passed. In contrast, individuals recruited by mobilizers may simply cease participating once their ties with the mobilizers have ended.

Employers typically focus on mobilization of their workers rather than organization. Unlike organizers, employers engaging their workers in politics do not usually grant them much autonomy or responsibility in the political process; workers are given very specific "asks," such as voting for particular candidates or contacting legislators about specific issues. Han notes that these sort of "discrete, easy requests that allow people to act alone . . . [without] any strategic autonomy" are highly characteristic of mobilizers.[31] The upshot of this difference is that we should not expect employer political requests to typically engender civic activism or participation beyond the workplace. That means even though specific employer requests may be very effective at spurring worker responses, these requests will not necessarily endure over time in the same way as participation spurred by successful civic organizers.

A similarly important caveat is that the political preferences of employers will not always be opposed to workers, even as employers hold economic power over their employees. Indeed there may be many situations in which workers and employers strongly share a common economic interest.[32] To give one example, both managers and workers in import-sensitive manufacturing sectors might oppose trade with low-wage competitor countries. And both managers and workers might support greater subsidies for their companies. In these cases of shared interests, employers may well be serving a role as a trusted "policy translator," helping workers to understand which policies and candidates are in a company's best interests.

The perspective I develop on economic power offers a number of predictions that I explore in subsequent chapters. If greater imbalances of economic power between employers and employees do indeed make political recruitment easier for managers—by increasing the likelihood that workers will respond to their bosses' requests, even if workers disagree—then we should expect that companies whose managers are less likely to expect backlash would be more likely to mobilize their workers. Employers should also be more likely to mobilize their workers, and to consider such recruitment as being more effective, when managers are closely monitoring their workers' political activities and behaviors. Such monitoring makes recruitment more likely to succeed, since managers can reward complying employees and potentially punish dissenters.

Workers, for their part, ought to be more responsive to employer political requests when they are more sensitive to the threat of job loss or wage and hour cuts or more fearful of political retaliation from their managers. Similarly, workers who perceive that they lack political privacy in the workplace should be more likely to respond to managers' requests than workers who do not believe their employers can discern their political opinions or behaviors.

Although this book is the first to systematically assess employer mobilization in the United States, my focus on the imbalance of power between workers and managers has important precedents in legal and academic work. For instance, the U.S. Supreme Court has recognized that speech from employers to their employees carries extra weight in the mind of workers given the economic control managers possess. In a 1969 decision on labor organizing, the Supreme Court argued that any free speech right held by managers needed to be balanced against the reality of "the economic dependence of the employees on their employer, and the necessary tendency of the former, because of that relationship, to pick up intended implications of the latter that might be more readily dismissed by a more disinterested ear."[33]

The idea underpinning the Court's opinion is that employees are especially attentive to speech from their employers—more so than other potential sources—because employees fear the economic repercussions of angering their bosses. Even the smallest suggestion an employer might make could change employees' behavior because of their fears of job loss, cuts to wages, and deteriorating working conditions. Accordingly this inherent imbalance of power between workers and employers has informed the way the National Labor Relations Board has approached employer involvement in union elections. The Board "is highly attuned to an employer's power to set agendas and manipulate institutional rules" in ways that might bias workers' opinions because of workers' desires to preserve their jobs and wages.[34]

Beyond the Supreme Court, several members of the Federal Election Commission have articulated similar logic in recent years. Those commissioners expressed concern that employer pressure on employees to hold particular political beliefs or engage in particular behaviors "is a real danger to our democracy—it puts citizens' right to express their political beliefs at the mercy of their employers."[35]

Conceptualizing employer mobilization in terms of this power imbalance also resonates with observations from civic participation experts Henry Brady, Kay Schlozman, and Sidney Verba in their canonical studies of political recruitment. Those authors argue that political recruitment is most successful when canvassers have leverage over their potential recruits. Having leverage over an individual gives that person a major incentive to consent to a canvasser's requests, especially when the recruiter can dole out punishments or rewards. The authors give employers as a prime example of such a recruiter, finding that individuals in a supervisory role over others were more effective at convincing their targets to participate in politics.[36]

And employer mobilization fits into older debates over the nature and exercise of political power in democratic societies. The two camps in this debate were, roughly speaking, the pluralists, who contended that political power was distributed relatively diffusely across American society, and the antipluralists, who argued that power was instead concentrated in the hands of economic and social elites.[37] A key distinction between them was the very different evidence they deployed to reach their conclusions. While pluralists tended to look at open competition between political factions, antipluralists claimed that the most important exercises of power were often not in outright political conflict but rather in the institutions, rules, and norms that structured political battles. Powerful political actors, the antipluralists argued persuasively, could use their resources to shape political structures in ways that benefited their own interests and disadvantaged their opponents, shutting out access to opposing groups. Elites could even use their privileged position to change the preferences of other actors. Lack of open political conflict thus did not necessarily mean that actors were in agreement; rather it might indicate that one side could not even muster the resources to enter into a debate.

Antipluralists distinguished among three different types, or faces, of power. The first face referred to open conflict between already organized actors, the domain typically studied by the pluralists. The second face involved changing the rules of the political game in ways that disadvantaged opponents—for instance, how the threat of a filibuster in the Senate might keep certain issues from even coming up for debate in the first place. And the third face of power referred to the ability of elites to change the preferences of their opponents in ways that went against opponents' material self-interests, a sort of false consciousness.

While these power debates were sometimes abstract, they had important implications for judging the health of American democracy. Where pluralists saw a well-functioning political system, antipluralists saw troubling inequalities, such as the fact that it was often the most economically disadvantaged citizens who were shut out of the political process. Employer mobilization contributes to these power debates in several ways. On one level, it provides a new avenue through which powerful economic actors (top corporate managers) can shape the preferences of their subordinates (workers). If employers can convince workers to change the way they think about politics, then employers have already won an important political battle. In this way, the concept of employer mobilization provides further empirical examples of the patterns John Gaventa documented in his extensive study of local communities in Appalachia as part of the power debates.[38] Gaventa found that politics in these communities was heavily tilted toward the interests of business because of the ways employers exercised both economic and cultural control over workers. Gaventa's key finding was that economic relationships can change how workers perceive their self-interest. That insight finds strong support in the recruitment practices I document in this book. Turning citizens into "employee voters," as one executive described them, fits with the notion of using imbalances of economic power between managers and workers to shift the preferences of workers over time—potentially against their own material interests.

Employer Mobilization and the Privileged Position of Business in American Democracy

Employer mobilization, especially the notion of employers using their control over workers' employment and wages to motivate changes in workers' political attitudes and behaviors, also resonates with the concept of the structural power of business—another important contribution to the older power debates in political science and sociology. Some of the antipluralists, especially Charles Lindblom, argued that in a capitalist democracy businesses possessed unique leverage over the policymaking process, a "privileged position" that other political actors could never attain.[39]

As Lindblom explained, in capitalist economies private businesses are ultimately responsible for employment, wages, and capital accumulation and investment. That gives policymakers strong incentives to keep the private sector happy, since "any change or reform [businesses] do not like brings to all of us the punishment of unemployment or a sluggish economy."[40] The market is, as Lindblom put it very memorably, "a prison" that restrains the actions of voters and politicians since no one wants to adopt measures that hurt the overall economy. Indeed the mere threat of unfavorable policy may be enough to trigger a negative reaction from businesses, pushing politicians away from even considering proposals that might impose significant costs on the private sector. Other actors, such as advocacy groups and unions, may also grumble about policy changes, but unlike businesses, the "dissatisfactions of these other groups do not result in disincentives and reduced performance that impose a broad, severe and obvious penalty throughout the society, which is what unemployment [in the private sector] does."[41]

Employer mobilization reveals a new mechanism for the exercise of this structural power of business, showing how the control that corporate executives and managers possess over the employment and wages of their workers can be converted into a political resource that companies can deploy to influence the policymaking process. In this way employer mobilization helps to flesh out the individual, worker-level mechanisms that reproduce the structural power of business that Lindblom described. When they communicate to their workers about the economic risks of electing a particular politician or passing a certain bill, companies are exercising their structural power in a capitalist economy. Similarly Lindblom's theory helps us understand how congressional offices respond to employee correspondence initiated by their managers. As it turns out, congressional offices that are more concerned about unemployment in their districts and states are much more attuned to employee correspondence than are offices that are less worried about joblessness—exactly what Lindblom would have predicted.

Situating Employer Mobilization as a Corporate Strategy and a Source of Political Recruitment

Why would managers become political recruiters? The answer to the question my colleague originally raised is that employer mobilization affords managers an opportunity to advance their political priorities through a variety of strategies: by supporting or opposing candidates for elected office, creating a grassroots lobbying force in favor of pending legislation, and changing the ideologies and political outlooks of their workers.

That brings us to the second question my colleague asked: Why would workers ever pay attention to the messages their managers send them? As this chapter has described, unlike the mountain of other political mailings that Americans receive every year, employer messages have the potential to carry extra weight in the minds of workers because employers—unlike other political groups or leaders with whom citizens might interact—are the ones cutting the checks for workers' wages and benefits. Workers thus have good reason to pay attention to their managers' political messages because managers can speak directly to issues that affect employees' workplace or industry. Workers also have a strong incentive to follow through on their managers' political requests because those requests contain a potential threat of retaliation. Just as an employer might fire or discipline a worker for refusing to participate in other workplace activities, so too might a manager punish a worker for failing to respond to political appeals. The looming threat of retaliation ought to be greatest for workers who are least secure in their employment and who perceive that their employer is more closely tracking their political preferences and actions. I will test each of these predictions in the coming chapters.

2

Methods for Studying Employer Mobilization in the United States

"Here's a Memo from the Boss: Vote This Way" ran a headline in the *New York Times* in late October 2012, just weeks away from the presidential election that November. In the article, veteran labor reporter Steven Greenhouse described how a number of large employers, including many I included in the introduction, had been actively campaigning for political candidates in their workplaces, taking advantage of a newly favorable legal regime. I was so surprised by the piece that I read it twice, not having realized the latitude employers had to recruit their workers into politics, nor the degree to which private-sector employees could be disciplined or even fired for their political views or actions on the job. In fact I had even made the common (but no less embarrassing) mistake of assuming that the First Amendment would protect the right of workers to speak their mind (or not) about politics in the workplace. (In reality the state needs to be involved in some capacity for the First Amendment to apply; the employment relationship between private-sector managers and employees thus does not count in the eyes of the Constitution.)

As a political scientist, my first instinct was to look for existing research that might indicate how common were the activities the *New York Times* detailed and how these practices might have shaped the 2012 election. To my surprise, I came up empty-handed. While journalists had documented the increasing tendency of employers to recruit their workers into political causes and campaigns, academics paid barely any attention to this topic. I could not find any academic polls that might indicate how frequently employers contacted their workers, or what workers thought about those messages. Even the major national surveys used by political scientists and other analysts—such as those from the Pew Research Center, the General Social Survey, the American National Election Studies, the Annenberg Election Survey, and the Cooperative Congressional Election Study—neglected to include a single question about employer political contact with employees.

The absence of previous work on employer political mobilization piqued my interest: here was a practice that was increasingly recognized by labor and political journalists as shaping politics, and yet it had not been studied in a rigorous way using the tools of social science. But I also realized that studying employer mobilization would require a substantial amount of original data to simply get a handle on the basic landscape of facts even before I could examine the consequences for politics and policy.

This chapter summarizes the strategy I developed to tackle these challenges, documenting the original surveys and interviews I fielded to better understand the prevalence, nature, and consequences of employer political communications to workers in American politics. While I have made an effort to keep the discussion as accessible as possible to a broad audience, readers who are less interested in the methodological foundations of the book should feel free to skip to the next chapter, where I begin summarizing the results of my analysis.

The Overall Approach

Because we know so little about employer mobilization, I opted for a research strategy that builds on many different types of evidence rather than simply a single source or approach. The bulk of my analysis relies on five types of data: surveys of workers, surveys of corporate managers, surveys of congressional staff, in-depth interviews with top corporate managers responsible for political affairs, and investigative journalism and media coverage. None of these sources on its own offers a complete picture of employer mobilization; however, each source can complement the strengths and weaknesses of the others. Surveys, for instance, are an excellent tool for establishing the overall prevalence of employer mobilization within a large and representative set of respondents. Surveys also permit me to understand how top legislative staffers in Congress—individuals responsible for providing information and opinions to lawmakers—might respond to the receipt of messages from employees. On the other hand, it is harder for a survey-based approach to capture detailed mechanisms, such as the varied considerations that corporate managers weigh when deciding to mobilize their workers into politics or how mobilization fits into broader corporate strategy. To gain a deeper understanding of these processes within particular companies, I supplemented the surveys with over 40 interviews with top corporate managers responsible for political affairs or government relations at a random sample of large American businesses and trade associations.

Surveys of American Workers

Early on in the project I realized that I was going to need a comprehensive picture of what employer mobilization looked like from the perspective of individual employees. Accordingly I contracted with SSRS, Inc., a well-respected polling company, to conduct an in-depth survey of American employees—that is, non-self-employed workers—in April 2015. With a response rate of 6.7 percent using live calls to landlines and cell phones, SSRS polled 1,032 employees on a variety of questions about their experiences with political messages received on the job, in addition to basic demographic, political, and economic information. This poll, which I refer to throughout the book as the *worker survey*, provides the data I will use to describe worker experiences with mobilization and also some of the data I will use to assess how workers respond to employer messages they have received. The appendix to this chapter provides the full survey instrument that SSRS used, along with a more detailed explanation of their polling methodology.

Although the SSRS survey offered a great deal of detail on employer mobilization from the perspective of workers, because of the high cost of live telephone surveys I was unable to ask all the questions I had hoped to field. I therefore added additional important questions about employer mobilization to the 2016 wave of the Cooperative Congressional Election Study (CCES), a collaborative academic poll fielded by YouGov. YouGov uses online survey takers who have been randomly selected to be representative of the American adult population. The 2016 CCES questions, fielded on 1,000 American adults during the fall of that year (both before and after the election), asked about employed workers' experiences with political contact from employers, unions, and parties and candidates, their political participation across a range of outcomes, and their attitudes toward an array of policy issues, permitting me to gauge the effects of employer, labor, and campaign messages on political participation and policy preferences. I also asked employed workers about their perceptions of political privacy and pressure at work and queried all respondents about their support for legal limits on various forms of employer mobilization. I refer to this sample as the *2016 CCES*. As with the SSRS worker survey, I reprint the full text of the questions I included on the CCES in the appendix to this chapter. Although I did not place questions on the 2014 CCES about employer mobilization, I use that wave of the survey to examine whether employees in states with more active employer recruitment drives were more likely to support Democratic Senate and gubernatorial candidates in the 2014 elections.

Aside from the SSRS and CCES surveys of workers, I also rely on evidence from two other national samples of employees at other points in the book. One is an original sample of 1,214 workers (including 1,014 private-sector workers) that I surveyed through SSI, Inc., an online polling company that selected survey takers who would be representative of employed American adults on a variety of characteristics. I used this sample to conduct an Internet-based survey experiment in September and October 2016, in which I randomly selected some of these workers to read messages that closely matched the sort of messages employers send to their workers about political issues. I used this survey experiment to see if such messages—about the minimum wage and a component of the Affordable Care Act—could actually change workers' political attitudes and behaviors. The full survey questions appear in the appendix to this chapter, and I also describe the survey experiment setup in more detail in chapter 6. By randomly selecting the workers who received the mock employer messages, I am able to show the causal effect of receiving such messages on employees' political attitudes and behavior—a powerful complement to the survey-based evidence on workers' self-reports in chapters 4 and 6. I refer to this sample as the *worker survey experiment*.

Last, I report on data from a survey that I did not design myself but that was fielded by the non-profit, nonpartisan Kaiser Family Foundation at the end of 2011. That telephone survey of 1,212 American adults asked where respondents had gotten their information about the Affordable Care Act and included employers as one such information source. I therefore use the *Kaiser survey* to examine the effect of having received employer messages on workers' perceptions of the health care reform law.

Surveys of American Employers

The surveys of workers represent only half the story. Managers are obviously the other actors in the employer mobilization process. To understand how managers decide to recruit their workers into politics and get a picture of what mobilization looks like from the perspective of corporate executives, I contracted with YouGov to survey over 500 top managers at American businesses. YouGov maintains a panel of these "top business decision-makers" that is broadly representative of the overall population of business organizations along characteristics like size and sector, which I polled to understand whether those managers' organizations had contacted their employees about politics, and if so, what that contact looked like. As I document in the appendix to this chapter, these top decision-makers had titles such as chairman or board member; partner or owner; president, CEO, or COO; CFO, controller, or treasurer; CIO or CTO; executive vice president, senior VP, general manager, or director or department head. The employers they worked for were in a diverse set of industries and of varying sizes, which I also summarize in the appendix. Altogether YouGov contacted 513 managers in December 2014 and January 2015 and successfully reinterviewed 395 of these managers at the end of August and the beginning of September 2015. I refer to these data as the *firm survey*. The full survey instrument for the first and second waves is available in the appendix.

In addition to the main firm surveys, I also had YouGov sample 518 managers in October 2016 to conduct a short survey experiment to test whether managers were underreporting their true mobilization practices in the first series of surveys, as well as to understand whether variation in worker economic power can explain why managers opt for mobilizing their employees over other political strategies when presented with an electoral threat.

I addressed the first question with a *list experiment*, which is a common survey design used to elicit truthful responses on sensitive topics.[1] In a list experiment, respondents are shown a list of several statements and are asked to indicate how many items they agree with. The twist is that half of respondents are shown a short list without the sensitive item or behavior the researcher is interested in studying, while the other half see a list with the sensitive item or behavior included. The true proportion of respondents agreeing with the sensitive statement or admitting to the sensitive behavior can be calculated by subtracting the average number of items selected among respondents who saw the full list and the average number of items selected by respondents who saw the short list. The idea is that no individual respondent has to reveal his or her own behavior: instead of indicating *which* items they agreed with, respondents simply provide a count of the items with which they agreed or admitted to. This design has helped researchers study the prevalence of many sensitive behaviors, such as electoral misconduct and racial prejudice.

For the list experiment I conducted, I gave all respondents the following prompt: "Businesses communicate to their workers about a variety of issues. Please review the following list and indicate how many of the things your business has done in the past. We don't want to know which things your business has done, just how many things your business has done in the past." I then gave managers the following list of control items, which all respondents saw: "Encouraged workers to learn about the costs of labor unions," "Encouraged workers to engage in environmentally friendly activities," "Encouraged workers to donate to charities," and "Encouraged workers to learn about financial literacy." The sensitive item was "Encouraged workers to vote for particular political candidates," which was shown to only half of respondents. After seeing either the short or full list, managers were asked, "How many of these things has your business done in the past?"[2] By subtracting the average number of responses given by the managers who saw the list without the sensitive item from the average number of responses from managers who did, I can estimate the proportion of managers reporting that their business had indeed mobilized their workers to vote for particular candidates in the past.

Aside from the list experiment, the *managerial survey experiment* on this survey gave respondents a brief vignette about an electoral contest in a state or district where their business operated. In that vignette I varied a number of characteristics of the election, including whether or not managers expected their workers to protest company efforts to send out information about the election in question. The vignette permits me to test the importance of worker backlash as managers consider whether or not to deploy mobilization of their workers as an electoral strategy. I spell out the full details for the managerial list and survey experiments in the methodological appendix.

Interviews with Corporate Managers

The firm surveys, including the managerial experiments, provide a detailed look at the mobilization efforts of American employers and how those efforts varied across employers of different sizes and industries. But these surveys were limited in their ability to help me understand how corporate managers thought about mobilization as a political strategy—especially the decision of companies to mobilize (or not) and the form that mobilization would take. To develop a richer understanding of decision-making processes within companies, I conducted semistructured telephone interviews with government affairs officers at large American employers and business associations. These interviews ranged in duration from 15 minutes to an hour and were typically around 20 to 30 minutes long. I conducted the interviews from January to May 2015.

The strength of these interview data is not in their representativeness (that is the comparative advantage of surveys), but I nevertheless attempted to sample a broad range of companies so that the interviews would be relatively generalizable. To do this I first compiled a list of the 1,000 largest companies operating in the United States by revenue. I then identified the top government affairs officer (or corporate communications officer if the company did not have a government affairs division) at each company and randomly selected 200 of these officers to email a request for an interview. In that email I explained who I was and why I was interested in conducting an interview, and importantly, I stressed that I was interested in interviewing them even if their company did not engage their workers in politics. I successfully interviewed 32 corporate executives from an array of different sectors. I list those sectors in the appendix to this chapter. Despite my best efforts to interview nonmobilizing companies, the majority of the interviews (80 percent) were done with mobilizing businesses.

The company interviews proved to be remarkably insightful, and respondents talked candidly about how and why their companies started mobilizing their workers into politics, cases of successful and unsuccessful mobilization, and factors like technology, regulatory exposure, and participation in trade associations that help to explain why companies mobilize and why they might have more success contacting some workers and not others. There were two elements to the interviews that I believe helped facilitate their success. The first was that I was flexible in the structure of the interview, permitting the corporate executives to begin the conversations on their own terms and expand on points or topics that were especially important to their narratives. The second aspect is that I offered interviewees the option of anonymity, which all of them took. I therefore refer to interviews not with specific companies by name but rather with companies from broad industrial sectors.

To get the perspective of trade associations, which are an important actor in promoting the spread of mobilization as a political strategy, I also interviewed executives at nine randomly selected business groups, using a list of business associations from Leadership Directories Online. These interviews focused on association representatives' perspectives of how their industries (or the business community in general) had adopted mobilization as a political strategy and how its intensity had changed over time. As with the business interviews, I also provided anonymity for the trade association representatives, describing the sector they represent in broad terms so they are not individually identifiable.

Survey of Congressional Staffers

The final survey I conducted was not with companies or workers but with top staffers working in the U.S. Congress. Given that companies indicated on the firm survey and in interviews that political recruitment of their workers was highly effective in changing public policy, I wanted to see if that perception was shared among policymakers themselves. I opted for surveying top legislative staffers rather than legislators themselves for two reasons. First, legislative staffers are typically the individuals who are interacting with businesses and other interest groups on a daily basis as the main conduit for information to their members of Congress—and the very top staffers are typically responsible for aggregating this information and presenting summary opinions to their member.[3] More practically, it is much easier to reach staffers for surveys than sitting members of Congress themselves. Accordingly, between August and September 2016, I conducted an online survey of top policy staffers in each congressional office in the House and Senate (typically chiefs of staff and legislative directors; this survey was done jointly with Matto Mildenberger and Leah Stokes). The survey was part of a broader project, which asked staffers about their experiences gathering information and deciding on policy proposals to present to their member of Congress. Crucially the survey asked staffers what they thought about different strategies businesses might use to contact their office and lobby for policy proposals, including having their employees contact the office to express positions on legislation. This survey also included an experiment that asked staffers to imagine that they had received correspondence from constituents on pending legislation and varied whether or not staffers were told that the correspondence came from employees at a large company in their district, ordinary constituents, or a non-profit citizens group. This experiment permits me to gauge the causal effect of employee letters—as opposed to ordinary constituent letters or messages from citizens' groups—on staffers' perceptions of constituents' opinions.

Out of 1,057 top staffers contacted to take the survey, 101 participated, for a response rate of 9.6 percent, consistent with other surveys of political leaders and of legislative staffers. (The Congressional Management Foundation, for instance, obtains response rates of around 15 percent in its surveys of staffers.) The survey received a range of responses from Democratic and Republican offices alike: 54 percent were Democratic staffers and 46 percent were Republican. As I show in the appendix to this chapter, the sample of responses looked quite similar to the overall distribution of top staffers on the Hill on a variety of important characteristics, including job title, their members' ideological orientation, members' seniority, and geographic region members represented. The appendix to this chapter also details the survey instrument fielded on legislative staffers. I refer to these data as the *legislative staffer survey*.

Investigative Journalism and the Media Record

The final data source I relied on comes from the important work of political and labor journalists who have uncovered specific cases of employer mobilization. I am particularly indebted to those journalists who have recovered leaked examples of mobilization materials that I use throughout the book to show readers exactly how employer recruitment works on the ground. Investigative work from Mike Elk (writing for *In These Times*), Steven Greenhouse (*New York Times*), Adele Stan (*The Nation*), Alec MacGillis (*New Republic*), Hamilton Nolan (*Gawker*), and Spencer Woodman (*Slate*) has been especially helpful in this regard.

Presenting Statistical Findings

Many of the conclusions that I will report rely on statistical analysis, including regression analysis. Where possible, I place the raw data underpinning those regressions in figures or tables, allowing readers to get a feel for the relationships and the distribution of the data themselves. To ease presentation of regression data, I include the full regression results and specifications in the appendices to each chapter, simply discussing the substantive interpretations of the regressions (including point estimates and statistical significance) in the main text. Readers interested in the full specifications should consult these appendices.

Pinning Down Cause and Effect

Social scientists are generating increasingly sophisticated tools for identifying causal relationships—that is, establishing that one factor is responsible for changing another. The gold standard for such an approach involves experimental manipulation: to show that X causes Y, we would ideally randomly assign some people to experience X and some not, and then evaluate whether Y is more prevalent in the former group compared to the latter. The logic is the same as a drug trial, in which participants are randomly assigned to receive either the real medicine or a placebo. Researchers then compare the outcomes of the participants in the drug group with those in the placebo group. Because of the random assignment of participants into those two groups, researchers can attribute any differences at the end of the trial between the groups to the drug itself and not other differences between the patients, such as their age or preexisting health conditions.

In studying employer mobilization and its causes and consequences, I take advantage of the logic of randomized experiments in several ways. First, I use the list experiment to test for the proportion of managers who admit that their business has encouraged workers to cast ballots for a particular candidate free from any concerns about openly admitting to this practice. I also use survey experiments to consider how the prospect of worker backlash changes the appeal of employer mobilization relative to other, more traditional political strategies for corporate managers. Switching to the perspective of workers, I test the effect of employer messages on workers' political attitudes and behaviors using the survey experiment fielded on American private-sector employees. I also deploy a similar approach to studying the effect of employee messages on top legislative staffers' opinions of their constituents and their decisions to pursue certain policy proposals over others, permitting me to study employer mobilization from the perspective of policymakers. These three sets of experiments—on corporate managers, employees, and congressional staffers—offer strong evidence of the causal effect of employer messages on both individual employees and policymakers, as well as evidence for the considerations managers bring to bear when deciding to mobilize their workers into politics.

Experiments, however, are not without important downsides. For instance, the worker survey experiment is limited in that the messages that workers were reading were not actually from their real employers—which, if my argument throughout this book is correct, will make an important difference in how employees should respond to messages. In a similar way, the legislative staffers I surveyed were indicating changes in their perceptions of their constituents. We do not get to observe changes in staffers' actual behaviors. Because of these limitations I also rely heavily on other strategies for understanding employer mobilization and its effects on American politics. For instance, I use the surveys of workers to understand how workers who report that they were actually contacted by employers ended up thinking about politics. Similarly I look at the relationship between geographic areas where employers engaged in more intensive employer mobilization drives and electoral outcomes, after accounting for a range of other potentially confounding factors.

These strategies of relying on observational data are, of course, not without their own drawbacks too. Most important, we cannot be completely certain that the relationships that emerge from these analyses are causal in the same way as with experimental approaches. At the same time, however, these observational approaches have the advantage of relying on cases where employer mobilization actually happened and observing variation in outcomes that are of direct substantive importance, like electoral results and policy changes. As a result of the strengths and weaknesses of these various approaches, readers should judge the conclusions in this book not on the basis of any one analysis but on the collected weight of all of these different types of evidence. My hope is that, taken as a whole, these diverse empirical strategies convince readers that employer mobilization is an important practice in contemporary American politics with significant consequences for both elections and public policy.

What Managers Say about Employer Mobilization

In the early morning hours of January 9, 2014, over 7,000 gallons of crude MCHM, a hazardous chemical used to process coal, poured into West Virginia's Elk River. Some 300,000 residents were promptly advised not to use their tap water for days, and over 100 West Virginians eventually sought treatment for symptoms related to the leaked chemical, including nausea and vomiting, rashes, sore throats, and eye pain.[1] In the wake of the spill, the state's legislature rushed to pass new rules regulating above-ground chemical storage. That bill had the potential to impose substantial new costs on companies that produced and stored chemicals across West Virginia. One major chemical manufacturer told me the bill would have considerably "impacted the way we do business in the state." Accordingly the company's legislative affairs division came up with a plan that satisfied the legislature's desire to take action while protecting the firm's operations in the state. Lobbyists then met with state legislators to promote the compromise proposal, which fit with the company's principles for chemical management, especially a risk-based approach to management.

But the firm knew that it would need more than just an inside lobbying strategy to win. To build further support for its legislative language, the company used its human resource records and an internal company website to contact its workers who lived within the districts of pivotal West Virginian representatives and senators. Those workers were then asked to contact their legislators to express support for the company's proposal. The company even provided a template that workers could use for their letters. The combination of inside lobbying with broad-based support from the company's West Virginia employee base worked, according to the government affairs officer I interviewed, and the bill signed into law by the governor contained the compromise text.

The power of employer mobilization was not a new discovery for the chemical manufacturer. Its executives had realized years ago that their workers could be a potent resource to deploy during legislative battles, and its government affairs officer reported that mobilization had been "hard-wired" into its political strategy at all levels of government. Indeed just a few years earlier, in 2008, the company's internal mobilization website had encouraged employees to vote in elections for West Virginia's state supreme court (it made similar appeals for state judicial elections in Louisiana, Michigan, and Texas), writing, "Just as it is important to care about who serves as your Governor or state legislator, the people who are elected to the West Virginia Supreme Court serve an important role within the checks and balances of state government." The website stressed that employees' votes could make a key difference, since "state judicial elections are often decided by just a handful of votes," yet "bad decisions by judges who substitute their own personal interests for the law can affect your children, grandchildren and future generations." As the website summed up, "When a business evaluates whether a state is 'business friendly,' one of the important things it considers is the state's litigation environment, and whether the law is fairly and consistently applied. A state with a history of judicial activism creates uncertainty and sends a warning against doing business there. This can have enormous economic consequences for employees."

In this chapter I draw on original survey and interview evidence to document how many other companies are using similar tactics to shape American politics (such as state electoral races) and policy (such as the battle over chemical storage legislation), what employer messages contain, what managers hope to achieve with those communications, how managers think about mobilization in comparison with other political strategies, and why some managers decide to deploy mobilization while others do not.

The Corporate Perspective on Mobilization

About 46 percent of managers included in the first wave of my firm survey reported that their company attempted some form of political engagement by providing a response to the question "To the best of your knowledge, has your firm ever contacted its workers about the following political issues?"[2] The options that managers could select included information about registering to vote; turning out to vote; endorsing a political candidate, a presidential candidate, a candidate for the U.S. House of Representatives, a candidate for the U.S. Senate, a candidate for state government, a specific issue or piece of legislation; contacting a legislator about an issue; donating to a political candidate; or "other kinds of political information."

Unlike with my telephone survey of workers, there are fewer ways to benchmark the results from my firm survey. The one outside source I identified is the Society for Human Resource Management (SHRM), a professional association.

SHRM has periodically surveyed a random sample of its members to ask about employer efforts to encourage workers to "vote in elections." The SHRM question therefore does not quite capture the same concept as my firm survey, which measures a broader range of firm activities related to politics and policy. In addition the SHRM sample does not represent all American employers, just those that have human resource professionals who are members of the group. Nevertheless the SHRM study does provide one benchmark against which we can compare my results. In 2004 SHRM found that about half—53 percent—of its members did at least one thing to "encourage employees to vote in elections"; that proportion increased to 57 percent in 2006, 58 percent in 2008, and 84 percent in 2016.[3] Thus, at least among well-institutionalized employers—those with a designated human resources division participating in SHRM—it appears that electoral efforts are relatively widespread and have increased considerably since the early 2000s.

That said, the most common mobilization reported by managers responding to my firm survey went well beyond getting workers to the polls. Of the firms that reported mobilizing their workers, only 29 percent reported providing exclusively information about registering or turning out to vote. The remaining 71 percent gave their workers more explicitly political information about candidates and policy issues (representing some 33 percent of all managers responding to my survey).

Some readers may wonder whether managers were responding truthfully to the firm survey. Might managers have been uncomfortable revealing detailed information about their companies' practices, especially mobilization? Fortunately the list experiment I described in chapter 2 can gauge the prevalence of mobilization when managers faced fewer concerns about social desirability bias. Recall that the list experiment estimated the proportion of managers agreeing that their business has, in the past, "encouraged workers to vote for particular political candidates" without managers needing to identify their own individual responses.

When given that privacy, about 28 percent of corporate managers revealed that their business actively encouraged workers to back particular politicians.[4] That amount is nearly the same as the proportion of managers who said they gave workers explicitly political information about candidates and policy issues when asked the direct question on my original firm survey. In short, it does not appear that managers were responding to the original firm survey with much hesitation about revealing their business's mobilization practices.[5] That fits with my experience interviewing top corporate executives: managers were quite open about their companies' political strategies.

Figure 3.1 illustrates the specific types of political information that employers provided to their workers. Managers were most likely to report that they gave information about policy issues to their workers—as the chemical manufacturer did in West Virginia. Information about contacting legislators, as well as information about political candidates, was less common but still frequent. Requests for political donations were least reported by firms, likely because most corporate contributions flow through political action committees (PACs), which most of the time are restricted by law from soliciting contributions from rank-and-file workers. Unlike with executives or shareholders, corporate PACs can only solicit rank-and-file workers for contributions twice a year—and even then, the request must be mailed (not done in person) and must ensure anonymity so that the company cannot reward or punish workers based on their donations to PACs. These limits were set by Congress out of fear of corporate coercion of ordinary workers yet have been undermined by the *Citizens United* Supreme Court decision in 2010, a point I revisit in chapter 5.

In general, transportation, utility, financial services, professional services, and extractive resource firms were most likely to report mobilizing their workers (see Figure 3.2). Political mobilization that went beyond simple get-out-the-vote reminders was most frequent in financial services, mining, and wholesale trade. Unlike by industry, there was not much variation in the prevalence of mobilization across companies by number of employees. Mobilization was common in

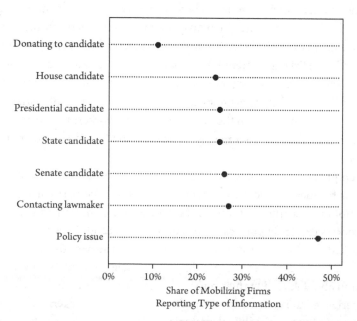

Figure 3.1 Political information in employer mobilization efforts. Data from 2015 firm surveys. Shares do not sum to 100 percent because managers could select more than one option. Denominator is all firms that reported mobilization (sample size: 237).

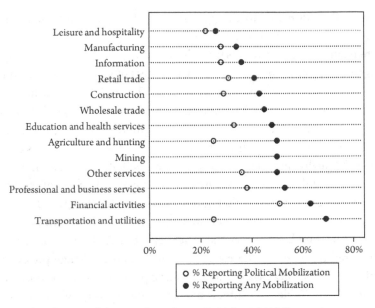

Figure 3.2 Employer mobilization by industry. Data from 2015 firm surveys. Denominator is all firms in a particular industry (sample size: 237). Political mobilization refers to content that goes beyond get-out-the-vote messages.

small and large firms alike. However, the character of mobilization varies greatly between firms of different sizes as we will see shortly.

Managers' Perceptions of the Benefits of Mobilization

How do managers perceive mobilization, especially in comparison with other political activities? Given that these surveyed executives are at the front line of corporate policy and management, it is useful to know whether they perceive mobilization to be more or less effective than other tactics that companies might deploy in politics. To answer this question, the firm survey asked managers to rank the relative effectiveness of the political strategies in which their firm engaged. The text presented to managers was as follows: "Businesses engage in politics in a variety of ways, including forming political action committees, buying political advertisements, hiring lobbyists, and joining business associations. Thinking about your firm's political activities, which of the following have been most effective at changing public policy? Please rank the following activities in descending order of how effective you think they are in changing government policy." The options included mobilizing workers, buying political advertisements, donating to campaigns, hiring lobbyists, and participating in various business associations.

When interpreting the results from this question, recall that I am asking about managers' perceptions of the *relative* effectiveness of various political strategies, not the effectiveness of mobilization overall. That point is important because while managers, and especially government affairs officers, might have an incentive to overstate the effectiveness of any given political strategy, I instead asked respondents about which political strategies were more important as compared to others.[6] Equally important to keep in mind is that this question asks about perceptions and does not necessarily capture the actual effects of mobilization on policy outcomes. (I revisit that question in more detail in part II.)

In all, 35 percent of corporate managers who reported mobilizing their workers ranked mobilization as their most effective tool for influencing policy as compared to the other strategies companies used to change policy, such as participating in business associations, making political contributions, and buying political ads. Table 3.1 explores managers' perceptions of the effectiveness of mobilization in more detail. The only strategy that was ranked higher than

Table 3.1. **Managers' Rankings of Most Effective Options for Influencing Policy**

For managers who reported engaging in mobilization	
35%	Ranked mobilization as most effective

For managers who reported lobbying	
24%	Ranked lobbying as most effective
21%	Ranked mobilization as most effective

For managers who reported donating to political candidates	
17%	Ranked donating as most effective
25%	Ranked mobilization as most effective

For managers who reported buying political ads	
3%	Ranked buying ads as most effective
21%	Ranked mobilization as most effective

For managers who reported membership in the U.S. Chamber of Commerce	
10%	Ranked U.S. Chamber as most effective
21%	Ranked mobilization as most effective

Data from 2015 firm surveys. Denominator is all firms that reported mobilization and other political activities (sample sizes: 244, 192, 210, 106, 184, respectively).

mobilization was hiring lobbyists; managers ranked mobilization as being more effective than donations to political candidates and substantially more effective than either purchasing political ads or participating in the U.S. Chamber of Commerce, a major national business association. The evidence from the firm survey thus indicates that business leaders consider mobilization to be a very effective means of influencing public policy.

How Mobilization Complements Other Corporate Political Activity

Even as businesses reported that mobilization was a very useful tool for moving legislation and regulation, managers were more likely to report engaging their workers in politics if their businesses were involved in other political activities. This suggests that employer mobilization is best seen as a complement to, not a substitute for, other forms of corporate political activity. We can see this in the firm survey data. Figure 3.3 plots the proportion of employers reporting mobilizing their workers into politics by the intensity of their other forms of political engagement (I grouped firms into three equal-size groups based on the count of political activities aside from mobilization in which an employer engages: low, medium, and high).[7] Employers in the first category did not engage in any other political activities. Only 27 percent of managers at these firms reported mobilization. In contrast, 50 percent of employers in the middle category of political activity (engaging in an average of one other political activity) reported mobilization. Even more strikingly, 61 percent of employers in the highest category of political activity (engaging in an average of six other political activities) mobilized their workers into politics. Clearly companies that do more in politics are also much more likely to mobilize.

My corporate interviews paint a nuanced picture of the relevance of other political commitments for mobilization, above all indicating that worker recruitment is not often a strategy pursued in isolation from hiring a lobbyist or making campaign contributions. If politics was not part of their business through these other activities, managers were unlikely to think of mobilization as a worthwhile investment. One communications officer at a semiconductor manufacturer conveyed this sentiment to me. "I joined four years ago and noticed the fierce intensity of our core manufacturing focus. . . . We are a very lean organization," she summarized. For a company like that, which viewed public affairs as being outside the scope of its core functions, mobilization was off the table. Similarly a manager at a national fast-casual restaurant chain answered me quite bluntly when I asked about mobilization at his company: "Do we engage our workforce in politics? We barely engage in politics at any level." And a manager at a mining

firm that had neither a PAC nor lobbyists reported that extensive worker engagement was unthinkable given the firm's strong desire to "stay off the radar": "We're
just keeping it simple.... Our shareholders aren't paying us to get involved up in
these [political] issues."

Worker political recruitment, then, was heavily concentrated among those
businesses that were already highly engaged in politics. For many of my interviewees, mobilization was valuable because of the way it complemented other
corporate strategies, making it clear that the relationship between mobilization
and other forms of political activity is not simply driven by other underlying
factors in a business. Rather the decision to engage in other political activities
created the opportunity—and often the necessity—to mobilize workers into
politics. Interviewees explained that mobilization can put additional pressure
on legislators with whom employers already had relationships because of PAC
donations and lobbying. A government affairs officer at a chemical manufacturer
said that she might ask workers to contact a key legislator during a debate in
Congress and then "take the data [on worker letters] to the members of Congress
that I know have been reached by our workers, and follow up with them about
the specific number of letters that were written."

A lobbyist for a telecommunications company reported using a similar
approach in meetings with members of Congress, saying that recruiting workers

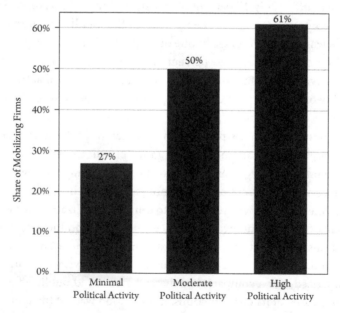

Figure 3.3 Other forms of corporate political activity and employer mobilization. Data
from 2015 firm surveys. Figure plots the proportion of mobilizing employers by terciles
of other forms of corporate political activity (sample size: 391).

to write to a member "creates a heightened sense of importance of an issue" and permits their lobbying team to bring those contacts up in one-on-one meetings with the member and his or her staff. The lobbyists might say, "We have 3,500 workers in your district and this is an important issue for them." Sometimes, if workers sent enough correspondence to the member, it might even be the elected official who asked the company's lobbying team about the issue.

Mobilization was also used to introduce candidates to workers around election time, such as in plant visits or town hall forums. Managers might also remind workers during campaign season that "we appreciate the support we've gotten over 20 years from Senator X," as I heard from a household appliance manufacturer. Such a tactic further strengthens the relationship between the company and an elected official. In this way mobilization can reinforce a business's decision to give to a political campaign to build a relationship with a political candidate.

Aside from complementing lobbying and PAC strategies, mobilization bolsters efforts by employers to join political coalitions with other companies and business associations. Take the example of when a group of CEOs came together in 2013 to press Congress to resolve an impending government shutdown. That coalition had CEOs send letters to their employees encouraging them to contact legislators to voice support for a budget deal. A steel producer similarly reported working closely with the Steel Institute (an industry trade group) and the National Association of Manufacturers to mobilize workers around issues related to U.S. trade with China.

How Companies Use Software to Deliver Messages and Track Participation

Managers now have access to a variety of applications that permit them to deliver political messages and requests to their workers in an inexpensive and highly targeted manner. More than two-thirds (68 percent) of mobilizing firms reported using such packages, according to the firm survey, which asked managers at mobilizing firms, "Does your firm use software to contact your workers about politics or political issues?" The options included using software from the Business-Industry Political Action Committee (BIPAC); a leading group helping firms to mobilize their workers, software from another business association or organization, or software developed in-house at the company.

Larger firms were much more likely than smaller firms to report the use of communications software. Only slightly more than half of firms (56 percent) with 100 or fewer workers reported using software to deliver messages, while 94 percent of firms with over 500 workers reported using such platforms. Firms mostly reported developing their own in-house software for mobilization, though about one-third of firms using software reported contracting with BIPAC to use their Prosperity Project platform. I discuss the pioneering role of BIPAC's platform in encouraging employer mobilization, especially in the post–*Citizens United* period, in chapter 5.

These software packages helped managers to specify the workers who would receive political messages and requests. The firm survey asked managers whether their companies delivered political messages to all workers or targeted workers to receive messages. The specific question managers answered was: "When your firm contacted its workers about politics or political issues, did your firm target the workers who received political information?" The options given to managers included targeting by workers' past engagement in political activities; workers' voter registration or turnout record; workers' position in the company; workers' residence; the location of a store, office, plant, or factory; workers' demographic characteristics; or any other targeting. In all, over three-quarters of firms reported that they targeted specific workers to receive political information, and firms that used software packages were more than twice as likely as those that did not to indicate that they targeted messages.

Figure 3.4 summarizes the worker characteristics used by managers to tailor political recruitment requests, expressed as a proportion of all employers that reported targeting their workers. Managers were most likely to report that they targeted messages based on workers' position in the firm, such as their occupation or job description. Nearly one-third of targeting employers reported

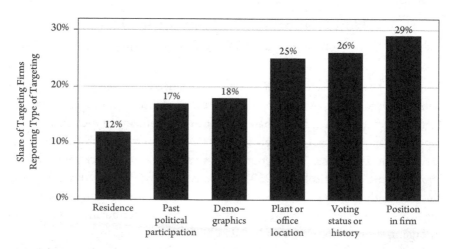

Figure 3.4 Targeting of political messages by worker characteristics. Data from 2015 firm surveys. Shares do not sum to 100 percent because managers could select more than one option. Denominator is all firms that reported targeting their workers (sample size: 120).

customizing their message by employees' position in the company. Closely behind this type of targeting was the use of workers' voting status or turnout history. Slightly over a quarter of targeting firms reported this kind of tailoring. It is relatively straightforward for firms to obtain this information by purchasing access to voter files, which contain records, by name and address, of Americans who have registered and turned out to vote in recent elections. The extent of information available in these records varies greatly by state, but the most comprehensive records include details on voter turnout, party affiliation, and race. (The candidates for whom voters cast their ballots are, of course, secret.) These records have become essential to political campaigns in recent years, which use the files to focus their recruitment efforts on specific subsets of citizens.[8] Companies can also simply poll their workers directly to ask if they have registered to vote or turned out to vote.

About the same share of targeting companies reported tailoring political information by the location of plants, offices, or stores. This would permit managers to deliver messages about an election to only their establishments that are plausibly affected by the political candidates in a particular race, or only the plants or stores subject to a given piece of legislation. Targeting by worker demographic characteristics, including age, race, sex, and education, as well as workers' past political participation in firm-sponsored activities and workers' residence, was the least common form of targeting reported by managers.

The reasons companies might target some workers and not others are relatively straightforward: not all political messages are relevant to a company's entire workforce, and not all workers are equally likely to be persuaded by a firm's messages. This means that rational managers can maximize the likelihood of success by ensuring that messages reach only those workers who are immediately affected by a policy or election, and within that group, only those workers most likely to respond to political requests. But not all means of targeting were equally useful to managers. I found that the most useful forms of targeting were based on worker voting status or voting history and on past participation in firm activities. Taking into account the other means of targeting, firms that tailored messages to workers based on voting records were 33 percentage points more likely to report that mobilization was their most effective strategy for changing public policy. Similarly firms that targeted based on workers' past political participation were 46 percentage points more likely to report that mobilization was most effective. Targeting by these characteristics permits managers to activate only those workers who are most politically responsive to corporate messages— and also those who thus pose a credible threat to lawmakers.

My conversations with managers heavily underscored the importance of tracking and tailoring messages to workers. One government affairs official at a large extractive resource manufacturing firm explained that "being able to target [political messages] to discrete audiences" was the biggest advance his firm had experienced in mobilization in recent years. That manager was able to send highly customized recruitment requests, for instance, even targeting "100 people that live on one street" out of the company's 45,000-person workforce. This, in turn, meant his firm's lobbying team could target mobilization requests or messages to only the employees working or living in the districts of pivotal lawmakers.

Tailored messages could be further reinforced with a "tele–town hall" for all of the employees residing in that district, delivered through the company's internal website. As that same government affairs officer put it, "We identify and target down to [say] five members of Congress that are critically important, and then [send political messages] to the employees in those districts." Those communications from workers get tallied up by members of Congress and are referenced by the firm's lobbyists in meetings the company might later arrange with members. The lobbyist summed up plainly, "Members of Congress are going to listen to their constituents, especially if they are registered voters who can threaten them in the next election." The ability to target workers thus has very real payoffs for companies. The firm's government affairs officer said that targeting made the difference in a recent legislative battle over the construction of a controversial oil pipeline project. It is for this reason, too, that the Public Affairs Council, a professional association that helps managers to mobilize workers, argues that a "system for identifying, tracking and communicating with your advocates is an essential component of any grassroots [worker engagement] program. It gives you the ability to target your communications and activate your people by district or state."[9]

Electronic software not only helps companies target messages to specific groups of their employees to maximize their political impact. Software platforms also permit managers to follow up on their messages to see which workers have responded to requests. That sort of tracking means that managers can reward workers who comply with political appeals—and, more troubling, potentially punish workers who do not.

We can see the importance of electronic monitoring—with attendant rewards for complying workers—in the following account from a manager at an extractive resource manufacturing firm. By merging his company's human resources records with the company's political mobilization software, this manager was able to send customized messages and to keep tabs on which workers responded to each political request. According to this manager, this recruitment technology means that he "can keep track of who is a champion, who has responded to every single request or letter." His company then promoted those employees who most consistently responded to employer requests as "political ambassadors" and "peer recruiters," who received free trips to their state capital or to

Washington, DC, to wine and dine with elected officials and media representatives. In covering the trend of rising employee political engagement at American companies, two Reuters reporters identified similar rewards for employees who participated in corporate political activities at BP and Walmart.[10] BP employees who donated at least 2.5 percent of their paychecks to the company's PAC were rewarded with better parking spots, and Walmart associates who donated to political campaigns got a two-for-one match for their giving to the company's internal charity program. (HP and Coca-Cola have had analogous incentive programs.)[11]

In a similar vein, an executive overseeing employee political participation at a Minnesota energy company reminded his corporate colleagues in a guide for employer mobilization that "employees may view grassroots participation as a career advancement opportunity," and as a result companies should not "disappoint them."[12] That same executive recommended, "When an employee helps out [with a mobilization campaign], make sure his or her boss knows. Hold recognition dinners or similar events at which grassroots volunteers are honored in the presence of senior executives and managers who might boost a volunteer's career. Grassroots participation should be a plus in promotion decisions."[13]

The pharmaceutical giant Glaxo Wellcome (now GlaxoSmithKline) has taken that advice to heart in its own mobilization efforts and developed a sophisticated system of tracking employee political participation and rewarding frequent participators. Through the Civic Action Network (CAN) the company "tracks the activities of employees . . . and offers awards to those who are the most involved."[14] "Employees earn points for each activity in which they participate," the CAN manager explained in a 2000 case study for other companies to follow.[15] For instance, "making a telephone call to an elected official concerning an issue the company has alerted employees about is worth 300 points. Presenting our 'Value of Medicines' video to an advocacy group—educating the group's members about the cost of pharmaceutical discovery—is worth 500 points. Meeting face-to-face with one of the employee's own state or federal elected officials is worth 600 points. And volunteering to help a candidate's campaign is worth 700 points."[16] The employee "who, at the end of the year has the most points for the sales region in which he or she resides, wins an all-expense paid trip to Washington. The winners—while given time to enjoy the city's sights—also meet with their elected officials and with senior executives in the company."[17]

One 2010 mobilization drive by Harrah's, the casino company, at their Las Vegas properties provides a nice example of how employers can closely track their employees' voting behaviors even without obtaining election records from the voter file.[18] A campaign staffer for Democratic senator Harry Reid, who was in a tight reelection contest that year, sent an email pleading for electoral help from the gaming company. Reid's campaign cited the fact that 1,100 employees from competitor casino MGM had already voted, while turnout among Harrah's employees remained low. After receiving the frantic message from Reid's campaign, Harrah's top executive for public policy urged her fellow managers, "PLEASE do whatever we need . . . [to] get employees out to vote." In response, one executive sent a follow-up message measuring turnout rates for each of Harrah's properties with a line-by-line spreadsheet for each employee at the company and their voting record for the election. Managers at each of Harrah's properties were told to follow up with employees who had not yet voted. One employee reported to the *National Review*, "We were asked to talk to people individually to find out why they had not yet voted and to fill in these spreadsheets explaining why."[19]

A major business association of manufacturers that helps its member companies mobilize their workers also reported using a dedicated Internet portal to closely track and monitor workers. The head of grassroots political affairs told me the following: "I can tell you who opened each email, how long they spent with the message, and whether they clicked through to additional materials." "We do everything when it comes to tracking," she said; it is "very easy" and very important for "unleashing the grassroots" within their member businesses. This point was reiterated by the top lobbyist at a telecommunications company, who reported that she tracked how successful each mobilization campaign was by "click-through" rates, or whether or not workers opened and read the messages sent to them. This company also encouraged employees to use social media to drive the conversation about major political issues affecting the firm, and reported monitoring how "employees . . . are blogging or tweeting about things . . . creating energy on social media" for specific campaigns. Such social media initiatives are an important way the company could shape "the environment and context in which [policymaking] happens . . . so that when [a] conversation happens, there is positive energy around that conversation" in ways that favor the business's policy objectives.

A public affairs executive at a health insurance company mentioned that his firm wanted to move toward a similar use of employee social media engagement as a lobbying device and said that doing so would require more infrastructure to monitor the mentions of the company by its employees. Close tracking and monitoring of employee responses, including voting and social media usage, are thus important ways for businesses to maximize the effectiveness of their political requests and, ultimately, their political campaigns.

Outside of my own interview data, recent reporting confirms that American businesses engage in extensive monitoring of their employees' social media accounts. In one striking example, Walmart retained the services of Lockheed Martin to track potential labor sympathizers within its stores. Although

Lockheed Martin is perhaps best known for building fighter jets and weapons systems for the U.S. military, it also houses an analytics division that can track online, open-source data produced by individuals to reveal their behaviors and attitudes. Its promotional material explains, "[Our product] provides automated data collection, advanced processing and knowledge management, and analysis and monitoring capabilities. It supports tracking, event monitoring, correlation, aggregation, and indexing of massive multi-language data from the Internet, including RSS feeds, news and information sites, subscription content information sites, databases, Web sites, Twitter, Blogs, and social networking sites."[20]

A journalist with Bloomberg has described how Walmart used Lockheed's analytics services in the run-up to labor protests at the company's annual shareholder meeting in Bentonville, Arkansas. A Lockheed analyst "was monitoring the social media of activists in Bentonville [for Walmart]. . . . He sent his updates to Walmart and copied Mike Baylor, who's named as a project manager on Lockheed's . . . website. On June 4, at 6:30 p.m., [the analyst] sent this update about the artist and activist Favianna Rodriguez to seven Walmart and five Lockheed managers: 'Favianna tweeted that OUR Walmart [an organization of Walmart protestors] is preparing for action "walmart headquarters." Tweet is 9 minutes old as of this e-mail.' "[21]

Walmart also used Lockheed's social media monitoring "to determine which stores are most at risk of labor unrest. These are dubbed Priority 1 stores, in need of extra training for managers and extra information sessions for employees. Several [Walmart organizers] have described Bentonville executives arriving suddenly in their stores with scripts in hand."[22]

Close employee monitoring clearly provides valuable benefits to companies, not only to control labor costs and boost productivity but also to track employees' social and political behaviors. "The payoff for well-designed workplace monitoring," one corporate consultant summed up for the *New York Times*, "can be significant."[23] Indeed the Public Affairs Council recommends in its "best practices" for employer mobilization that managers "track" their employee advocates and that "all your grassroots advocates should receive rewards and recognition for their efforts."[24]

What Do Employers Hope to Accomplish with Mobilization?

Survey responses about the type of information that managers are sending to their workers provide some sense of what employers are trying to achieve in their mobilization drives. But we can also ask managers directly what they hoped to accomplish with their messages to workers. Figure 3.5 lists the share of

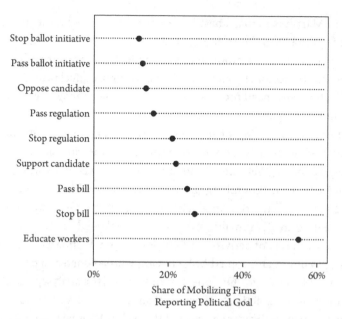

Figure 3.5 The political goals of mobilizing firms. Data from 2015 firm surveys. Shares do not sum to 100 percent because managers could select more than one option. Denominator is all firms that reported mobilization (sample size: 249).

mobilizing firms reporting particular goals for their mobilization efforts, drawing on responses to a question on the survey that asked managers, "When your firm contacted its workers about politics or political issues, what were the goals your firm hoped to achieve?" The options included passing or stopping legislation, passing or stopping state ballot initiatives and referenda, passing or stopping regulation, supporting or opposing political candidates, educating workers, or other, unspecified goals. If managers selected legislation or regulation, they were further asked if this regulation or legislation was at the state, local, or federal level, and if they selected supporting or opposing political candidates, they were given options for state or local, U.S. House, U.S. Senate, or presidential candidates.

By far the most frequently cited goal was to educate workers about particular policies or issues. Of course, as I explained in chapter 1, education efforts often bleed into other goals. Companies typically began education campaigns with the intention of later "activating" employees with specific requests around policy battles or elections after they have invested in educating their employees about broader issues and ideas. For instance, a manager at a major pharmaceutical company I interviewed mentioned that they were "starting to educate workers now, three years out, [to eventually lobby for extensions on] patents that are expiring on [our] three biggest drugs." And a grassroots political engagement officer at a manufacturing firm underscored that your "first ask [to employees] isn't for money"; instead you "start with information, why this [politics and elections] matters," and you develop that message before making specific requests.

The next cluster of goals involved stopping and passing bills, which were listed by a little over a quarter of managers. Supporting political candidates and stopping regulation were the next most commonly cited goals, at slightly over a fifth of all firms. Addressing ballot initiatives—whether by supporting or opposing them—was the least cited goal. Yet even though ballot initiatives were the least mentioned item on the survey, there are still a number of high-profile state referendum battles involving employer mobilization efforts. In Ohio, for instance, the state Chamber of Commerce encouraged employers to mobilize their workers to oppose a 2008 ballot initiative that would have created a new employee paid leave benefit. Writing to their members at the time, the Chamber said that it "highly encourages business leaders to educate their employees on this issue. A few e-mails, a payroll stuffer or a simple conversation will go a long way [to defeating the paid leave policy]."[25] The Chamber even created a website for Ohio employers to use in that education initiative against the paid leave benefit. In the face of strong business opposition, among other factors, the pro–leave benefit campaign stopped their efforts.[26] (I also examine the role of mobilization in more detail around an Alaska ballot measure in chapter 7.)

Mobilization around regulations might come as a surprise to some readers. While it is clear that mobilized employees can make a difference in legislative deliberations by sending correspondence to pivotal lawmakers or in elections by providing votes for candidates, it might be less clear how employees can affect the regulatory process. One good example comes from battles over the Obama administration's proposed rules about "net neutrality," or whether Internet and telecommunications providers would have the power to control the content and services viewed by end-users. Could Comcast, for instance, charge its cable Internet customers extra to stream television shows on Netflix, a major competitor, or even block user access to streaming services altogether? The Federal Communications Commission (FCC), the agency in charge of regulating telecommunications, was set to revamp its principles on this issue in 2009, and telecommunications companies wanted to make sure they retained as much control as possible over the traffic that ran through their networks.

The trade group representing wireless service providers warned that moves to expand net neutrality regulations to their industry would create "unintended consequences" and might even reduce "investments from the very industry that's helping to drive the U.S. economy."[27] AT&T, one of the largest wireless service providers in the country, wanted a bright-line exemption from the rule and was not shy about asking for it. The company thus organized a letter-writing campaign from their employees to the FCC during the period when the agency was soliciting comments from the public about the proposed measure. The FCC soon found itself "overwhelmed with thousands of comments, not the typical five or 10" they usually received on rules, in part as a result of AT&T's push among its employees.[28] As we have now seen is quite common, the senior vice president at AT&T in charge of legislative affairs provided clear talking points to employees that they were supposed to use in their messages to the FCC. Such correspondence from businesses can make a crucial difference as federal agencies deliberate over proposed regulatory measures; as two scholars of agency rulemaking have concluded, "a greater proportion of business interests within the public comments [on proposed federal regulations] allow business commenters to better pursue their preferred level of government involvement in agency rules."[29] Employer mobilization can vastly increase the number of pro-business comments that regulatory agencies receive, and in so doing help companies to shape regulatory policy in their favor. This can happen even on issues that seem fairly technical and obscure. A staffer at a major business association boasted to me that he helped a financial services company generate 100,000 employee letters opposing a proposed rule issued by the Department of Labor expanding the fiduciary responsibility of investment advisers to their clients.

There is a convincing argument to be made that we should see companies mobilizing most frequently at the state level, given that businesses are more likely to be politically successful when they are operating in legislative debates that receive less public scrutiny, and state political debates tend to be much less visible to ordinary citizens than national politics.[30] Yet we do not observe this pattern in the survey results. Companies were, in general, more likely to mobilize at the federal level than the state level. The reason for this difference is made clear in the interviews I conducted with managers, who repeatedly told me that they mobilized where there were significant threats from public policy. Given that motivation, it is no surprise that most mobilization is happening at the federal level, which presents a much greater risk of public policy to businesses. That said, I did hear from businesses, even large businesses, that mobilized in the states when there were relevant policy debates at that level of government. Several health insurers, for instance, reported that they were very active in state-level politics, given that governors and state legislatures have significant authority to regulate the pricing and sale of insurance plans, and this was further reinforced after the passage of the 2010 health care reform law.

How Mobilization Is Spurred by Policy Threats

We can examine the importance of policy threats for employer mobilization more systematically by combining the survey data and interview results. Using data from George Mason University's Mercatus Center, I divided the managers in my firm survey into those operating in heavily regulated sectors (such as extractive industries, pharmaceutical manufacturing, and energy production) and those that are not (such as wholesale trade). I found that more heavily regulated companies are much more likely than are less regulated firms to mobilize their workers into politics. Only 43 percent of employers in minimally regulated industries mobilized their workers, compared to nearly 60 percent of employers in more tightly regulated sectors (see Figure 3.6).

The interview data also provide very strong support for the findings about threats from government action. A software developer reported to me that the fact that her business was only weakly exposed to government policies meant there was no clear reason to invest in mobilization: "Because we're in the soft ware industry, we are not a highly regulated industry, [so] there is not much of a need to get involved in government."

A government affairs executive of a computer peripherals company reflected on the difference between his business and other companies with which he had worked, saying that in his experience mobilization tended to occur within "highly regulated, focused industries, like a coal company, that has very well-defined interests. They get the crap beaten out of them by the regulatory

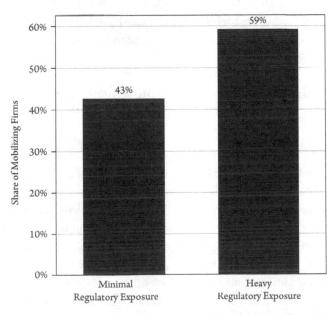

Figure 3.6 Exposure to regulation and employer mobilization. Data from 2015 firm surveys. Figure plots the proportion of mobilizing employers by the regulatory exposure of firms, coded by industry (sample size: 356).

agencies, like the EPA, and they want Republicans on the Hill in order to keep their business going."

A representative of a major retailer agreed with that sentiment, stating that the main reason his firm began mobilizing was it was being "hit on the head" by regulation after regulation from state and local governments. And a government affairs officer at a health insurer told me that the most recent national mobilization campaigns launched by his company involved changes to Medicare payment schemes: "We're a large provider for the Medicare program so the rates are something we are interested in, and so as part of that campaign there is certainly an employee activation piece of that."

A typical example of the importance of regulatory threats for initiating workplace mobilization comes from a food manufacturer, whose government affairs officer told the story of a worker recruitment effort around a state ballot initiative for GMO labeling in Oregon. The company worried that the measure would raise production costs, forcing them to close baking and packaging operations in that state. According to the interviewee, "We educated our employees about the issue. . . . We have a ballot initiative here that will greatly increase—if it were adopted—a threat to our company, reduce the competitiveness of the [plant in this state]. The reason is that it would . . . raise costs of packaging at that plant relative to all of the other locations." The state-level mobilization campaign included information on the company's intranet, as well as discussions between plant managers and their employees. The company has similarly advised workers periodically about elections in which political candidates have "a very clear stance on an issue that matters to us," either for or against the company's bottom line.

The Importance of Economic Power for Employer Mobilization

One of the underlying themes I developed in chapter 1 was that the difference in economic power between employees and employers deeply structures managers' political requests of workers. When workers are more fearful of losing their jobs and wages, they should be more likely to respond to managers' requests. That makes it easier for employers to make political requests of their workers. In contrast, when workers are less fearful of losing their jobs, they should be more likely to resist or protest employer recruitment efforts with which they disagree. Under those conditions, political recruitment is costlier for managers since there is a greater chance that workers will ignore their messages—or even actively oppose them. Can we find evidence for this proposition in the firm survey?

Since it is hard to directly ask corporate managers about the economic power they possess relative to their workers, I instead opted for a survey experiment of managers participating in my October 2016 firm survey. The idea behind this experiment is that I could see if managers who were prompted to think about the possibility of their workers protesting or resisting political messages—a consequence of greater worker economic power—would be less likely to say that they would attempt to mobilize their workers.

The experiment thus presented respondents with a short vignette that described a politician who was running for elected office in a district or state where the business operated. The politician in the vignette was proposing a policy that could affect managers' business operations. Here is an example of the vignette shown to respondents:

> Suppose that there was a Democratic politician running for the U.S. House of Representatives in a district where your business operates. The politician is proposing a policy that would hurt your business. Your business has many of its workers in the constituency of the politician, who is a challenger.
>
> The election is receiving a lot of media attention. Other businesses in your sector have backed the candidate. You anticipate that the election will be very close. Your workers are mixed in their support for this candidate.

After reading the vignette, half of the respondents were shown the following text: "You are worried that some of your workers might protest if you communicate about the politicians in this election." Half of respondents did not see that text. I then asked the managers to describe how likely they would be to donate to candidates in that election, to donate to political organizations involved in the election, to tell workers about candidate positions in the election, and to encourage workers to vote for a particular candidate in the election. Managers rated the likelihood of each alternative on a 1–5 scale, ranging from "very likely" to "very unlikely." (The prompt was "Thinking about this election, how likely is your business to"; see the appendix to this chapter for the full survey instrument.) The advantage to asking about a range of corporate political activities is that I can compare worker political recruitment against other potential strategies a company might deploy.

If managers were indeed concerned about potential worker protests to their mobilization efforts, then managers who saw the prompt about worker protests ought to have ranked the more traditional political strategies (donating to the political candidates or other organizations) as being more likely than communicating with their workers about the election or encouraging workers to vote for a particular candidate. That is precisely what we see. Managers who saw the description about potential worker protests were about 7 percentage points

more likely to say that their business would deploy traditional election donations compared to mobilization strategies. Twenty-two percent of managers who
did not see the prompt about potential worker protests said that they would be
more likely to use traditional strategies over employee mobilization, compared
to 29 percent of managers who saw the prompt, an increase of over 30 percent.[31]
Figure 3.7 shows this difference.

Managers' fears of workers either ignoring employer messages or, worse,
protesting them, came up repeatedly in my interviews. I found across multiple
interviews that if employers reported having a predominantly white-collar and
relatively autonomous rank-and-file who might protest messages, they were less
likely to report mobilizing their workers. Moreover, when they did mobilize
their workers, companies tended to use far less partisan forms of contact.

When asking managers of white-collar businesses about their lack of mobilization, for instance, my interviewees often cited the fact that they expected their
workers to resent or protest more extensive and partisan recruitment efforts.
A manager at a software consulting business explained, "The other [reason for
not mobilizing] that I see is that we have a very highly educated workforce. . . .

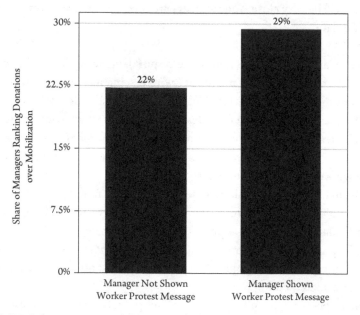

Figure 3.7 Worker protest against employer messages and employer mobilization. Data
from 2016 managerial survey experiment. Figure plots the share of managers saying their
business would be more likely to engage in traditional electoral activities (donating to
campaigns and organizations) than to mobilize their workers into an election (telling
workers about the candidates or encouraging workers to vote for particular candidates),
depending on whether managers were shown a warning that their workers might protest
mobilization efforts (total sample size: 508).

This is an employee base that would not take kindly to having their employer telling them how to channel their political inclinations and activities." In a similar vein, a manager at a major financial services business explained that his company had a "light-touch" approach to mobilization because "most of our workforce is white collar, college-degreed, involved in the financial services sector for a long time. It's a highly educated workforce. . . . It's a delicate area because our employees often times resent any kind of pressure or input from senior management to the rank and file to vote, or to vote a certain way."

Another way that high worker economic power makes mobilization costlier for businesses is by making it harder for managers to predict the speech and activities of workers. An executive at a computer peripherals business with a largely high-skilled engineer employee base reported that she did not want the company's workers to participate in political outreach because they "are comfortable being very candid, [and] they could write some diatribe about a politician or the administration. . . . I don't want our employees to contact someone in Congress—I don't know what they're going to say!" It is riskier for companies to mobilize workers if managers cannot be sure that workers are going to express the preferences held by the firm.

I also observed the economic power explanation at play within companies, as corporate representatives considered the ease with which they could recruit different segments of their workforce. One manager at a pharmaceutical products manufacturer I spoke with explained that the highly autonomous and skilled research scientists at his business were much less likely to respond well to mobilization efforts ("It is harder to get them to toe the company line"), whereas the less autonomous and lower-skilled sales and administrative support staff were much better political representatives of the business ("All of those kinds of enabling function workers are much more engaged [in mobilization efforts]")— exactly what we would expect given the differences in economic power between the research scientists working at the bench to develop new drugs, and staff supporting those scientists and selling the company's products to doctors and hospitals.

Similarly a government relations official at a major movie studio reported that his business did not mobilize any of their own full-time workers but did engage the part-time independent contractors the company used when filming on location across the United States. "If we want to film movies in a particular city . . . we want the state legislatures to support that," the manager explained. To get state and local governments to support tax credits or other breaks for filming on location, the studio would get independent contractors, such as caterers and florists, to lobby city or state officials. It is precisely these sorts of contractors who we might expect would have less economic power than the full-time workers at this movie studio, who thus would be more receptive to employer requests for political participation. Of course these contractors also had the benefit of being locally employed in the cities and states in which the movie studio was seeking more favorable tax treatment, which could potentially make them more persuasive lobbyists on behalf of the company as well.

While managers' descriptions of worker autonomy often aligned with employ-ees' education, at other times they did not, providing evidence that economic power (and managers' corresponding fear of backlash) was not entirely driven by the skills possessed by workers. At one large regional bank, the government affairs manager reported extensive mobilization of branch officers, which were typically well-educated employees. But despite being corporate officers, they did not have much power within the company. "We have [thousands of] offi-cers," the government affairs official explained; by comparison, "Ford maybe has a hundred." These individuals were granted the corporate officer title because the bank needed several officers at each branch location to authorize loans. So despite having a college degree and an impressive-sounding title, these workers were still very much dependent on the bank's top management and were not all that autonomous—again, the very workers who likely would be more worried about retaliation from their bosses.

"Many companies are in a war for [top] talent," summed up one association executive. As a result you "want to be careful that you don't alienate [that tal-ent]." Managers are simply not in a position to send potentially controversial messages to these highly mobile workers, "even if [they] wanted to." But not all workers are equally well positioned to threaten to leave their job, and so we should expect more mobilization—and more intensive mobilization—in com-panies where workers have less of this economic power relative to their manag-ers, as the interviews and experiment have shown.

Understanding Employer Mobilization from Inside American Businesses

About half of the managers in the firm survey reported that they did something to recruit their workers into politics. But what does that mobilization look like in practice? And what explains whether employers fell on one side of that divide or the other? Drawing on the insights of top corporate managers them-selves, both through survey data and in-depth interviews, I have described what mobilization looks like from the perspective of individual corporate managers. I showed how employers contacted workers, which issues they discussed, and what employers hoped to achieve with their recruitment efforts. I also explored some of the factors that led companies to rely more heavily on mobilization as a political strategy: highly regulated businesses or businesses facing a specific policy threat were more likely to mobilize than were less regulated companies; more politically active companies were more likely to mobilize than were less politically active firms, as employee recruitment provided an important complement to existing political engagement strategies; and managers were more likely to opt for mobilization when their workers had less economic power and thus there was less risk of backlash.

Employer efforts to change worker behavior—for instance, by encouraging workers to contact lawmakers or attend events—are less effective, however, when managers cannot actually observe whether or not workers are following through on their requests. As a result companies rely heavily on new software platforms that can help them target specific workers and also check which workers actually follow through on political appeals. As we will soon see, it was the development of this new technology that opened the door for more expansive mobilization efforts in recent years.

Studying corporate managers' perspectives on mobilization is only half the story, though. To fully understand how and why mobilization works, we need to examine workplace recruitment from the perspective of workers.

4

What Workers Say about Employer Mobilization

On August 14, 2012, GOP presidential hopeful Mitt Romney visited a coal mine outside of Beallsville, Ohio, to deliver a speech attacking the energy policies of his Democratic opponent, Barack Obama. "We have 250 years of coal, why in the heck wouldn't we use it? And so, I want to take advantage of those energy resources," Romney told the assembled crowd of mineworkers. Throughout his speech he was flanked by miners dressed in blue overalls and hardhats, some with coal-stained faces from an earlier shift that day, making for a striking visual complement to the content of his remarks.

A campaign stop such as this one might not seem that unusual in the midst of a heated presidential election. But this event was different, as the owners of the coal mine had told their workers that attendance at the rally would be both mandatory and unpaid.[1] An executive with the mining company later attempted to clarify that management "communicated to our workforce that the attendance at the Romney event was mandatory, but no one was forced to attend."[2] The mineworkers felt differently about this distinction. They told reporters that they showed up to the rally even if they opposed Romney out of fear of losing their jobs or being disciplined in some other way.[3] The wife of one miner explained that her husband "felt like [his managers] were pushing the Republican choice on him and he felt a little intimidated by that."[4]

It turns out that the miners were justified in their concerns. Almost immediately after Obama was reelected, the Murray Energy CEO announced over 100 layoffs, blaming the decision on the "war on coal" being waged by the Democratic administration.[5] In announcing the layoffs, the CEO lamented that the "American people have made their choice," and in the process the "takers outvoted the producers."[6] As a result Americans "will pay the price in their reduced standard of living and, most especially, reduced freedom."[7]

Journalists who had covered midwestern politics in the past explained that the corporate owner of the mine, Murray Energy, had a long history of pushing its employees to support Republican causes.[8] One investigative reporter put it bluntly: the business had "for years pressured salaried employees to give to the Murray Energy political action committee (PAC) and to Republican candidates chosen by the company. Internal documents show that company officials track who is and is not giving [and] those who do not give are at risk of being demoted or missing out on bonuses."[9] A miner expanded on that description: "There's a lot of coercion. I just wanted to work, but you feel this constant pressure that, if you don't contribute, your job's at stake. You're compelled to do this whether you want to or not."[10]

One leaked document shows how Murray's management emphasizes to employees just how closely bosses monitor their political choices. In a March 2012 memo to his workers expressing disappointment at low political fund-raising totals, the firm's CEO included a list of workers who did not attend recent events, calling them out by name: "I do not recall ever seeing the attached list of employees . . . at one of our fund-raisers."[11] Some employees felt that the threat of dismissal or discipline for not participating in company political activities was very real, reporting that failing to back firm-favored candidates could hurt their jobs.[12] One former Murray foreman recently sued the company, alleging that she was terminated in part due to her lack of participation in company-sponsored political fundraisers. The lawsuit went on to argue that she was fired to send a message to other employees who refused to back Murray's favored candidates, that "by firing [foremen] . . . [Murray's CEO] knows and understands that he can and does create a concern among the remaining foremen that, if they fail to contribute to his candidates, they may also lose their jobs."[13]

Whatever Murray Energy was doing, it has been unquestionably successful. Since 1992 the company has raised over $5 million in political donations, nearly entirely for Republicans. And the business has held a string of large fundraisers for GOP stars such as Scott Brown, Rand Paul, David Vitter, Carly Fiorina, and Jim DeMint.[14] (As the 2016 GOP presidential nominee, Donald Trump also held an event with Murray.)[15] During his remarks at the 2012 rally, the firm's CEO earned high praise from Romney, who declared to the crowd, "I tell ya, you've got a great boss. He runs a great operation here."[16]

How common are the efforts deployed by Murray Energy, especially the more coercive practices? And what do workers have to say about employer messages like the ones from Murray? This chapter explores those questions, laying out a landscape of employer mobilization from the perspective of workers, drawing on new national surveys of employees I have fielded over the past few years. The picture that emerges from these surveys largely parallels the findings from my previous look at the business side of mobilization. Not only is mobilization prevalent across many sectors of the American economy, but workers report that employer messages often affect how they think about political issues. Employees receiving employer political messages say they have decided to register to vote, turn out to vote, contact lawmakers about pending legislation, and even cast ballots for particular candidates as a result of those messages.

While I find that most employees do not experience the kind of pressure the Murray miners did, I do identify nearly a third of workers who either think that political retaliation might be likely or have observed such retaliation firsthand—and among lower income workers the share is much higher. I also document an even broader set of workers who report that they either perceive a lack of privacy at work when it comes to their political decisions or choices or say that their employers have in fact discovered aspects of their political attitudes and votes. These findings raise the concern that employer mobilization may indeed be coercive in many businesses.

I conclude the chapter by evaluating whether employer mobilization moderates the stark inequalities in civic participation that exist across Americans of different socioeconomic standing. On the one hand, employer messages do help close the gap in voter registration and political volunteering between lower income and higher income workers. But at the same time, employer mobilization exacerbates inequalities by income in who donates to political candidates and contacts their elected officials. What is more, it tends to be lower income workers who are disproportionately persuaded by employer messages to change their vote choices or stands on political issues; higher income workers are much less likely to report such persuasion. Yet lower income workers were no more likely to agree with their employers than their higher income counterparts. This introduces the possibility that lower income workers are being pressured into supporting their employers' favored stances and candidates, which tend to skew to the right and the GOP.

Workers' Perspective on Mobilization

How many workers report receiving political messages from their bosses? And how do workers perceive those messages? Turning to the worker survey, I found that about one in four American employees (or about 34 million Americans, if we extrapolate from the survey results) reported ever experiencing some form of political contact with the top managers at their main job as of spring 2015. That population is nearly the size of California, though employees who are contacted by their bosses are of course spread out all over the country. That in turn means that workers collectively represent a potent political force for lobbying legislators and changing elections. As numerous managers reminded me, every politician represents an "employee constituency."

I arrived at the overall estimate of employer mobilization by combining worker responses to two questions intended to capture the different varieties of mobilization that occur in the workplace. The first question asked about top management endorsing political candidates or parties, like the coal mining company and casino owner I mentioned in the introduction, "Do the top managers in your main job make it clear which political candidates or party they prefer?" Respondents who answered yes to this question were coded as having experienced employer mobilization. In all, 16 percent of workers responded affirmatively to this question.

A second question asked about more specific varieties of employer mobilization that had ever occurred in the workplace: "I am going to ask you about specific situations where your managers and supervisors may have contacted you about politics or political issues, such as contacting you about voting, political candidates, or public policies. Have you ever. . . ?" The pollsters then asked workers if they had received an email about politics from managers and supervisors, received a letter about politics, received a phone call about politics, seen a posting on a company website about politics, had a meeting about politics, been asked to attend an event about politics, been asked to volunteer for a political campaign, received paycheck messages about politics, seen posters or flyers about politics, or had any other contact about politics. About 14 percent of workers responded affirmatively to these more specific items.

The combined worker survey estimate of mobilization (a fourth of employees) jibes well with a 2014 nationally representative telephone survey from Allstate and the *National Journal*, which found that about a third of employed workers reported that their employer had ever been vocal about their opinions on politics and legislation.[17] Of course it is important to note that my worker survey and the Allstate–*National Journal* poll looked at whether employees had *ever* been exposed to political communications from their managers. Even setting aside the targeting that many employers do (as we saw in the last chapter), employer mobilization efforts vary from year to year as employers deal with specific policy threats or become involved in particular electoral battles.[18] There is undoubtedly a greater proportion of workers contacted during years with more policy decisions or elections at stake. Results from the 2015 national Cooperative Congressional Election Study indicate that fewer than 10 percent of American employees heard from their top managers and supervisors in that year.[19] In contrast, the 2016 version of that survey (the results of which I explore in more detail later in this chapter) indicates that the share of workers reporting political contact from their top managers and supervisors may have increased to at least 30 percent around the 2016 election.

How Employers Deliver Political Messages to Workers

About one in four American workers reports ever receiving messages from their employers. How did workers receive these communications? Figure 4.1 examines the various ways employers contacted their workers with political messages. Employers were most likely to convey political messages through company websites, posters, and emails. Letters, political events, and meetings were less common. Websites and emails are exactly the sort of contact employers reported coordinating through specialized software that can easily be targeted to a subset of workers based on predefined characteristics. The least common methods of contact included paycheck messages and phone calls. Still, these modes of contact were not entirely unheard-of. The U.S. Chamber of Commerce, for instance, produced materials in 2012 that it encouraged employers to stuff in the paycheck envelopes of their employees supporting candidates in the upcoming election.[20] According to ABC News, the Chamber said it reached "7 million members, distributing payroll stuffers, posters, and postcards for businesses to turn out employees and sway their votes." One such payroll stuffer included a newspaper clipping explaining why candidate Elizabeth Warren (now a Democratic senator from Massachusetts) was "catastrophically antibusiness."[21]

There was substantial variation in the medium of employer messages by company size. Separating workers by whether they reported working at companies either under 500 workers or with 500 or more workers (as reported by workers themselves), we see that the larger companies are much more likely to use websites, posters, and email messages. Indeed the rate of website contacting is more than twice as high for larger companies. In contrast, smaller companies were more likely to use in-person meetings. Businesses were about equally likely to deploy paycheck messages, phone calls, and recruitment at political events regardless of size. Smaller businesses, interviews reveal, are more comfortable using in-person meetings to discuss politics, and such meetings are also simply more practical than in a larger company. Larger companies, in contrast, are much more likely to rely on internal websites to communicate with their workers about politics, consistent with the survey evidence.

One important consideration for how companies deliver political messages to workers is whether workers have on-the-job access to corporate Internet and email accounts. Some employees regularly use computers to do their work (such as white-collar service workers), while others may not (say, manufacturing workers on an assembly line). Many mobilization packages offered to companies take this difference into account. In an "E2E [employer to employee political communication] Training Introduction" video produced by the Job Creators

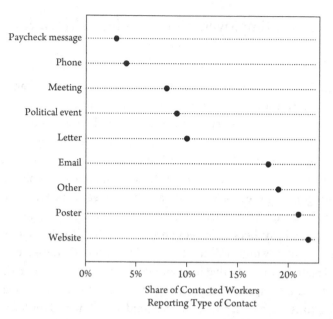

Figure 4.1 Methods of employer mobilization among contacted workers. Data from 2015 worker survey. Shares do not sum to 100 percent because workers could select more than one option. Denominator is all workers who reported employer mobilization (sample size: 273).

Network, a right-leaning business group encouraging mobilization, the narrator explains that for managers to "reach off-line employees, you just need a place to show videos, a good printer, and some imagination. Most of our E2E tools are printable, so print and share where it makes sense, like a breakroom, mailboxes, paycheck envelopes, or newsletters. Queue up videos on your laptop, head to the breakroom and hit play during some downtime, or during a staff meeting. Have the boss treat everyone to pizza, then show videos, circulate print-outs, and get employees talking."[22]

Similarly, at another large manufacturer, election mobilization involved marshaling not just content on the company's internal website and email messages but also "Why Vote?" posters, slides on the internal company TV channel, flyers, branded promotional items (such as T-shirts, Post-it note pads, stickers, and USB drives), monthly conference calls, weekly stories in the company newsletter, and on-site events with pizza—all strategies that could reach off-line workers.[23] As this training video and manufacturing business examples make clear, in-person meetings, flyers, and posters are much more important for businesses in which workers do not have regular access to email or other electronic communications. Companies can also produce online content for workers to read on their own time at home, as Menards did with the online civics and economics course their owners created (see chapter 1).

Issues Discussed in Employer Political Messages

What did employers discuss with their workers about politics? The specific question posed to workers on the survey was as follows: "What did your manager or supervisor mention to you when they contacted you about politics or political issues?" Respondents had the option of choosing from a similar set of answers as in the managerial survey, including information about registering to vote, turning out to vote, about a presidential candidate, a candidate for the U.S. House, a candidate for the U.S. Senate, a candidate for state government, a bill or policy issue, contacting a lawmaker, donating to a political candidate, or another kind of unspecified message. Figure 4.2 graphs these responses from contacted workers.

We can summarize the political intensity of employer messages that workers reported in the following way. At one end are efforts that consist of relatively nonpartisan activities, such as helping workers register to vote or turn out to vote,

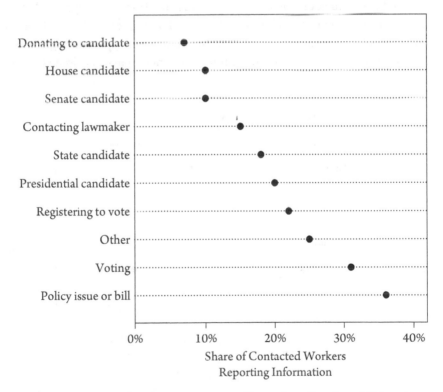

Figure 4.2 Employer political messages reported by workers. Data from 2015 worker survey. Shares do not sum to 100 percent because workers could select more than one option. Denominator is all workers who reported employer mobilization (sample size: 273).

while at the other end are more explicitly partisan activities that urge workers to support specific candidates during elections. About 11 percent of all American employees experienced get-out-the-vote mobilization that only discussed voter registration and turnout and was plainly nonpartisan. Another 6 percent experienced mobilization that discussed political issues (such as bills under debate in a legislature), but not political candidates. The final 7 percent experienced mobilization that went beyond political issues to discuss candidates.

As with the means of contact, there was also considerable variation in the type of information offered by employers by company size. Compared to smaller businesses, larger businesses were much more likely to distribute messages about policy issues, bills, and contacting legislators. Smaller businesses were more likely to discuss messages about presidential candidates. The biggest difference in this comparison is thus the much more central focus of larger companies on policy.

What kinds of policies did employers discuss with their workers? Another question tapped into this dimension by asking the following of workers: "What issues did your manager or supervisor mention to you when they contacted you about politics? Did your manager or supervisor mention . . . ?" Figure 4.3 summarizes the answers to this question, showing that employers tended to most frequently address health care, followed by education, taxes, and regulations. Workers heard least about trade and unions from their managers. Some of these

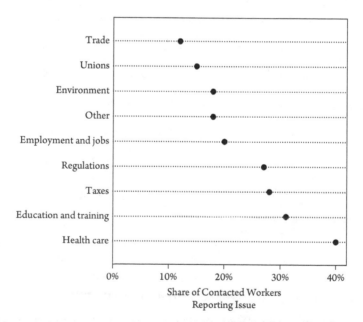

Figure 4.3 Employer political messages by issue. Data from 2015 worker survey. Shares do not sum to 100 percent because workers could select more than one option. Denominator is all workers who reported employer mobilization (sample size: 273).

differences may be due to recall effects; workers might be more likely to remember receiving messages about issues that were more prominently featured in the news around the time of the survey (such as health care reform) or that were especially memorable. A more conservative interpretation of these results would thus read them as the issues that employers included in their messages and that workers found to be most salient.

Another way of considering variation in issues discussed by employers is to divide messages by whether or not they were electorally focused. Electoral messages—those discussing candidates or parties—were much more likely to mention taxes than were nonelectoral messages. The reverse was true for messages about education and training, which were much more likely to be discussed in nonelectoral messages. Still, in practice these categories blur together, and a single electoral message from an employer might combine multiple issues. Consider the message in a pamphlet from the Job Creators Network distributed to managers during the 2012 election. That document described how GOP presidential candidate Mitt Romney supported a "flatter, simpler, fairer tax code for all Americans that will help businesses, and families to prosper," while Democratic opponent Barack Obama "would increase many types of taxes, including those on businesses that file taxes as individuals," especially through his new health care reform program.[24] That message clearly combined both health care and tax issues with particularly important implications for small businesses that would face higher taxes on the revenue they passed through the individual income tax code.

Threats of Economic Consequences in Employer Messages

A final way to divide employer messages is by whether they include threats of job loss or wage and hour cuts if particular candidates are not elected or policies are not passed, as in the case of the Murray Energy workers at the start of this chapter. Twenty percent of contacted workers—or about 7 million, extrapolating from the survey—reported that their employer had ever issued at least one such warning, responding affirmatively to the question "When your manager or supervisor discussed politics or political issues with you, did your manager or supervisor ever mention changing or cutting worker hours because of politics, mention changing or cutting jobs because of politics, or mention closing offices or plants because of politics?" These threats made workers uncomfortable: workers who received at least one threat were three times more likely to indicate that they were uncomfortable with employer messages compared to workers who did not receive threats when asked, "How comfortable or uncomfortable are you with the contact you had with your manager or supervisor about politics and political issues?"

Workers who received threats were also substantially more likely to report that they feared for their jobs. While only slightly over 50 percent of workers who did not receive threats from their employer reported concerns about their job security, 70 percent of workers who did receive threats reported such concerns. (The question was "To what extent, if at all, do you worry about the possibility of losing your main job?") This suggests that workers take economic threats about jobs and wages from their managers quite seriously. Companies too recognize the importance of economic warnings. One corporate executive overseeing political mobilization at a midwestern energy company recommended that other businesses use warnings about economic losses to motivate greater employee participation in politics, explaining that "one of the broadest incentive categories" to appeal to workers "is economic self-interest, including job security, paychecks, employee benefits, promotions, raises, bonuses, profit sharing, stock dividends and pensions. Economic interests may be manifested as fear or anticipation."[25]

Table 4.1 outlines how the incidence of economic threats varies across the topics and issues discussed by employers. Threats about the economic consequences of politics or policies were most likely in messages about political candidates (especially for the U.S. House and the presidency) and about unions and trade, and were least likely to appear in messages about state government candidates, turning out to vote, bills or policy issues, and regulations and health care.

Threats can come in a variety of forms. Sometimes employers merely remind their workers that their job is on the line in upcoming elections. The Job Creators Network has taken such a tack. In the materials the Network distributes to its members, it explains that voting "is an important way for you to not only do your civic duty, but to protect your job."[26] In other cases, managers make a more explicit link between the election of particular candidates and workers' jobs and wages. David Siegel, a timeshare mogul, sent a message to his workers before the 2012 elections warning, "The economy doesn't currently pose a threat to your job. What does threaten your job however, is another 4 years of the same Presidential administration."[27] In a similar vein, many companies have made the connection between specific policies and workers' jobs to motivate participation. When Congress was considering major legislation to address climate change in 2009 and 2010, Tesoro, a large oil processor, dispatched its CEO to tour the company's refineries to explain to workers how the legislation "could force many domestic companies"—including his own— "out of business" and

Table 4.1. **Economic Threats by Message Topics and Issues**

Type of Message	Share of Messages with Threats (%)	Issue Mentioned	Share of Messages with Threats (%)
House candidate	45	Unions	46
Presidential candidate	40	Trade	40
Contacting a legislator	39	Employment or jobs	34
Donating to a candidate	38	Taxes	29
Senate candidate	37	Environment	28
Registering to vote	32	Education/training	26
Bill or policy	27	Health care	26
Voting	27	Regulation	25
State candidate	24	Other	27
Other	25		

Data from 2015 worker survey. Denominator is all workers reporting employer mobilization and a particular topic or issue (total sample size: 273).

created a website for employees to learn about the "negative impact" the bill would have on their jobs. The website also encouraged workers to write to their lawmakers to oppose the climate legislation.[28]

More detailed examples of these threats can be found in the material that Georgia Pacific (a paper products manufacturer) and Cintas (a uniform and corporate supply company) provided to their workers during the 2012 election, which included warnings that the companies might need to lay off workers if particular politicians were not elected. Table 4.2 summarizes excerpts from both of these messages.

Employer threats and warnings pose some tricky issues from the standpoint of my research. In an ideal scenario I would know whether a worker had received some kind of warning about changes to wages, employment, or working conditions from their managers that was tied to elections or policy debates, and I would also know whether that warning was sincere, in the sense that managers actually did think there was a strong probability that their business would need to adjust operations in response to politics. (This is in contrast to empty threats managers might make to workers intended to change workers' political behavior.) Unfortunately it is difficult, if not impossible, to gather this sort

Table 4.2. **Examples of Employer Messages with Threats of Job or Wage Loss**

Cintas	*Georgia Pacific*
"The upcoming Election on November 6th is one of the most important Elections of our time.... It's important for each of our voices to be heard this Election because the decisions that are made and the policies that are set by our government impact each of us personally as individuals.... These decisions and policies could also have a significant impact on Cintas—on our ability to run our business effectively and efficiently, on our ability to attract and retain customers and on our ability to provide the level of benefits, opportunities, and development we believe our partners want, need and deserve.... According to the Supreme Court, the new health care law amounts to the single largest tax on Americans and business in history.... Under the new law, we estimate that our health care costs will increase by over $50 million, taking the total we would need to spend to provide the same level of coverage we are currently providing to $188 million.... Finally, while some government regulation is needed for all businesses, the current economic uncertainty faced by many of our customers prevents them (and Cintas) from growing in the way we would like. The over-regulation that business is facing today from the various administrative agencies ... is suffocating many companies. This uncertainty felt by many of our customers about their ability to run and grow their businesses prevents them from adding jobs which hurts our ability to grow and add jobs." (Quoted in Jamieson 2012.)	"While we are typically told before each Presidential election that it is important and historic, I believe the upcoming election will determine what kind of America future generations will inherit.... If we elect candidates who want to spend hundreds of billions in borrowed money on costly new subsidies for a few favored cronies, put unprecedented regulatory burdens on businesses, prevent or delay important new construction projects, and excessively hinder free trade, then many of our more than 50,000 U.S. employees and contractors may suffer the consequences, including higher gasoline prices, runaway inflation, and other ills." (Quoted in Elk 2012b.)

of information, even if I were able to survey both workers and their managers simultaneously. Business decisions about layoffs and changes to workers' wages and working conditions are inevitably driven by a mix of factors, and it would be hard to pin down the contribution of any single change in policy on executives' thinking about labor policies.

In addition managers often have a strong incentive to *overstate* the role of politics in their decision-making as a bargaining strategy with policymakers.[29] Dramatizing the potential effects of policy on unemployment or wage cuts can help managers gain leverage in negotiations over legislation, echoing the lesson from Charles Lindblom about the "structural power of business" I quoted in chapter 1. For instance, during deliberations over national health reform in 2009 and 2010 a number of employers issued dire predictions that they would be forced to drastically cut health care benefits in a bid to reduce their obligation to provide coverage to workers or pay a fine. Yet, as a *New York Times* analysis uncovered six years after the passage of the reform law, those predictions were generally wrong. Most companies, and especially big employers, have continued offering health insurance to their workers.[30] Similarly the timeshare mogul in Florida who threatened layoffs if Obama were reelected in 2012 ended up giving his workers across-the-board raises in 2015 after experiencing "the best year" in the company's history, despite the gloomy predictions of the effect of Obama's policies on the economy.[31]

To be sure, there are some clear-cut cases of businesses whose economic success is directly tied to public policy. Coal-fired power plants, for instance, are directly threatened by environmental regulations that tighten standards on their carbon dioxide emissions. On the other side of the environmental policy debate, wind energy producers rely heavily on generous federal tax credits to lower the cost of constructing and operating wind turbines, and as a result the wind industry actively mobilizes its employees to support renewal of that tax credit. The expiration of those credits would deal a serious blow to the financial viability of wind energy.

From the perspective of my analysis, however, distinctions about the accuracy and sincerity of the threats, warnings, or predictions that employers might make to workers about politics are somewhat beside the point. Regardless of the accuracy or sincerity of the threats, what matters is the fact that workers recognize that employers are uniquely positioned to act on those predictions. As long as there is a chance that an employer might act on those threats, these messages ought to weigh heavily on the minds of employees. The best parallel is to the threats made during union drives: even though most of the time employers do not end up closing plants, stores, or factories after successful union elections, the mere mention of those threats is often enough to sway workers into opposing the union, especially when made in concert with other threats of wage or benefit cuts.[32] Employer warnings about politics can be similarly powerful.

Worker Agreement and Comfort
with Employer Messages

Having laid out the descriptive features of employer political recruitment, I turn to workers' subjective perceptions of managers' messages. Did workers agree with employer messages, or were they generally opposed to the information? I found that employees were divided over whether they agreed with their employers' political material: about 47 percent of workers contacted by their bosses reported that they agreed with the messages, while the remaining workers either had no opinion (28 percent) or disagreed (25 percent; the exact wording of the question was "How much did you agree or disagree with the messages that your manager or supervisor provided to you about politics or political issues?" and workers selected from a 5-point scale of agreement).

Workers were similarly divided over whether or not they felt comfortable with managers' messages: 55 percent reported that they were either very comfortable or somewhat comfortable with their employers' political recruitment efforts; 15 percent were very or somewhat uncomfortable; and 29 percent had no opinion. (The exact wording of the question was "How comfortable or uncomfortable are you with the contact you had with your manager or supervisor about politics and political issues?" and workers selected from a 5-point scale of comfort.) Workers found employer messages about donating to candidates to be least comfortable, and were most comfortable with requests to contact legislators. Information about political candidates and voter registration and turnout fell somewhere between these extremes. Looking across issues, workers found messages about unions and employment and jobs (such as the minimum wage) to be least comfortable, and those about trade and the environment to be most comfortable.

These patterns may reflect the fact that trade policy frequently unites the interests of managers and their employees, as do environmental regulations that potentially impose costs on companies. In contrast, unions and labor regulations (such as the minimum wage) more clearly divide the interests of workers and management and therefore could make workers more uncomfortable. Extrapolating broadly, I estimate that some 42 percent of all the workers who were contacted by employers received messages that we might think united the natural economic interests of workers and managers. I arrived at this estimate by combining workers who received messages about the environment, trade, and education and training—three areas where we might think policies that were good for the company would be largely good for individual workers too (at least from a purely economic perspective). These are the issues that chemical manufacturer DuPont, for instance, argues are ones that workers too should "care about," along with managers: "Issues that have an impact on the way DuPont conducts its business and the company's profitability have a direct impact on all our shareholders, including DuPont employees, retirees, and their families. . . . DuPont employees and retirees reap the benefits of a successful company."[33]

The Ideological Orientation of Employer Messages

According to the worker survey, 43 percent of employees reported that their employers' messages were ideologically conservative and 27 percent reported liberal messages (the remaining workers reported ideologically moderate messages). (The exact wording was "When your manager or supervisor contacted you about political issues, what were the political views of your manager or supervisor's message?" and workers could choose from a 5-point scale of political ideology.) Most workers received messages that differed from their own personal ideology. Only 30 percent of contacted workers received messages that exactly matched their ideology on the same 5-point scale. About 66 percent of contacted workers, in contrast, received messages that differed from their own position; that is, liberal workers who received conservative messages, conservative workers who received liberal messages, and moderate workers who received either liberal or conservative messages. Workers were most likely to rate messages about health care as conservative and to rate messages about education and training as being relatively more liberal.

Employers' partisan slants were similarly conservative. When employees reported that their employer had a favored party, it was much more likely to be the Republicans rather than the Democrats. (The exact wording of the question was "Were the political candidates discussed by your manager or supervisor mostly Democrats, mostly Republicans, or were the political candidates evenly divided between the two parties?" Respondents chose from options that included all Democrats, mostly Democrats, evenly split between the parties, mostly Republicans, or all Republicans.)

Worker Responses to Employer Messages

Employers differ greatly in how they deliver messages to workers, the content of those messages, and how their workers perceive and interpret those messages. But what do all of these communications add up to? Did employees report that these messages mattered to their political attitudes and decisions? To begin to answer this question, the worker survey asked respondents whether employer messages influenced a range of their behaviors and attitudes, specifically, "Did the political information you received from your manager or supervisor change your mind about politics or voting?", and gave workers the following choices to answer that question: "made you more likely to" register to vote, turn out to vote, vote for a particular candidate, volunteer for a political campaign, change your mind about a particular issue, contact a lawmaker about an issue, donate to a political candidate, or any other effect not previously specified. Figure 4.4 summarizes the responses to this question. In all, nearly half of contacted workers (47 percent) reported that employer messages changed at least one of these political practices or beliefs.

Workers were most likely to report that employer political messages made them more likely to turn out to vote or to register to vote (32 percent and 24 percent of contacted workers reported these effects, respectively). Fifteen percent of contacted workers reported that their bosses' political messages made them more likely to vote for an employer's favored candidate, and another 15 percent reported that the message made them more likely to write to or call a legislator about a policy issue on behalf of an employer. Although these self-reports do not provide direct evidence of an effect of employer messages on political behavior

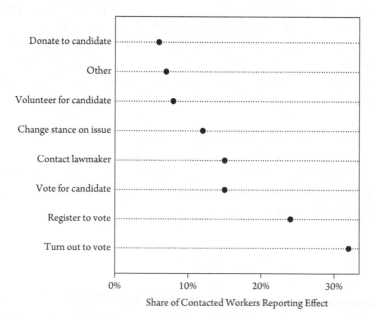

Figure 4.4 Self-reported effects of employer mobilization on worker political behaviors. Data from 2015 worker survey. Shares do not sum to 100 percent because workers could select more than one option. Denominator is all workers who reported employer mobilization (sample size: 273).

on their own, they do indicate that a number of contacted workers perceive that employer messages are shaping the ways they are thinking about politics. (I conduct a more rigorous test of these effects in part II.)

Most of the potential effects reported in Figure 4.4 are relatively straightforward; we can easily imagine how an employer's political message might push a worker to register or turn out to vote, or even to change his or her support for a candidate. But what do political volunteering requests look like in practice? One example comes from the Associated General Contractors of America (AGC), the national trade group representing general contractors. AGC actively encourages its member businesses to deploy mobilization, and one especially promoted activity is the "meet and greet" event with aspiring or elected officials.[34] As the AGC describes it, "Developing relationships with a candidate can be a real help in influencing future public policy decisions. Since a strong personal relationship with policymakers is essential to successful grassroots advocacy, hosting such an event is an effective tool in building long-term relationships."[35] One benefit construction companies and contractors can offer politicians, AGC notes, is the opportunity to ask for support from workers and to leave behind information on how a worker can contribute to or volunteer for a campaign.

Contrasting Unions and Employers as Political Recruiters

How distinctive are employers as political recruiters? In chapter 6 I directly compare the effectiveness of union, party, and employer appeals on workers' political behaviors. For now, we can compare employers to the other major political actor in the workplace—unions—by asking workers about their perceptions of the effect of union and employer messages. Despite also mobilizing workers in their identity as employees, union political contact is quite different from employer mobilization. About 12 percent of employees reported ever experiencing political contact from a labor union in their workplace, or about half the share of employees who reported ever receiving political messages from their employers. It is clear from this comparison that employer voices far outweigh labor voices at work, which should come as no surprise given the dramatically weakened position of labor in the U.S. economy. The share of wage and salary workers participating in unions steadily declined, from 24 percent in 1973 to 11 percent in 2016, according to the Current Population Survey.

Workers responded to labor messages differently from employer messages. Recall that in all, 47 percent of workers who received messages from their employers reported that those messages changed at least one of their political behaviors. By comparison, a slightly greater share—54 percent—of workers who received messages from a union reported that they had been affected by labor communications. Still, given that far fewer workers received labor messages than received employer messages, the overall number of workers affected by union messages was much lower. About 12 percent of all American employees (or perhaps some 17 million Americans, extrapolating from the survey results) were affected by employer messages, while only 6 percent of employees (or about 9 million Americans) reported an effect from labor messages.

Aside from the overall differences in the behavioral effects reported by workers, there were also striking contrasts between the sort of effects associated with employer and labor messages. Figure 4.5 compares workers' self-reports of the effect of either employer or labor messages on political behaviors and attitudes. Union messages were much more likely than employer messages to spur workers to contact their legislators: 34 percent of union message recipients reported such an effect, compared to only 15 percent of employer message recipients. Union messages were also more likely to change workers' vote choices: 24 percent of union message recipients reported an effect on vote choice, while the comparable share for employer messages was only 15 percent. One area where employers appeared to be more effective than unions, at least according to workers' self-reports, was voter registration: 24 percent of employer message recipients

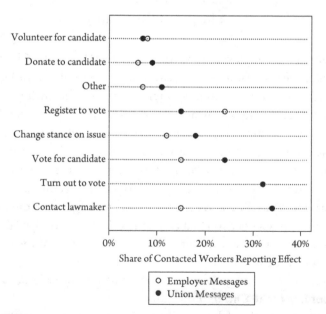

Figure 4.5 Self-reported effects of employer and union messages. Data from 2015 worker survey. Denominator is all workers reporting either employer mobilization or labor mobilization (employer messages sample size: 273; union messages sample size: 75).

reported that they were more likely to register to vote as a result of employer mobilization, compared to only 15 percent for union mobilization targets. The fact that unions are less effective with voter registration likely reflects the fact that union members are already much more likely to be registered to vote than nonmembers, so there is not much more that labor unions can do to affect this behavior.[36]

Coordination between Labor and Employer Mobilization

I have described union and employer messages as if they are conducted separately from one another. But in some cases employers do coordinate with unions on political mobilization efforts. This is especially true for regulatory and trade issues. For instance, a manager at a railroad company reported working closely with his industry's union on "economic regulatory issues, passenger issues . . . and railroad retirement and unemployment insurance programs." The railroad company and the union also collaborated on anything that might endanger the economic health of the industry. "It's basically self-preservation," explained the executive. Similarly a major metal manufacturer, also heavily unionized, reported working with the union on safety issues and other regulatory changes that brought together the interests of workers and employers.

In general, however, interview evidence suggests that corporate coordination with unions was relatively uncommon, even in businesses with a substantial union presence. In fact one government affairs executive at a heavily unionized telecommunications firm told me he thought that collaboration with the union on political mobilization went against the union's collective bargaining agreement. After checking with the union, I discovered collaboration was not prohibited, but the fact that the top government affairs executive at the company believed it to be so is revealing, indicating that coordination is simply not something that was on his radar.

The worker survey also provides evidence that most workers are not exposed to coordinated messages from employers and unions. Most workers who reported union mobilization (68 percent) did not also report employer mobilization. In fact the worker survey results suggest that unionized workers were more likely than non-unionized workers to receive anti-union messages. These results indicate that unionized businesses are more likely to be sending conservative messages to their workers criticizing the labor movement rather than collaborating with unions.

Not only can managers send out political messages that go against union efforts, but companies also have the legal right to squelch any labor political recruitment that is not directly relevant to workplace issues. Although employee on-the-job mobilization related to working conditions, wages, and employment is shielded against employer retaliation by federal labor law, no similar protection exists for more general political messages not pertaining to the workplace. As one labor law expert has explained, "if a union wanted to hand out political materials in the workplace not directly relevant to the workers' interests—such as providing a list of candidates to support in the elections—the employer has the right to ban that material." Employers can "even prohibit its distribution on lunch breaks or after shifts, because by law it's the company's private property."[37] Far from being equal partners, most employers and unions keep each other's mobilization at arm's length.

Political Monitoring, Pressure, and Coercion at Work

One of the concerns looming behind employer mobilization is whether managers are using implicit or explicit threats of economic retaliation to spur workers to participate in politics in certain ways. The example of Murray Energy is one extreme case of such pressure, with workers reporting that their managers were closely tracking their participation in company-sponsored political requests and then threatening to punish defiant employees. How common is such monitoring and pressure?

Unfortunately my 2015 worker survey did not ask respondents about these aspects of employer mobilization. But a subsequent battery of questions, which I fielded on the 2016 CCES, did ask employees about precisely these issues. I asked non-self-employed workers—the same population I targeted for my 2015 telephone survey—about the following issues (the exact survey question wording appears in parentheses next to each item):

- Whether employees thought their employers could monitor their political choices and actions. ("How likely is it that your main employer can track your political views and actions, such as keeping track of whether you voted or which candidates you support?" Responses: "very likely," "somewhat likely," "somewhat unlikely," "very unlikely," and "don't know.")
- Whether employees said their employer had actually discovered something about their political choices. ("Has a manager or supervisor at your main job ever discovered whether you voted or which candidates you support? Check all that apply." Responses: "discovered whether I voted," "discovered which candidates I support," and "discovered something else about my politics.")
- Whether employees thought their employer might punish them for their political views or actions. ("How likely is it that you might miss out on

opportunities for advancement or promotion at your main job because of your political views or actions, including which candidates you support?" Responses: "very likely," "somewhat likely," "somewhat unlikely," "very unlikely," and "don't know.")

• Whether employees said their employer had actually punished workers for their political views or actions. ("As far as you can remember, have any of the following things happened to someone at your main job in part because of his or her political views or actions? Check all that apply." Responses: "someone was fired," "someone missed out on a promotion," and "someone was treated unfairly.")

Figure 4.6 plots the top-line responses to each of these items, expressed as a proportion of all non-self-employed workers. Looking first at employer monitoring, 35 percent of workers perceived the possibility of at least some employer surveillance; these workers said that monitoring was "very likely" or "somewhat likely" or that they did not know one way or another. (This estimate is 21 percent excluding workers who said they did not know.) A nearly identical proportion of workers—39 percent —said their employer had actually discovered their political actions or beliefs in the past. In chapter 3 I showed that employers often tracked the political participation of their workers in order to establish whether workers followed through on their political requests. It thus appears that many workers do in fact recognize the possibility of this sort of tracking and that their employers have indeed discerned their political views and actions. Though it is perhaps surprising—and worrisome—that so many employees doubt the secrecy of their votes in the workplace, my results are consistent with past polling that indicates that over 40 percent of Americans believe it would

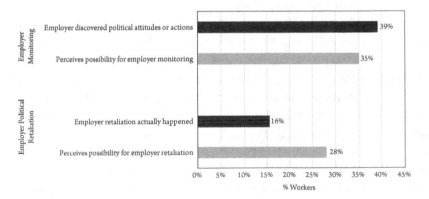

Figure 4.6 Workers reporting perceptions and actual occurrences of employer political monitoring and political retaliation. Data from 2016 CCES survey. Denominator is non-self-employed workers (sample size: 459).

not be difficult for "politicians, union officials, or the people you work for to find out who you voted for, even if you told no one," and that over 10 percent of Americans reported that "a politician, union official, or someone you work for" had "ever found out who you voted for" because of imperfections or errors in the voting process.[38]

Of course employer monitoring on its own is benign: employers might simply be using this information to assess the effectiveness of their campaigns. What makes employer mobilization coupled with close monitoring more concerning is the possibility that employers would punish workers for failing to participate—or participating in ways contrary to managerial preferences. Figure 4.6 indicates that 28 percent of workers perceived that they might miss out on a promotion or other possibility for advancement because of their political views or actions. (This is the proportion of workers reporting it was "very likely," "somewhat likely," or that they did not know one way or another.) Though lower than the proportion of workers who said that monitoring might be possible, it is still striking that so many employees think their political views and actions could affect their treatment at work by their managers.

Perhaps even more striking—and worrying from the perspective of employer mobilization—16 percent of workers said that political retaliation *had in fact occurred in their workplace.* That is, someone at their job was treated unfairly, missed out on a promotion, or was fired as a result of political views or actions. Combining workers who perceived the possibility of employer political retaliation with those who had actually seen such backlash at their jobs, we can say that a full 34 percent of employees might be subject to employer political pressure one way or another.

Figure 4.7 zooms into the actual instances of employer monitoring and retaliation that workers reported in the survey. Looking first at monitoring, we see that about equal proportions—just shy of 20 percent of all workers—reported that their employers had discovered whether they voted at all and for which candidates. Thus for a nontrivial proportion of the American labor force, there is not actually a secret ballot—at least at work. A much lower proportion of workers (just 6 percent) reported that their employers had discovered some other aspect of their political participation. Turning next to employer retaliation, we see that roughly similar proportions of workers—about 5 to 7 percent—reported each of three employer actions punishing workers for political views or behaviors: firing workers, passing workers over for a promotion, or treating workers in an otherwise unfair manner. Together these responses, totaling 16 percent of the employed labor force, represent the most troubling aspects of employer mobilization, raising the worry that workers are being pressured into toeing their company's political line and thus sacrificing their own political autonomy.

It is important to consider the fact that the full ramifications of an employer retaliating against an employee for political views or actions go well beyond the

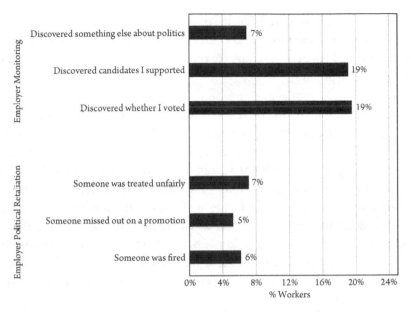

Figure 4.7 Workers reporting actual occurrences of employer political monitoring and political retaliation. Data from 2016 CCES survey. Denominator is non-self-employed workers (sample size: 459).

individual worker who was punished. As with the example of Murray Energy, the punishment or dismissal of even a single employee for political reasons sends a strong message to the remaining employees to get with an employer's agenda—or leave the company altogether. Indeed the mere suggestion of economic consequences for incorrect political choices might be enough to convince wavering employees to support the company's political program, especially if employees perceive the potential for monitoring, as we saw earlier. It is likely no coincidence, then, that 63 percent of employees who perceive the potential for economic retaliation at their job also perceive the possibility of employer monitoring. (Contrast that figure with just 24 percent of employees who did not perceive the possibility of economic retaliation.) Monitoring and the threat of retaliation, then, tend to go hand in hand.

Does Employer Mobilization Moderate Civic Inequalities?

The final issue I consider in this chapter is how employer political mobilization changes the landscape of civic participation in the United States. Extensive past work in political science has shown that lower income and lower educated workers are much less likely to participate in politics in nearly every way, from voting to donating to campaigns to following political news.[39] These inequalities in participation, in turn, are thought to contribute to inequalities in representation, since politicians have few incentives to represent citizens who do not make their voices heard in politics.[40]

Are employer messages—and worker responses to those messages—exacerbating or moderating these civic inequalities? One way of answering this question is to examine income differences in who responds to employer messages. If we see a negative relationship, with lower income individuals more likely to change their behavior as a result of employer mobilization, that would suggest employer messages are mitigating income disparities in participation, pulling lower income individuals into politics. On the other hand, if there is no relationship between responses to employer messages and income, then we might think employer messages do not do much to reduce civic gaps by class. And a third possibility is that it is only the most advantaged workers who are responding to employer requests for participation, worsening income inequalities in civic participation.

Figure 4.8 begins to answer this question by considering the income gap in worker responses to employer messages, returning to the 2015 worker survey data. Each bar shows the share of workers in each of four income quartiles who

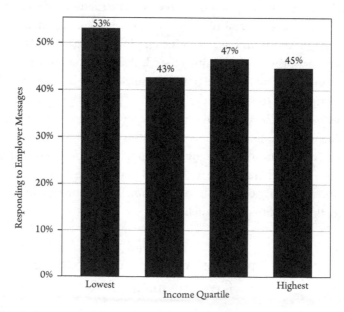

Figure 4.8 Worker responses to employer messages by income quartile. Figure shows the share of each income quartile responding to employer messages (i.e., reporting an effect). Data from 2015 worker survey. Denominator is all workers who received employer messages by quartile. Income is measured by total family income (sample size: 249).

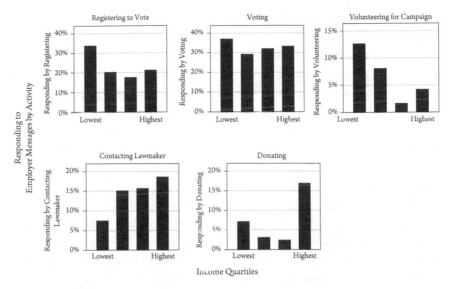

Figure 4.9 Worker responses to employer messages by income quartile for each political activity. Data from 2015 worker survey. Figure shows the share of each income quartile responding to employer messages by political activity. Denominator is all workers who received employer messages by quartile. Income is measured by total family income (sample size: 249).

responded to employer messages. There is not much of a pattern across income groups. Workers in the lowest income quartile (with family incomes averaging about $25,000 to $30,000) had a slightly higher rate of response than other quartiles, but the relationship is not a strong one. (The highest quartile represents families averaging incomes over $150,000.) At least in the aggregate, then, employer messages are not moderating civic inequalities—but nor are employer messages increasing them.

The picture changes substantially when we turn to income gaps in specific political activities, as in Figure 4.9. Each panel shows the relationship between income (in quartiles, as before) and a specific political response to employer messages. Lower income workers were far more likely than higher income workers to respond to employer messages by engaging in two of the activities: registering to vote and volunteering for political causes. Employer messages thus appear to reduce inequalities in participation for these political behaviors, disproportionately encouraging lower income workers to register and turn out for political causes. The relationship is especially striking for political volunteering. It is likely that higher income workers were already volunteering and registering at very high rates even without employer messages, tempering the effects that employer mobilization could have on these groups.

But lower income workers were not universally more likely to respond to employer messages. Workers with the highest family incomes were substantially more likely than workers with the lowest incomes to respond to employer messages by contacting their lawmakers and donating to political campaigns (though these findings are less certain than those for volunteering and registering). The difference was particularly large for legislative contacting. For these activities, then, employer messages were exacerbating the existing tendency of wealthier workers to participate more than poorer workers. And in the case of voting in general, there were no differences at all in responses to employer messages by income.

The cross-cutting effects of employer messages by income thus make it difficult to take away a single message about the implications of employer mobilization for civic inequalities. While these messages reduce income gaps in some areas of political life, especially volunteering, they reinforce gaps for other activities, like legislative contacting. A further complication of this analysis is that it does not consider *for whom* workers are casting their ballots or which issues and candidates workers are supporting as a result of employer mobilization. I address this question in Figure 4.10, which examines differences by income in whether workers reported changing their vote choice or changing their stance on an issue as a result of employer messages. In both cases we can clearly see very sharp income differences. Lower income workers are more likely than higher income workers to report that they changed their preferences and attitudes. In

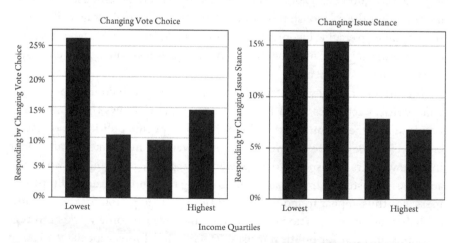

Figure 4.10 Worker responses to employer messages by income quartile, political persuasion. Data from 2015 worker survey. Figure shows the share of each income quartile responding to employer messages by type of political persuasion (changing vote choice or issue stance). Denominator is all workers who received employer messages by quartile. Income is measured by total family income (sample size: 249).

both cases workers in the lowest quartile were around twice as likely as those in the highest quartile to report changing their political positions as a result of employer messages.

Is the disproportionate effect of employer messages on lower income citizens indicative of greater support for employer messages among poorer Americans? To the extent that I can answer this question with the existing survey data, it seems the answer is no. Poorer workers were no more likely to report agreeing with their employer's political stances compared to wealthier workers, and if anything, wealthier workers were slightly *more* likely to agree with their bosses, as reported in Figure 4.11.

Lower income workers were more likely to change their vote choices and issue stances to match their employers. Were these mostly liberal workers changing to conservative positions, or vice versa? Figure 4.12 shows the share of workers who reported changing their issue or candidate support in each quartile that were either liberal workers receiving conservative messages from their bosses or conservative workers receiving liberal messages. (The remaining category, which I do not plot, consists of workers who received messages that were aligned with their ideology, such as liberal workers receiving liberal messages.) Across the bottom three income quartiles it was much more likely

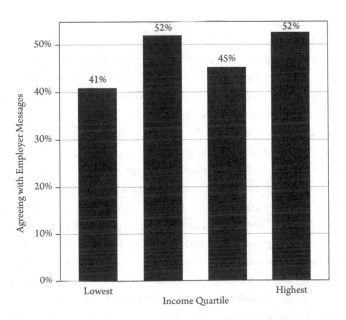

Figure 4.11 Share of workers agreeing with employer messages by income quartile. Data from 2015 worker survey. Figure shows the share of each income quartile agreeing with employer message. Denominator is all workers who received employer messages by quartile. Income is measured by total family income (sample size: 249).

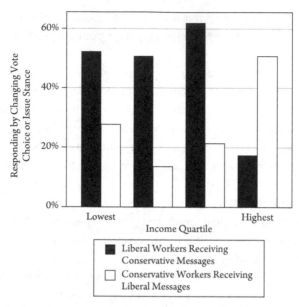

Figure 4.12 Ideological cross-pressures from employer messages by income quartile. Data from 2015 worker survey. Figure shows the share of each income quartile who reported changing their vote choice or issue stance and who were either liberal workers receiving conservative messages (solid black bars) or conservative workers receiving liberal messages (hollow bars). Income is measured by total family income (sample size: 249).

to be left-leaning workers who reported receiving—and subsequently switching to—conservative positions than it was conservative workers switching to liberal positions. It was only among the wealthiest workers that we were more likely to see conservatives switching to liberal positions.

The considerable persuasion of lower income workers to conservative and Republican stances raises potentially worrisome questions. Should we think about these persuasion effects for lower income workers as closing inequalities in political knowledge and participation? Or should we be concerned that the new political activities and preferences of lower income workers are not reflective of workers' "true" preferences or self-interests? These issues harken back to older debates in political science and sociology about the distribution of political power I described in chapter 1, in which some scholars argued that elites in society had the power to change the preferences of citizens to go against their own self-interest, much like the concept of false consciousness.[41]

One way of pushing forward with this issue is to return to the 2016 CCES data to see if lower income workers are more concerned about political retaliation than are higher income workers. If lower income workers are no more likely to fear political pressure from their bosses than are higher income workers, then we might be less concerned that lower income workers are being coerced into supporting their employers' positions against their interests. But if lower income workers fear punishment from their employers more than their higher income counterparts do, then we would have stronger reasons to think that poorer workers are being pressured into changing their political stances and practices against their self-interest.

Figure 4.13 evaluates this question and shows that worries of political retaliation at work are much more prevalent among lower income workers than higher income workers. (I divide workers, as in the telephone survey, into four equal-size groups based on their self-reported family income.) The figure plots workers who either reported the possibility of political retaliation from their managers or who said they had actually witnessed such retaliation.

There is a strong negative relationship between family income and the proportion of workers reporting the possibility of political retaliation at their jobs. About 50 percent of all workers in the lowest income quartile either reported a concern about retaliation or said that such retaliation had happened before. That proportion fell to 40 percent of workers in the second quartile, 31 percent in the third quartile, and just 26 percent in the highest income quartile.

Figure 4.13 suggests that lower income workers might be much more likely to be pressured by their employers into changing their political preferences and

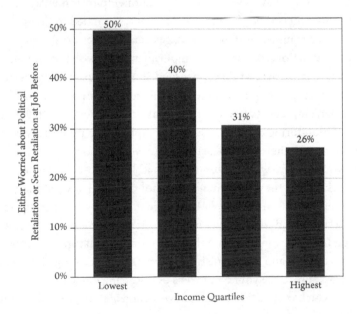

Figure 4.13 Workers reporting perception or actual occurrence of employer political retaliation at their job by income quartile. Data from 2016 CCES. Income is measured by total family income (sample size: 495).

practices than are higher income workers, raising the concern that the shifts from left to right I identified in Figure 4.12 might represent coercion just as much as persuasion. Ultimately, however, the survey evidence I have presented cannot adjudicate between these very different conclusions, which turn on how one defines workers' self-interest—an impossible task to do in an objective manner. And some skeptical readers might wonder if the low-income workers who are indicating large effects of employer messages are simply reporting "nonattitudes"; that is, employer messages did not really change workers' preferences so much as simply introduce a transient consideration that workers pulled from the top of their heads when queried by pollsters.[42] Still, the fact that lower income workers are no more likely than higher income workers to report agreeing with their employers and yet report changing their behavior to match the conservative positions espoused by their bosses strongly suggests that economically vulnerable workers may be pursuing right-leaning stances with which they disagree in order to hold on to their employment and wages.

Turning Americans into Employee Voters

Drawing on original surveys of workers, this chapter has complemented the picture of employer mobilization I provided from the perspective of managers in chapter 3. We have seen the prevalence of employer messages, as well as the forms those messages take and how workers responded to them. At least by workers' own accounts, employer messages can be a powerful source of political beliefs and actions. Yet even as employer messages shape worker political behavior, there are reasons to be concerned about some—though certainly not all—efforts at employer political outreach. A significant proportion of workers, nearly 40 percent, reports that their political choices are not actually private at work. That monitoring opens the door for employers to potentially reward and punish workers for their political actions, and we saw that nearly a third (28 percent) of workers were worried about just that. Even more distressingly, 16 percent of workers said they had actually seen political retaliation at their jobs.

Those perceptions of privacy, or lack thereof, should make a big difference in how workers respond to employer messages. If you think your bosses are keeping tabs on how you vote, whose political campaigns you support, or which lawmakers you contact and may punish you for making the wrong choices, you will likely feel pressure to toe your employer's political line much more closely than if you believe you have political privacy at work and are not worried about potential retaliation.

I also showed that it is difficult to come to a clear conclusion about how employer mobilization shapes civic inequality. While employer messages close some gaps in political participation by income—such as for volunteering—employer messages reinforce other inequalities. We also saw that it tended to be lower income Americans who were most likely to have their preferences and stances changed by managers and that this persuasion had a heavily conservative and Republican slant. When business associations and companies talk about turning Americans into "employee voters"—Americans who see their political interests through the lens of their workplace—it tends to produce voters who favor the causes most closely associated with the GOP and the conservative movement.

This raised other thorny issues about whether workers were becoming more informed, or whether employer contacting is convincing poorer workers to oppose their own interests and support corporate-favored causes and candidates, potentially because of the fear of economic retaliation. Available evidence points to the latter, more pessimistic conclusion, given that lower income workers were no more likely to agree with their employers than were higher income workers and that lower income workers were also much more concerned about political retaliation than their higher income counterparts. But ultimately, regardless of which of these assessments holds, it remains the case that employer mobilization helps companies to obtain concrete benefits from public policy and politics, as we will see in part II. For now, I turn to the question of how employer mobilization has changed over time—and why we are in a period when mobilization is an increasingly appealing strategy for corporate managers.

5

The Return of Employer
Mobilization to American Politics

When I finished my first surveys of employer mobilization, I met with one of the leading historians of American elections, Alex Keyssar, to discuss my results. Keyssar's reaction to my finding that employers were trying to change the political behavior of their workers was: What else is new? Employers, Keyssar reminded me, had engaged in such practices since early elections in the United States. And had I heard of a man named Lemuel Boulware, he asked?

A generation ago, General Electric was not just bringing good ideas to life. The company was also investing heavily in bringing conservative, pro-business ideas to their employees, thanks to the relentless vision of a corporate political guru by the name of Lemuel Boulware.[1] Boulware served as VP of labor and community relations for GE from 1956 to 1961, and during that period he launched a huge campaign to inspire support for the free market across the company's nearly 200,000-person workforce.

The face of that campaign was a charming movie actor named Ronald Reagan. Boulware hired Reagan to barnstorm the country, giving speeches to GE employees to foster a greater sense of corporate community and to promote the virtues of the free market and the evils of government spending and the labor movement. The time Reagan spent at GE was a smashing success for the company, as workers and their families clamored for more programming with the popular actor. Reagan's service at the company was also critical to building a national profile for his later political career. Despite its achievements, GE's free-market evangelism was unusual, as employer mobilization was relatively limited during that era. "Few other companies during the 1950s made such a radical attempt to shape a political corporate culture," noted historian Kim Phillips-Fein in an extensive study of the GE program.[2]

Although the company's aggressive political efforts were not recognized by its corporate contemporaries in the 1950s, nearly six decades later, Reagan's GE advocacy was being held up as a model for other businesses to follow. At one recent annual gathering of Americans for Prosperity, a libertarian grassroots advocacy group, a speaker took to the stage to remind the gathered crowd of conservative activists that Reagan regularly promoted free-market economics across GE's workforce and that companies now had the tools—and the obligation—to do the same.[3] Managers, the speaker argued, should run courses for their workers on the importance of the free-market system, just as Reagan did.

One executive of a Wisconsin-based manufacturer then described to the crowd how well a Reagan-inspired economics curriculum had worked at his own company, saying that the material had helped his employees to understand the dangers of union organization, cap-and-trade legislation to address climate change, and Obamacare. According to the publisher of the curriculum, managers "need to help [employees] to be able to sift through all that they are hearing and help them to discern the truth. So that when they hear 'Oh yeah, you know, higher taxes will help provide benefits'—well where do the taxes come from?... Do they stop to think that profits aren't bad? That profits are necessary to run a business and provide jobs?... Why are we demonizing the people that have been successful?"[4] Another employer has said that he is "thankful" for the curriculum since, "as [a] responsible employer," he could "no longer stand on the sidelines while the very foundations that made our country great—free enterprise, entrepreneurship, and the ability to take risks for greater rewards are under attack." Having this program helped him to educate his employees so that they would become "informed voters." The wealthy industrialists Charles and David Koch, who founded Americans for Prosperity, now make it a point to encourage hundreds of their fellow businessmen to educate workers on the benefits of the free market and the costs of government intervention at their annual political seminars as well.[5]

How did we get from early elections in the United States, where electoral coercion (including coercion by employers) was common, to the 1950s, when GE was practically alone in its workplace political education efforts, to the present day, when Reagan-style free-market evangelizing has become standard practice for many companies? This chapter offers a brief overview of the history of employer mobilization, focusing especially closely on its return to the American political scene in recent decades. My presentation is necessarily limited by the fact that I lack historical data on the prevalence of employer mobilization. Instead I turn to secondhand sources, including newspaper accounts and business association records, to pin down just how mobilization efforts have changed over time.

Shifts in the law, technology, corporate culture, and employer-employee relations form an important basis for explaining why employer mobilization has become a more frequent corporate practice in recent years after a notable absence from American politics throughout the mid-twentieth century. Yet, independently of those long-run shifts, I also identify a central role for business associations in the emergence of employer mobilization. If those economic, legal, and political shifts were necessary conditions to lay the groundwork for employer mobilization as a strategy that companies could again pursue, business associations were the decisive actors responsible for convincing managers that this new strategy was both legal and desirable. Given that top corporate managers are often risk-averse and cautious in adopting new strategies, savvy business associations were essential in educating companies about the importance of mobilization and the ways managers could recruit their workers into politics without running afoul of campaign finance law.

A Brief Sketch of Employer Mobilization throughout American History

Industrialization of the U.S. economy transformed the relationship between labor and management. Large corporate conglomerates came to dominate the social and economic lives of many American cities, with a single employer responsible for the economic livelihood of an entire community. "Big railroad systems, Big industrial trusts, Big public service companies; and as instruments of these Big banks and Big trust companies," summed up the progressive legal luminary Louis D. Brandeis in a chapter titled "The Curse of Bigness."[6] That "bigness" gave corporate managers a great deal of leverage to dictate the behavior of their workers, leverage that some owners used during election time.[7] During the 1896 presidential election between pro-business Republican William McKinley and populist William Jennings Bryan, for instance, several newspapers described efforts by business owners to convince their communities of the economic imperative to vote Republican. *The Public*, a progressive weekly, wrote of a manager at one large company in Cadillac, Michigan, who gathered his employees shortly before the election and gave the following speech: "Now, I am not here to talk politics. . . . We have no desire nor right to interfere with any man's politics. . . . [But here] are orders enough to run our mills all Winter. . . . If you will look at them you will see that every order is contingent on McKinley's election. Now then, we haven't got any business in sight if Bryan is elected, and we will be forced to shut down. That's all I've got to say."[8] The reporter alleged that the threat of lost sales made the difference in tilting an otherwise populist constituency of blue-collar workers for the GOP. When Bryan ran for the presidency in 1908 against Republican William Taft, *The Public* again documented similar practices, with managers reminding workers that business and employment would be hurt if Bryan were elected.[9]

Variations on these coercive practices were traced throughout other company towns as well. John Fitch, a sociologist who studied Pittsburgh-area steel towns at the turn of the twentieth century, wrote that he was repeatedly "told that workmen have been discharged . . . for refusing to vote the way the company wishes."[10] But Fitch also found that in many other cases outright threats were unnecessary because the workers were already so dependent on their employers for their economic livelihood that they would have voted for company-favored candidates anyway.[11] Employer pressure extended beyond manufacturing towns. In *The Right to Vote*, Keyssar recounts an episode from the 1914 elections in which Colorado Republicans, working with several coal-mining companies, had drawn electoral lines so that a number of precincts would fall on land owned by the mines. Armed guards employed by the companies refused to let labor sympathizers onto company property to vote on Election Day, thereby ensuring support for the antilabor Republican candidates favored by the mine owners.[12]

Such employer threats were especially effective during the first century of U.S. politics, when Americans did not vote in secret. No stalls with flag-adorned curtains were available. Instead voters sometimes publicly pledged their support for a candidate in front of their friends, neighbors, bosses, and party representatives. In other cases, voters would cast distinctive ballots printed by the parties, which had the advantage of making it clear to the poll minders (and anyone else watching) whom the voter supported. Given the public nature of voting in this era, it is no surprise that coercion, bribery, and intimidation were rampant—and that employers had the means of closely monitoring their employees' political behavior and rewarding or punishing workers accordingly.

Though the later adoption of the secret ballot and voting protections curbed the incidence of outright workplace intimidation, employers continued to pursue mobilization of their workers well into the twentieth century. Following GE's efforts in the 1950s, however, it is difficult to establish much evidence of extensive employer recruitment of ordinary workers outside of a few isolated episodes until the 1990s and 2000s. Even in his definitive study of outside lobbying published in 1998, for instance, political scientist Ken Kollman found that companies were not very likely to engage their rank-and-file workers in politics. During the high-stakes 1993 debate over the North American Free Trade Agreement, Kollman found that political insiders laughed at corporate America's outside mobilization on behalf of the trade bill, explaining that "corporations and trade associations are very bad at grass roots. . . . They're not good at all at getting their employees to contact Congress."[13] It was not until 2004 that one campaign finance and corporate lobbying reporter was able to argue that employer political recruitment had "entered the mainstream," where companies that did not engage their workers in politics were now considered to be the "exception."[14] Similarly the head of the Public Affairs Council explained in an interview that he thought it was not until the early 2000s that grassroots engagement of employees really took off.

To be sure, since the growth of corporate PACs in the 1970s, companies have asked their top managers to participate in the political process. In some cases companies were quite aggressive in recruiting their management to donate to these committees and also to help lobby members of Congress. As Dan Clawson, Alan Neustadtl, and Mark Weller note in their study of corporate PACs in the 1980s, when it comes to PAC contributions, "neither stockholders nor union members can be coerced to contribute—the organization doesn't have power over them, they have power over the organization." "Managers," on the other hand, "can be coerced. . . . If your boss comes to you and asks for a contribution, saying he or she hopes that all team players will be generous, it's not easy for you, an ambitious young manager, to say no."[15] What is different about employer mobilization as I describe it in this book is that it is now not just the top managers who are being pressured into participating in political causes for their company; it is ordinary, rank-and-file workers as well.

Clearly, then, businesses' current efforts at engaging rank-and-file employees in politics are relatively new. Some of the unusual cases of employee political recruitment from midcentury are informative, however. In a 1962 article in *Time*, one of the rare sources of evidence of mobilization from that period, a business reporter expressed surprise at the executives who were mounting campaigns to "educate employees in the vagaries of politics."[16] There were some businesses, *Time* reported, in which politics permeated all levels of employee activities, such as Houston's Continental Oil Company. Continental's president started workshops to teach employees and their families to participate in politics, even giving workers time off to volunteer with campaigns. At General Electric, U.S. Steel, and Monsanto the programs more frequently revolved around teaching workers about important policy issues—closer to what companies are doing today. The *Time* article hinted at an important reason more managers were not engaging their workers in politics during this period: managers feared that mobilization might invite backlash—perhaps from the then-powerful labor movement, politically sensitive consumers, or politicians.

Although most companies were wary of these practices, other observers recognized the enormous potential that employer mobilization could have for politics. One political strategist implored large businesses to get their act together in the face of the onslaught of new regulations coming from the federal government in the late 1970s. "Corporations can participate legally in a wide variety of political activities," wrote the author, a scholar at the conservative American Enterprise Institute, yet "typically they are much more reluctant than labor unions to do so." The author pointed out that companies do indeed have the right to tell certain employees "how they should vote," but "in practice, very few attempt to exercise that right to develop and communicate their view on specific candidates." Unions, he noted dryly, "show no similar shyness." What business needed was to "be as politically active as possible" to "mold public opinion."[17]

While we lack rigorous survey data on employer political recruitment over time, there is suggestive evidence that employer mobilization is much more common now than in previous years. For instance, the Business Roundtable, an association of about 150 of the largest and most prominent firms in the country, estimates that the share of its members contacting workers about politics has increased from a mere handful in 1978 to 18 percent in 2002 and 66 percent in 2004.[18]

Using its own polling, BIPAC, which helps managers mobilize their workers, estimates that the share of employee voters hearing from their bosses about politics has risen from 7 percent in 2000 to 10 percent in 2010, 31 percent in 2014, and 27 percent in the 2016 elections.[19] We should be cautious in reading too much into these polling results since they were produced by an organization with a vested financial interest in motivating businesses to mobilize their workers. Still, a final data point hinting at a dramatic rise in the incidence of employer mobilization comes from the observations of campaign finance experts, who were baffled by a slew of news stories in 2010 and 2012 indicating that employers were actively campaigning for political candidates in the workplace. "We've never seen something like this before," said one partner at a Philadelphia-based labor law firm in response to a story about how Las Vegas casino conglomerate Wynn Resorts was encouraging its workers to vote for specific candidates in the 2012 election.[20]

So what changed? How did companies overcome the "shyness" bemoaned by the American Enterprise Institute pundit to begin sending political messages to their employees in the early 2000s? Thinking about the reemergence of employer mobilization as a classic whodunit mystery, I will show how managers' motive, means, and opportunity converged to make employer mobilization into the widespread corporate practice it is today.

Motive: Business Gets Its Act Together in the 1970s

Whether we approve of it or not, we tend to take it for granted that businesses are deeply involved in the political process. But this was not always the case. Five decades ago a leading corporate lawyer could write credibly, if dramatically, that

> as every business executive knows, few elements of American society today have as little influence in government as the American businessman, the corporation, or even the millions of corporate stockholders. If

one doubts this, let him undertake the role of "lobbyist" for the business point of view before Congressional committees. The same situation obtains in the legislative halls of most states and major cities. One does not exaggerate to say that, in terms of political influence with respect to the course of legislation and government action, the American business executive is truly the "forgotten man."[21]

It was easy for business executives to write themselves off as the "forgotten man" given that most did not pay much attention to politics—nor did trade groups, for that matter. The National Association of Manufacturers, for instance, as late as 1960 did not have a government affairs operations and was headquartered in New York City, far from policymakers in Washington, DC.[22] The U.S. Chamber of Commerce was not much more involved either. As late as 1970 the Chamber did not have a full-time permanent president, nor did it dedicate much of its efforts to politics and policy.[23]

All that was to change as the business community began to face down the prospect of mounting regulation—including new environmental and workplace safety rules—and an increasingly disruptive labor movement. Both of these changing features of the American political economy are captured in Figure 5.1, which plots the number of pages in the *Federal Register* on the left and the number of major strikes (involving 1,000 or more workers) on the right.

The *Federal Register* is the official journal of the federal government, publishing proposed and final rules and regulations as well as public notices from federal agencies. The number of pages published each year in the *Register* thus provides a relatively straightforward indicator of the overall regulatory activity of the federal government. Accordingly, Figure 5.1 gives a sense of the explosion in rule-making during the late 1960s and early 1970s as Congress created a number of new agencies to protect environmental and consumer rights, including the Environmental Protection Agency, the Occupational Safety and Health Administration, the National Highway Traffic Safety Administration, and the Consumer Product Safety Commission. These new costs of doing business gave corporate managers good reason to get involved in politics so as to scale back an enlarged regulatory state.

So too did heightened levels of labor unrest, represented by the jump in major work stoppages involving 1,000 or more workers during the 1960s and early 1970s. This new wave of mass strikes provided a clear reason for business leaders to fight for policies to weaken their labor foes, as businesses came to view unions as the prime source of rising inflation and weakening international competitiveness. As one business historian has put it, "for most industrialists [during the late 1960s], the chief villain was the price of labor. When powerful unions won new contracts that raised workers' pay faster than productivity increased . . . industrial executives claimed that they had no choice but to pass along the higher costs

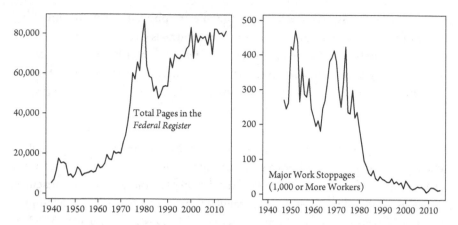

Figure 5.1 New pressures on American businesses from federal regulation and the labor movement in the 1960s and 1970s. *Federal Register* data from the Regulatory Studies Center at George Washington University. Major work stoppage data from the Bureau of Labor Statistics.

by raising the end prices of their products."[24] Having diagnosed the problem, the solution was simple: corporate managers would need to lobby lawmakers to hobble the too powerful American labor movement.

New regulatory and union pressure was thus a central motivation for businesses to start organizing politically during the 1970s and 1980s. In response older trade groups like the National Association of Manufacturers and the U.S. Chamber of Commerce beefed up their presence in Washington. The NAM moved its headquarters to Washington, DC, and created a new government affairs division, while the Chamber increased its membership nearly fourfold and scaled up its electoral contributions and lobbying efforts.[25] Individual businesses started to get in on the action as well, forming their own PACs and engaging in personal lobbying efforts outside of their trade group memberships. In the early 1970s one chief executive officer warned his colleagues, "If you don't know your senator on a first-name basis, you are not doing an adequate job for your shareholders."[26]

Thus, just as business became much more involved in politics through lobbying and funding electoral campaigns to scale back an encroaching federal government and labor movement, so too did firms invest in new methods of mobilizing the public around their favored policies and candidates through grassroots engagement, including eventually recruiting their own workers into politics.[27] One association executive summed it up neatly for me: "There was a growing sense that political involvement, including grassroots [employee engagement], was good for businesses' bottom lines." Still, pinning down a motive gets us only a third of the way to solving the puzzle of the return of employer mobilization. Like any good detective, we need to establish means and opportunity as well.

But the story of means is not so simple: before mobilization could really take off, companies needed to secure a new economic terrain, a series of technological breakthroughs, and favorable legal rulings.

Means: Weakened Economic Power for American Workers

As we consider the means that employers amassed to begin mobilizing their workers into politics, no transformation is as significant as American workers' loss of economic power and voice in the workplace. It is certainly true that workers in the United States never had the clout of their counterparts in many Western European countries. Levels of union membership and political power in the United States have long lagged behind our Continental and Scandinavian peers. Even so, by the early postwar era many U.S. employees had established a modicum of bargaining power with their managers thanks to tight labor markets, a powerful labor movement, and a government that was friendly to, if not always supportive of, rising working standards.[28] By the 1970s and 1980s, however, that balance of economic power between labor and management had begun to tip increasingly in capital's favor, and it has eroded ever since.

One clear symptom of this imbalance in economic power between workers and employers is the stagnation of workers' wages relative to the productivity of the overall economy. Figure 5.2 traces the evolution of wages for rank-and-file production workers and productivity from 1948 to 2013, showing that while the economy as a whole became much more productive (growing by over 240 percent over this period), wages and benefits for the typical production worker grew by only 109 percent. Put differently, ordinary workers outside of the executive suites are reaping less of the fruits of their labor now compared to previous decades. Another sign of reduced worker power is the declining quality of working conditions for many employees, such as record levels of wage theft by managers, misclassification of workers to evade taxes and regulations, and the rise of on-call positions, whereby employees are not notified of their schedules until just before they are required to report for work.[29]

A range of factors is implicated in the decline of worker economic power, especially the collapse of a formidable labor movement in the private sector that once could defend the interests of private-sector workers before corporate management (shown in Figure 5.3). But workers have also suffered from increased competition with lower wage economies overseas and from nonunion states within the United States, the failure of government to update relevant labor protections, and greater pressure on managers to generate high quarterly returns for their shareholders by slashing labor costs.[30]

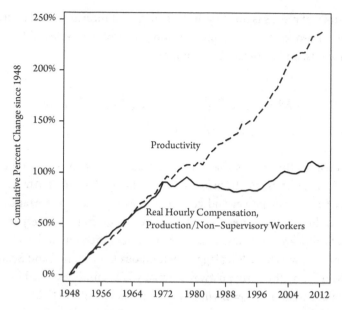

Figure 5.2 The growing productivity-wage gap. The Economic Policy Institute's State of Working America: "Cumulative Change in Total Economy Productivity and Real Hourly Compensation of Production/Nonsupervisory Workers, 1948–2013." See Mishel, Bivens, Gould, and Shierholz 2012.

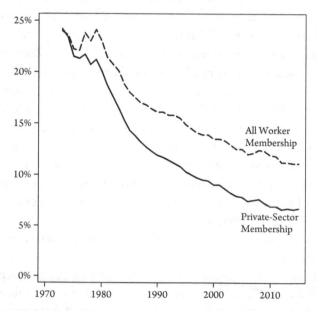

Figure 5.3 The collapse of the American labor movement. Union membership as a share of wage and salary workers. Data from the Bureau of Labor Statistics.

The upshot of all of these trends is that workers are in a far weaker position to resist demands that their employers place upon them. In previous decades, for instance in the immediate postwar period, workers might have been comfortable refusing to participate in employer-led political activities, given that they felt secure in their employment. When faced with an employer's political request with which she disagreed, a worker might go to her union representative to complain, knowing that she would be shielded from retaliation by the union. And even if that worker were not employed at a union company, she might still feel confident challenging management's political demands, given executives' fear of inviting labor unrest. It is much less likely that workers today would feel as comfortable resisting employers' political demands.

Not only are unions now virtually absent from the private sector, but employees recognize that if they protest workplace conditions, they may simply be replaced with a worker who is willing to comply with managers' demands. The insecurity faced by the contemporary American workforce thus ought to amplify the pressures employees experience to comply with employers' political requests. That, in turn, ought to increase the likelihood that employer mobilization will succeed in getting workers to accept managers' favored political positions and candidates. Declining worker economic power, then, was one important means for the spread of political mobilization at work.

Means: New Communications Technology in the Workplace

Apart from diminished voice and power at work, employer mobilization efforts have also been facilitated by new advances in technology, the second means that figures in our whodunit mystery. In the 1950s General Electric printed tens of thousands of free-market brochures, held in-person reading groups and courses, and sent Reagan cross-country to disseminate its free-market messages to employees. The same sort of corporate campaigns are now much easier and less expensive to implement. Top corporate managers explain in interviews that a company might now launch a mobilization effort around a particular policy with a series of emails to workers, then with online town halls, and finally with electronic requests for workers to visit a website that helps them to send prewritten messages to their elected officials.

Because many companies now possess electronic human resources records for their workers, managers report that they can create political content that is highly tailored to individual workers' jobs and geographic locations, as

I discussed in chapter 3. All of these technologies permit managers to deliver more and richer messages, such as videos and presentations, to a broader array of workers more cheaply.

Of course more traditional methods of reaching workers are still relevant. In interviews, corporate managers emphasized that they still use in-person meetings, booths or tables in break rooms, and posters to reach workers during especially intensive campaigns, or for offline employees. But technological innovations afford managers the opportunity to mobilize their workers much more regularly than in previous eras. Summed up one executive involved in employee mobilization efforts, "The ease of using these communications has created a new corporate culture to talk about these [political] issues. Companies support new voter outreach measures—handing out voter guides and other materials that they wouldn't have done before. The issues were already there. Technology just made it easier."[31] The head of grassroots mobilization at a major business association concurred in an interview with me, stating, "[The] ability to go from 30,000 to 1.2 or 1.3 million letters [from employees] was a sea change for us." Their goal was to reach a scale where employee messages would "bite [elected officials] in the ass" when engaging in legislative debates—and they accomplished just that.

Importantly, as I detailed in chapters 3 and 4, these technological advances also permit employers to closely track the workers who read and respond to political requests. Employers can easily see, for instance, whether a given worker opened a particular email about politics, clicked through to websites with additional information, and followed a manager's request to write a letter to a given legislator. This sort of tracking helps employers design recruitment campaigns that will be most likely to garner a high success rate, as employers draw from past experiences to design messages to which workers will respond. Consider the advice a government affairs officer at International Paper, the largest paper products manufacturer in the United States and a very active mobilizer, offered to other companies about employee political engagement:

> Figure out what works, what doesn't work with your programs and don't keep doing something because that's the way it's always been done or that's what everyone else is doing. Know your audience. . . . it will pay back dividends in committed and enthusiastic grassroots and PAC members.[32]

As an example, the head of employee political engagement at one manufacturing company shared with me the statistics she was collecting on her company's mobilization website, shown in Table 5.1, which allowed her to monitor how successful her company's recruitment campaign had been on an individual worker-by-worker basis. She then used those statistics to design future campaigns.

Table 5.1. **Examples of Employer Mobilization Statistics**

- Emails sent to 49/50 states with voting-eligible employees (no voting-eligible employees in the remaining state)
- 56.8% of employees opened the message
- 2,061 employee visits to site
- 9,365 page views
- 4.54 pages visited per visit by employees
- 3:15 average duration per visit
- 88% new visits; 12% returning visits

Source: Author interview with large manufacturing firm during 2015 mobilization drive.

Employers are simply in a better position to monitor their workers' personal preferences and behaviors than they once were given the preponderance of computer usage, with many American companies reporting that they carefully track their employees' Internet, social media, and email activities.[33] My own firm survey, for instance, indicated that 44 percent of managers reported that their organizations monitored at least some of their employees' Internet activities. This tracking means that even if a company does not monitor responses to its political campaigns, it could still discern the political behavior and attitudes of its workforce—both on and off the job—by keeping tabs on workers' online identities and activities. Many workers seem to recognize the possibility of this monitoring, especially as it relates to political activity; as we saw in the previous chapter, some 20 to 30 percent of workers thought their employers could keep track of their turnout records and vote choices.

The erosion of worker power in the labor market and the emergence of new technology thus opened the door for new and widespread mobilization in recent decades. "It is hard to imagine a well-organized grassroots campaign without a software platform [that can send and track requests]," one association executive and grassroots consultant said to me. But it would take one final means for employer mobilization to explode as it has in recent years: a new legal terrain for companies after 2010.

Means: A New Legal Terrain after 2010

"If there was one [Supreme Court] decision I would overrule, it would be *Citizens United*," proclaimed Justice Ruth Bader Ginsburg when asked about the

Court's worst ruling. "I think the notion that we have all the democracy that money can buy strays so far from what our democracy is supposed to be. So that's number one on my list."[34] In decrying the Court's 2010 decision in *Citizens United v. Federal Election Commission,* Justice Ginsburg reflected a common sentiment on the political Left. By ruling that the government may not ban political spending by companies in elections, so the theory on the Left goes, the Court opened the floodgates for a tidal wave of corporate cash that will drown out any other voices and corrupt democracy. President Obama articulated this theory well when he called *Citizens United* "a major victory for big oil, Wall Street banks, health insurance companies and the other powerful interests that marshal their power every day in Washington to drown out the voices of everyday Americans."[35] But six years after the decision, scholars of corporate political activity have been hard-pressed to find concrete evidence of the flood of corporate political cash that liberals had originally predicted. (Noncorporate funding from wealthy individuals, on the other hand, has indeed exploded since 2010.)[36] Most companies did not immediately rush to take advantage of their newfound ability to spend unlimited sums from their treasuries on the election or defeat of political candidates. Some evidence even suggests that shareholders actually became warier of companies making electoral contributions following the 2010 decision.[37]

The irony is that *Citizens United* may have indeed reshaped corporate political activities—but in a different way. Instead of introducing a wave of new corporate spending in elections, the ruling actually expanded the permissible scope of employee political recruitment, the final means to explain the spread of mobilization in recent years. In permitting companies to spend directly from their treasuries on political activities, *Citizens United* also allows managers to use employee time (a corporate resource) in campaigning and politics, so long as those activities are not explicitly coordinated with a candidate or a party.[38] "[Electoral mailings to workers] is certainly a post–*Citizens United* invention," one corporate lawyer explained.[39] Another consultant agreed: "I don't recall seeing companies suggest to their employees who they should vote for [before that decision]."[40]

Coupled with the fact that there are no federal legal protections for employees who are fired or retaliated against for refusing to participate in political activities, *Citizens United* creates the legal possibility for political coercion. Because the vast majority of private-sector employees are employed "at will," they can generally have their hours or wages changed, or can even be fired, without cause, as long as it is not for a narrowly defined set of legally protected reasons, such as religion, race, or gender.

While some states have protections in place for private employee speech or political activity, not all do.[41] Moreover many of the state-level political freedom laws protect an employee's own speech or activities only during off-work hours rather than political coercion from a manager while a worker is on the job. Figure 5.4 summarizes the current landscape of state laws based on my reading of state statutes and shows that 28 states have some sort of provision in place about political views and speech in the workplace. Yet of those 28 states, only 11 have statutes that explicitly protect workers against political coercion on the job, while the rest do not mention limits on employer pressure.

Even within the 11 states that have provisions in place to protect workers' political views and speech from managerial coercion, it is unclear whether those laws are actually affording workers any real protection, according to one leading legal expert I spoke with. Workers might not know about those laws, and even if they do, they might be afraid to use them. And looking at the data from my own worker survey, I find that workers in states with laws in place intended to protect private employee speech or even workplace political coercion were no less likely than workers in states without such laws to report uncomfortable or potentially coercive employer political messages.[42] While not definitive proof of the failure of these state laws—it might be the case that rates of threatening employer mobilization would be even higher in states without workplace freedom rules on the books—this does suggest that such laws do not rule out coercive contact altogether, a disconcerting landscape in the wake of the *Citizens United* precedent. As one expert on labor law has summed up: "Before *Citizens United*, federal election law allowed a company like Koch Industries to talk to officers and shareholders about whom to vote for, but not to talk with employees about whom to vote for. . . . Now, companies . . . are free to send out newsletters

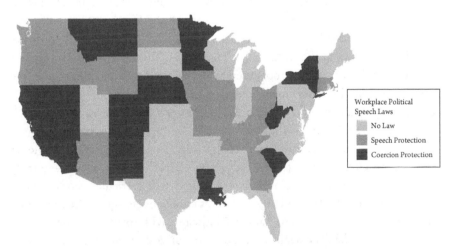

Figure 5.4 States with workplace political speech laws in place. Author's review of state laws. Alaska has no protections and Hawaii has speech but not coercion protections.

persuading their employees how to vote. They can even intimidate their employees into voting for their candidates. It's a very troubling situation."[43]

Importantly, these developments largely affect private-sector workers, not employees of federal, state, or local government. While private-sector workers in the United States possess only limited protections against political discrimination in the workplace, employees in the public sector have enjoyed much more robust safeguards since the passage of the Hatch Act in 1939.[44] Given fears of political patronage and machine politics, good-government reformers sought to impose strict limits on the ability of public-sector supervisors to recruit their employees into politics. Despite vigorous debates over its scope and legality throughout the twentieth century, the Hatch Act remains in effect today.

At present nearly all federal employees are restricted from engaging in a range of political activities, including running for partisan office, using their office to influence elections, and soliciting support or contributions for a party, candidate, or group. While most of these restrictions focus on the use of public resources for political ends—the prime target of progressive reformers—special attention in the Hatch Act is directed toward situations where managers and supervisors in government might use their position of authority to solicit or compel political activities from their subordinates. Even after substantial reforms in 1993, Congress retained and even bolstered the provisions of the Hatch Act that prevent political coercion of federal employees, declaring, "It shall be unlawful for any person to intimidate, threaten, command, or coerce, or attempt to intimidate, threaten, command, or coerce, any employee of the Federal Government . . . to engage in, or not to engage in, any political activity." And Congress did not limit coercion based only on voting; it included a wide range of other political activities as well, such as making contributions and working on campaigns. The penalties for disobeying the anticoercion provisions of the Hatch Act are stiff, with threats of fines and jail sentences for each violation.[45] Many states and localities passed similar laws in the wake of the Hatch Act. These statutory protections for public workers are further bolstered by their First Amendment rights to free speech; because the government is the employer of these workers, it cannot limit their speech beyond the Hatch Act restrictions or compel them to participate in politics against their will.

Table 5.2 summarizes the major changes in the laws governing employer mobilization after *Citizens United* for private-sector workers. Here "explicitly partisan" refers to corporate activities in support of particular candidates or parties—the sort of activities that companies could not engage in directly before the *Citizens United* decision. As Table 5.2 indicates, while private-sector employers could fire or retaliate against workers for political activities in most states even before *Citizens United*, the Supreme Court decision opened the door for employers to combine explicitly partisan recruitment of workers with threats of

Table 5.2. **Summary of Employer Mobilization Law before and after *Citizens United*, Private-Sector Workers**

Tactic	Pre–Citizens United	Post–Citizens United
Intimidating employees in the voting process	Illegal	Illegal
Sending explicitly partisan messages to rank-and-file workers	Limited	Permitted
Compelling workers to participate in explicitly partisan activities	Illegal	Permitted in many states
Retaliating against workers who do not comply with employers' explicitly partisan requests	Not possible	Permitted in many states
Retaliating against workers for their political views or partisan affiliations	Permitted in many states	Permitted in many states

changes to working conditions or employment.[46] That is, while employers could have dismissed workers for political views or participation before 2010, they could not pair explicitly partisan electoral messages along with cuts (or threats of cuts) to wages or benefits, job loss, or dismissal. Thus, in conjunction with the lack of federal protections for firing or punishing private-sector workers on political grounds, *Citizens United* permits businesses to require their workers to participate in partisan politics in particular ways on pain of dismissal or other changes to their employment.

Subsequent actions (or, rather, inactions) by the Federal Election Commission (FEC) have further expanded the set of permissible actions private-sector managers can take to engage their workers in partisan politics. In 2015 and again in 2016 the FEC heard complaints related to Murray Energy, the Ohio-based coal-mining company and fifth largest producer of coal nationwide from chapter 4.[47] Those complaints alleged that Murray managers had violated federal election law by coercing employees to attend political events and contribute to the company's political action committee. On party-line votes, the FEC deadlocked over whether to investigate those charges against Murray, essentially signaling to companies that engaging in similar practices would not result in FEC action.

The three Democratic FEC commissioners expressed concern that the latest Murray complaint "strikes at the heart of one of [the] key values of the American workplace: that employees should be free to maintain their personal political beliefs and not be compelled to participate or contribute based on their employers' interests."[48] One lawyer from a firm specializing in campaign finance and lobbying summed up the implications of the FEC's inaction on this case for employer mobilization more generally: "There is no doubt the standard as articulated, and the application of it to the facts here will be seen as moving the line significantly for those employers who ask: 'Will I get in trouble with the FEC for doing this?' . . . The statement [from the FEC] makes clear that, for many companies, a decision to be far more aggressive in requesting contributions from employees will not be second guessed at the FEC."[49] A former general counsel with the FEC agreed with that assessment, arguing that when legal compliance and corporate government affairs officers at a business see a decision like "the Murray case, they'll be like, 'Why are we being so conservative about [political mobilization]? Why don't we get more aggressive?'"[50] A similar reflection came from the lawyer in charge of the political practice group at Skadden, a major corporate law firm: *Citizens United* and later FEC decisions "made corporations more comfortable with giving all employees educational materials or 'voter guides' that make their political positions clear [to the employees]." Before the 2010 decision, he explained, companies were much more cautious to "make those things not slanted and not favor one candidate over another. Now I think they're pretty clear as to where they're going with those communications."[51]

Even before *Citizens United* and the subsequent FEC Murray Energy cases, however, employers had already begun to engage in some practices that resembled those that would be legalized after 2010. For instance, companies have long used "captive audience" meetings, or mandatory workplace presentations, to discourage workers from supporting labor unions.[52] Leading companies and business associations had even started to hold captive audience meetings about a broader range of political issues, including some related to political candidates, in the early 2000s, as Walmart did in attempting to discourage votes for political candidates who supported expanding union organizing rights.[53]

Both the First Amendment and the National Labor Relations Act, which governs private-sector labor organizing, permit captive audience meetings on labor-related issues and offer no protections for employees who are disciplined or fired for refusing to attend, leaving early, or even asking questions. And it is important to underscore the fact that communications—including posters, emails, town hall forums, and rallies—unrelated to elections or candidates were always legal for employers, even before *Citizens United*. So long as employers were talking about policies and not calling for the election or defeat of specific candidates or parties, they were well within their legal rights to talk with their employees—and even to connect changes in those policies to changes in employee working conditions, wages, benefits, and employment. In many ways, then, the most significant consequences of *Citizens United* did not necessarily involve the direct expansion of legally permissible mobilization activities in which managers could engage. Instead the case sent a clear signal from the judiciary that political communications between employers and employees were on safe legal terrain.

That brings us to the last piece in the whodunit mystery: the opportunity. We have now seen that businesses had the motive to seek out new means of changing politics and public policy following the onslaught of regulations and union pressure during the 1960s and 1970s. Business also had new means to expand political mobilization facing an increasingly pliant workforce and armed with new technologies for communicating with and tracking their workers. And the legal context has only grown more favorable to expansive communication efforts. But before they could reap the fruits of these shifts for political recruitment, managers needed to be convinced of the usefulness of mobilization in general and to be sold on the technology they would need to deploy mobilization drives in their own companies. That's where the opportunity comes in. Business associations—and above all BIPAC—played an essential role in providing precisely that opportunity to managers.

Opportunity: BIPAC Borrows Labor's Playbook—Again

In the early 1960s American business executives were bemoaning the influence of a new labor political action committee, the AFL-CIO's Committee on Political Education (COPE), that had begun to invest in labor-endorsed political candidates starting after the AFL and CIO merger in 1955. Business needed a counterweight to COPE that would support conservative politicians friendly to corporate America.[54] A small group of politically attuned managers at the U.S. Chamber of Commerce and the NAM, two of the oldest national business groups in American politics, began to discuss a business alternative to COPE as early as 1958. The proposed group, the Business-Industry Political Action Committee, would be a joint venture of the Chamber (representing business) and the NAM (representing industry) that would fund corporate-backed candidates each election cycle. Ultimately Chamber executives rejected the operation because they feared it would compete with their own burgeoning initiative to recruit executives to participate in politics. The NAM thus went at it alone and funded the creation of BIPAC in 1963. BIPAC leaned heavily on the NAM in its early years for everything from financial support to furniture and staff. Initially headquartered in New York, BIPAC moved to Washington in 1970 as the group developed credibility and no longer needed to be quite so geographically close to its donor base.[55]

BIPAC focused its attention in these early decades on supporting House and Senate candidates, given that Congress was the center of policymaking in those years and was the place where liberals and labor had been most successful.[56]

Although the group grew quickly—commanding a budget of well over $3 million (in 2015 dollars) by the 1970s—it still paled in comparison with its labor foe. The AFL-CIO's COPE was spending more than twice as much as BIPAC. Despite failing to match labor's political clout, BIPAC still played an important role in mobilizing corporate executives into politics. As business historian Benjamin Waterhouse points out, the group funded "political education efforts" for business owners and executives, "publishing a newsletter to explain the political process, the dynamics of specific local and national races, and the importance of voting, especially on 'business' issues and for 'business' candidates."[57]

By the 1970s, as we have already seen, businessmen had come around to BIPAC's message as they faced a barrage of new and costly regulations imposed by an increasingly activist government, as well as an ever more strident labor movement. Combined with clearer campaign finance regulations after a favorable 1975 FEC decision, corporate leaders responded to this reshaped legal and economic terrain by creating a slew of political action committees for their own companies. Those new committees could help elect politicians that would protect the interests of the private sector by cutting regulations, lowering taxes, and making it more challenging for labor unions to organize and engage in collective action. Companies were now free to solicit political contributions from their shareholders and management and, under certain limited circumstances, from their rank-and-file employees.[58]

As a result the four years between 1974 and 1978 saw the number of business PACs jump from under 100 to nearly 800, while the number of labor PACs stayed relatively constant, increasing only from 201 to 217.[59] The upper panel of Figure 5.5 plots the explosion in corporate PACs over this period compared to labor committees. We see a broadly similar gap between labor unions and businesses looking at the total amount of PAC spending over time in the lower panel of Figure 5.5. (These totals adjust for inflation.) After an initial increase in the early 1980s, labor PAC spending on Congress flattened, while corporate PAC spending continued to grow. By 2014 corporate PACs were spending more than five times as much as they did in 1978, and nearly four times as much as labor-affiliated political committees.

Thus by the late 1970s and 1980s BIPAC had in some ways outlived its original mission, as corporate America found its political voice and enjoyed "days of wine and roses—or champagne, even, and orchids ... in Washington," according to the *New York Times*.[60] As a consequence BIPAC's funding dwindled, and by 1990 the gap between AFL-CIO and BIPAC contributions had grown threefold, tripling to ninefold by 2000, even as union membership rolls eroded in the private sector. Figure 5.6 plots the steady decline in BIPAC's spending against increasing donations from the AFL-CIO over these years.

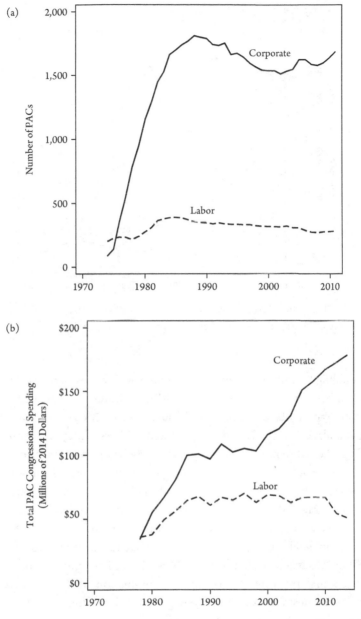

Figure 5.5 The evolution of corporate and labor PACs. Total number of PACs (top panel) and PAC spending on congressional elections (bottom panel) from the Federal Election Commission.

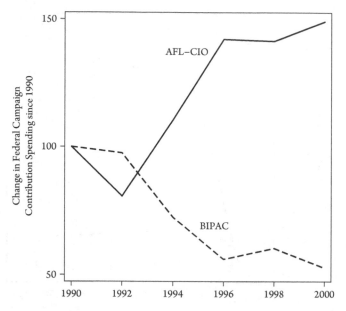

Figure 5.6 Change in BIPAC and AFL-CIO donation activity, 1990–2000. Donation data from the Center for Responsive Politics.

Scrambling to find a comparative advantage amid a crowded field of business PACs and other political associations, BIPAC's leaders turned once again to their labor opponents for inspiration.[61] "Business simply didn't have a grassroots strategy in place, but the Left did, and long did," Greg Casey, a veteran head of BIPAC, explained to me. Casey recognized early on that a business-based grass-roots strategy could be critical to breaking through the "explosion of PACs and campaign spending" that had occurred and made it harder for any one business group (including BIPAC) to reach voters and legislators. BIPAC would thus pro-vide the same grassroots mobilization of workers for employers that the unions had long provided for liberals. "Employers need to talk to their workers the same way that unions reach out to their members," Casey has summed up.[62]

BIPAC's first move was to conduct an evaluation of the potential effects of employer messages on employee political behavior.[63] That evaluation concluded that

> only a little more that [*sic*] thirteen percent of the American work-force is unionized, but seventeen percent of the electorate had heard about the elections from a labor union. Forty-seven percent of union members—and forty percent of union households—said they had heard from unions. Unions carefully targeted their communications to their members—voters who had an affinity to the labor organization

and a natural receptivity to its message. Only seven percent [of employee voters] had heard from an employer. Business has been slow to utilize the same tools as labor, even though elections law allows the same tools to each.[64]

BIPAC's evaluation further noted that employers have a unique role to play in communicating about politics to employees, since "the employer is the new safety net as the provider of family wages, family benefits, and family retirement security through investments," and its internal polling found evidence that "seventy-eight percent of respondents either wished their company would provide information on government and politics, or were open to receiving the information."[65] BIPAC's polling indicated that workers in swing congressional districts were even more likely to want employer political messages. Money that corporate groups were spending on issue advocacy advertisements, BIPAC reported after conducting this intensive evaluation, could be better spent on grassroots get-out-the-vote efforts among workers.[66] "This is why labor gets more while spending less," BIPAC's report later summed up. "It focuses on techniques that actually win elections. The business community has never done that in an organized fashion."[67]

BIPAC formally started their grassroots worker engagement campaign in the 2000 election with the launch of the Prosperity Project, or P2, which was piloted that year in several large companies, including Halliburton, Procter and Gamble, and Exxon-Mobil.[68] P2 offers companies the technical capacity to field mobilization drives among their workers, as well as consulting services to help corporate government affairs officers craft effective messages. But P2 is more than simply a new software system. BIPAC has also built a coalition of hundreds of other business associations and individual companies to coordinate efforts at mobilization around particular ballot initiatives, policy debates, and elections, and counts affiliates in all 50 states.

At the heart of P2 is an Internet platform that companies and associations use to provide information to workers about pending policy debates, encourage workers to contact their elected officials, and help workers register to vote. This platform can be customized for each business or trade association so the site retains the look and feel of other corporate web pages, with content that is tailored to each worker and organization. Figure 5.7 provides an example of BIPAC's site for John Deere, the farm equipment manufacturer. John Deere GAIN, or Government Action Information Network, lists a worker's elected officials and a summary of each official's sponsored bills and votes that have either benefited or hurt Deere operations.

BIPAC sites offer a diverse set of benefits to members depending on how much a company or association is willing to pay P2. Some of the most notable

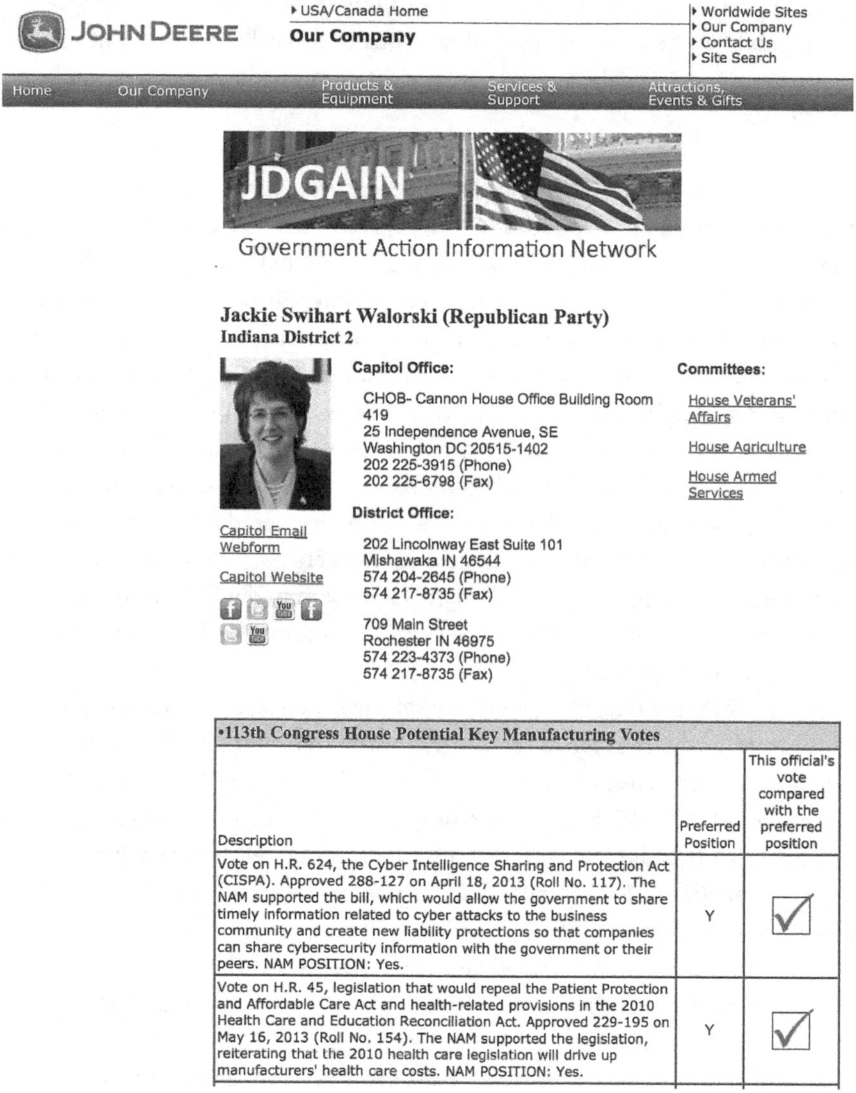

JOHN DEERE

▸ USA/Canada Home

Our Company

▸ Worldwide Sites
▸ Our Company
▸ Contact Us
▸ Site Search

Home | Our Company | Products & Equipment | Services & Support | Attractions, Events & Gifts

JDGAIN

Government Action Information Network

Jackie Swihart Walorski (Republican Party)
Indiana District 2

Capitol Office:

CHOB- Cannon House Office Building Room 419
25 Independence Avenue, SE
Washington DC 20515-1402
202 225-3915 (Phone)
202 225-6798 (Fax)

District Office:

202 Lincolnway East Suite 101
Mishawaka IN 46544
574 204-2645 (Phone)
574 217-8735 (Fax)

709 Main Street
Rochester IN 46975
574 223-4373 (Phone)
574 217-8735 (Fax)

Committees:

House Veterans' Affairs

House Agriculture

House Armed Services

Capitol Email Webform

Capitol Website

•113th Congress House Potential Key Manufacturing Votes

Description	Preferred Position	This official's vote compared with the preferred position
Vote on H.R. 624, the Cyber Intelligence Sharing and Protection Act (CISPA). Approved 288-127 on April 18, 2013 (Roll No. 117). The NAM supported the bill, which would allow the government to share timely information related to cyber attacks to the business community and create new liability protections so that companies can share cybersecurity information with the government or their peers. NAM POSITION: Yes.	Y	✓
Vote on H.R. 45, legislation that would repeal the Patient Protection and Affordable Care Act and health-related provisions in the 2010 Health Care and Education Reconciliation Act. Approved 229-195 on May 16, 2013 (Roll No. 154). The NAM supported the legislation, reiterating that the 2010 health care legislation will drive up manufacturers' health care costs. NAM POSITION: Yes.	Y	✓

Figure 5.7 BIPAC's P2 site in action. John Deere Government Action Information Network website. Accessed May 16, 2015.

features appear in Table 5.3, arrayed by membership level. The highest contribution level (Database Membership, at $50,000 per year) guarantees an organization access to highly customized websites that can track user activity and generate reports that the organization's leaders can use to monitor the success of their mobilization campaigns. Some of these websites are accessible to the public, while others are not.

Table 5.3. **BIPAC Prosperity Project Membership Benefits and Features**

Leadership-Level Membership ($5,000)	*Founder-Level Membership ($25,000)*	*Database-Level Membership ($50,000)*
• One customizable grassroots website and assistance in the creation of eight customized pages • Issue information: provided by BIPAC's national network and in-network partners • Election information • Legislative information • Political content for publication, political analysis, articles, and information on BIPAC portal • Voter registration, absentee ballot, information, and election data • Elected official voting records • Letter writing tools • Annual review	• Creation and maintenance for unlimited number of customized pages • Candidate comparisons • Customized GOTV messages • Tailored projects • Custom political analysis and articles available upon request • Design and drafting of custom materials • Capture relationships with elected officials • Newsletters	• Founder-level benefits • User-specific data: the system recognizes individual users and displays information tailored to them • Track email opens • Map and profile participation • Track website actions • Relationship tracking

Source: Excerpted from "P2 Tools & Services," BIPAC, accessed May 16, 2015, http://www .bipac.net/bipacorg/p2-services/.

BIPAC has enjoyed rapidly growing participation in P2. According to its own records, P2 had only 50 companies and associations participating in 2000, but that figure increased to 7,317 by 2014.[69] Similarly the number of messages delivered through the P2 website grew from 1.5 million in 2000 to 238 million in 2014, while employee letters to policymakers delivered through P2 platforms jumped from 286,000 in 2004 (when the service was introduced) to 3.2 million in 2014, and voter registration forms provided through the P2 platform grew from 147,000 in 2000 to 1.3 million in 2014.[70] BIPAC now estimates that P2 reaches about a fifth of the private-sector workforce.[71] The most frequent users of P2 services are individual businesses, which accounted for 62 percent of BIPAC customers in 2009.[72] The remaining users were mostly local or state business associations (representing 33 percent of BIPAC's customers in 2009). Only 5 percent of P2 users were national business associations, which generally had established mobilization packages of their own by that point.[73]

Early victories helped BIPAC's growth. Just four years after its launch in 2000, the Republican National Committee singled out BIPAC for helping to put the GOP "over the top in Ohio, Iowa and other key states by getting corporations involved in grass-roots campaigning."[74] In fact BIPAC succeeded in communicating with more than 21,500 new employee voters in Iowa alone, a figure that represented nearly 1.5 percent of all voters who cast ballots in 2004 and more than twice the eventual vote margin between GOP presidential candidate George W. Bush and Democrat John Kerry. (I estimate the contribution of BIPAC's mobilization efforts to Republican electoral prospects during the 2014 election more rigorously in chapter 6.)

Unions initially dismissed BIPAC's efforts as a pale imitation of their long-standing grassroots outreach, with the AFL-CIO arguing that the Prosperity Project "won't compare to labor's plan, which includes nearly 5,000 paid organizers nationwide and more than 100,000 volunteers on election day."[75] But as BIPAC's president has noted, the AFL-CIO started a program not dissimilar to the Prosperity Project, called Friend-to-Friend. As BIPAC's head explained, this is "where they try to have their union workers talk to their neighbors, or talk to their relatives who may not even be union employees—they might work for non-union companies."[76] Noting labor's dismissive reactions in the past to BIPAC, he laughed and argued that the unions "might want to scoff at our mission," but "ask them . . . why they're doing the Friend to Friend program."[77]

Another important reason for the success of P2 was early and frequent survey research evaluating the effects of employer mobilization on workers' behaviors and attitudes. CEOs and other top corporate executives are highly conservative and risk-averse in their behavior, explained BIPAC's head. This "political correctness" of CEOs and other executives thus kept managers from considering mobilization in the past. In particular, managers were concerned about the potential backlash to mobilization efforts, whether legal or political in nature—even if mobilization was well within corporations' First Amendment rights. Managers did not want to be seen as being "too political" or "too coercive," especially given the perceived "dicey" legal status of mobilization in "the very litigious world" companies face. "Legally, employers can be quite aggressive in talking politics with their workers, but corporate reticence has been a major barrier to making business more of an electoral force," one BIPAC representative explained to a reporter in the Prosperity Project's early years.[78] In a similar vein, a business lobbyist has remarked about BIPAC's initial difficulties in recruiting companies that "it's just easier to write a check, it's easier to contribute to a candidate, a party. There is discomfort in many businesses about talking to employees generally about policy issues."[79]

As a result of this hesitation on the part of business, it was important for BIPAC to be able to offer credible polling that workers were receptive to employer political messages, that workers found those messages to be useful in making decisions about which candidates and issues to support, and that employer messages actually had an effect on workers' behaviors. BIPAC has been able to produce polling data that reassured managers of precisely those points. BIPAC's biennial research report from 2012, for example, claimed that employees ranked their employer as being the "most credible source of information about political issues and elections affecting their job, company, and industry" and that "an overwhelming number of respondents" said they found "employer-provided information useful."[80] BIPAC leaders could thus take these polling results to corporate executives skeptical about participating in P2 to show them that employer mobilization could offer their businesses a valuable return on investment at little legal or political risk—and a huge upside as companies could build relationships with parties and candidates to support business-friendly public policy. It also does not hurt, BIPAC has found, to remind managers that whether they like it or not, unions have been doing, and are continuing to do, exactly this kind of on-the-ground mobilization of workers to support Democratic candidates and liberal policies. If reluctant corporate managers tell BIPAC's head, "I don't know if this is something I want to do. . . . I don't want to communicate with my employees—they really won't like it," BIPAC's head will remind them, "[Mobilization is] up to you. But please know that the AFL-CIO and all of their member unions are trying to do the same thing every single day to affect the political process and determine who is elected."[81]

Interviews with top corporate managers involved in corporate communications and government affairs further confirm the role of trade associations, especially BIPAC, in educating companies about the possibilities for employer mobilization. Interviewees described how BIPAC not only provided the logistical infrastructure for mobilization but also opened up the possibility of mobilization as a strategy that their company should be thinking about in the first place. One large telecommunications company, for instance, reported using BIPAC's services nearly right from the start, since 2005. BIPAC's services were appealing to this company because it offered a package that was a "known" quantity that wouldn't invite legal and political criticism from workers or other stakeholders. Said the manager, "We looked at [creating our own mobilization infrastructure], but we weren't sure what issues people cared about. Also we were worried about backlash from how we might describe the issues or candidates in each election." Using BIPAC's platform solved both problems. A manager at a manufacturer of heavy equipment explained that their mobilization initiatives were driven by a desire to be "first in class" when it came to their political activities. This company had a "top-50 corporate PAC," and to maintain that level of political activity, managers realized they needed to start mobilizing their workers. That company's government affairs division thus bought BIPAC's services to engage their workers.

Even when managers were not users of BIPAC's P2 platform, they still acknowledged the importance of BIPAC in motivating their forays into mobilization and in providing a target for their activities. A computer peripherals manufacturer reported that although they didn't work with BIPAC given their specific needs, the association's services provided a good benchmark for the manufacturer's own proprietary political mobilization system. Similarly a railroad company reported their industry's trade group developed a grassroots engagement effort inspired by BIPAC (called GoRail) that prompted many industry members to mobilize their workers.

The Rest of Organized Business Gets On Board with BIPAC

In some ways BIPAC's most significant effect on employer mobilization was not directly through P2. Rather the biggest consequence of BIPAC's shift into grassroots worker engagement was a broader signal that employer mobilization was not only legal but also desirable for business. It was a cultural sea change. In a testament to the success of BIPAC's efforts, a host of other business associations began employer mobilization efforts of their own. Shortly after P2 launched, the U.S. Chamber of Commerce announced that they would be starting their own effort, called VoteForBusiness.com, that managers could offer their workers as a resource to learn about issues affecting the business community, to see Chamber ratings of political candidates, and to register to vote. Unlike P2, the Chamber was offering its website free to companies and associations.

Where BIPAC and the Chamber ventured, so went the rest of corporate America. By 2004 a majority of the 100 largest trade associations had established their own versions of mobilization programs.[82] Explained one major association representative in an interview, "To the extent that trade associations are helping to organize the voice of a single industry, I think that they have to play the role of teaching firms to do this sort of grassroots mobilization." Another association leader used similar language to explain why his industry had begun to mobilize its workers: "A lot of it is education, finding ways to educate the [members] of our association" about the importance of mobilization.

So many trade groups had begun to offer mobilization services that several "best practice groups" emerged to provide advice to newcomers.[83] By the mid-2000s, then, employer mobilization had taken corporate America by storm. As one association executive explained, although the employer mobilization movement had been building for some time, during this period it was "achieving critical mass."[84] A testament to the success of this movement was its rapid adoption among the blue-chip Fortune 500 firms, which often set the trends for the rest of their respective industries to follow. In 2002 only 27 out of the 150 largest firms reported engaging in mobilization activities. Two years later all but 51 firms were mobilizing their workers.[85]

Like those "best practice" working groups, the Public Affairs Council offers another long-standing resource to companies that are trying to start mobilization efforts. Through conferences, workshops, training sessions, and various publications, the Council gives guidance to corporate managers who are trying to build up their "employee political engagement" programs. For instance, in *Winning at the Grassroots*, a hefty volume published in 2000, the Council provided a manual to guide companies "along the road to building, managing and measuring the success of your grassroots efforts," with chapters such as "In the Beginning: Considerations for Launching a Grassroots Program," "Politics Matters! Getting Your Employees to Believe It," and "You *Can* Make a Difference: How Glaxo Wellcome's Awards Program Encourages Employee Involvement."[86]

The NAM, for its part, launched a service in the late 2000s that aimed to reach all 12 million of the employees in the manufacturing sector.[87] The Job Creators Network, started in 2011 by Home Depot's cofounder Bernie Marcus and GOP presidential candidate Herman Cain, provides another resource for companies to educate their workers "about the real dangers of Obama/Democrat policies—about the real threat to their jobs and to their livelihoods."[88] "America's employees, particularly non-union employees, are an untapped reservoir of support for free enterprise," explains the Job Creators Network in its pitch to prospective members.[89] Participating CEOs now include executives from companies as diverse as BB&T, Sunshine Gasoline, Best Buy, Sergio's Family Restaurants, Liberty Power, and Food Lion Stores. Other employers currently on track to implement Job Creators Network–based outreach to their employees include the Las Vegas Sands resorts and burger chain White Castle.[90]

Even the secretive seminars organized by the billionaire industrialists Charles and David Koch, which bring together several hundred wealthy conservative donors twice a year to discuss politics and invest in political advocacy organizations, now promote employer mobilization in support of their libertarian causes,

as I described in the opening to this chapter. The leaked agendas of these meetings reveal that the Kochs encourage other corporate executives who attend the
seminars to engage workers "in the cause of freedom," based on the model the
Kochs have perfected at their own company, Koch Industries, and its subsidiar-
ies, such as Georgia Pacific.[91]

The end result of business associations' embrace of mobilization was a fundamental shift in the culture of government affairs divisions at major American
firms. "Companies have been reluctant to do this for decades, but now it's not
just acceptable, it's desirable. The potential here is very big, even transforma-
tional," reported one NAM executive in response to the change.[92] Corporate
managers often shift their behavior in packs, and business associations helped to
start the current wave of employer mobilization.

Business Associations Help Get Out the Word about *Citizens United*

Nearly a decade after the P2 initiative launched, business associations, including
BIPAC, again played an important role in mediating the effect of *Citizens United*
on employer mobilization efforts. Although BIPAC had long defended its mobilization activities as legal through the First Amendment free speech rights of
managers and the companies they worked for, its executives recognized that the
2010 Supreme Court decision could make businesses more comfortable doing
more in their mobilization activities—even as few other groups or individuals
recognized that possibility. The Supreme Court's deliberations on the case, for
instance, barely made any mention of employer communications to workers,
and such concerns were not even raised by the numerous advocacy groups and
legal experts filing amicus briefs with the Court, including labor unions. Indeed
I was told in interviews that not even campaign finance lawyers working on this
case were aware of its implications for employer mobilization.

Yet following the decision, BIPAC released a message welcoming the ruling
on the grounds that it would "increase the discussion on economic issues in the
2010 elections, which is a very good outcome."[93] Explained Greg Casey, head of
BIPAC at the time, "The Supreme Court's ruling frees American business from
the yoke of second class citizenship. It returns the right of American business
to talk about workplace issues and hold candidates accountable. . . . This ruling
allows us to more effectively execute a public issue education and advocacy strategy already in place."[94] That sort of signaling by BIPAC is important because,
as one progressive political activist has noted, one major reason more employers had not been engaging in more explicitly partisan recruitment of workers

was that managers "weren't sure it was legal." "Corporate lawyers," that activist explained, "are extremely risk averse and want to avoid litigation. If they give the green light to action that ends up in court, the company will probably get another lawyer. Better to play it safe."[95] BIPAC helped firms understand that more partisan mobilization was in fact legal after all.

Other business groups soon followed BIPAC's lead. In a conference call with small business owners organized by the National Federation of Independent Business in June 2012, GOP presidential hopeful Mitt Romney implored, "I hope you make it very clear to your employees what you believe is in the best interest of your enterprise and therefore their job and their future in the upcoming elections." Romney then took pains to assure the business owners that there is "nothing illegal about you talking to your employees about what you believe is best for the business"—and, as we have seen, Romney was exactly right in the post–*Citizens United* era.[96]

Small businesses were also the target of a national tour by Herman Cain on behalf of the Job Creators Network during the 2012 election.[97] Cain was organizing dozens of lunchtime meetings for the owners of small businesses in swing states, often leveraging the networks of local Tea Party groups. He began each event by reciting a standard litany of business complaints against President Obama, then pivoted to making the argument for why the assembled owners should mobilize their workers on behalf of Romney. "The left has been the only ones organizing in the workplace," lamented a speaker at one of the lunchtime sessions, "while those who sign the paychecks are scared to speak." Like Romney's message on behalf of the National Federation of Independent Business, the Job Creators Network outreach effort stressed to small business owners that partisan mobilization was entirely legal in the wake of *Citizens United*.

Not all companies needed encouragement from business associations to ramp up their activities in the wake of *Citizens United*, however. Just nine months after the Supreme Court justices handed down that decision—and one month before the midterm elections determining control of Congress—Koch Industries sent packets to nearly all of its workers with endorsements of its favored candidates for elected offices, ranging from state legislatures to the House and Senate. "As Koch company employees," the company's president wrote, "we have a lot at stake in the upcoming election. Each of us is likely to be affected by the outcome on Nov. 2. That is why, for the *first time ever*, we are mailing . . . helpful items to the home address of every U.S. employee" (emphasis added).[98] It likely helps that Koch Industries was no stranger to aggressive employee political education and, perhaps more important, that the political advocacy of the two major owners of Koch Industries—Charles and David Koch—was critical in bringing the *Citizens United* case in front of the Court in the first place.[99] If any company was well positioned to take immediate advantage of the new legal regime, it was Koch Industries.

Assessing the Change in Mobilization
since *Citizens United*

How much has mobilization changed over time, especially in the wake of the 2010 *Citizens United* decision? We saw some preliminary evidence from BIPAC polling that mobilization had increased since the 2000s, and especially since 2010. But we should be somewhat skeptical of these data given that they came from an organization with a financial interest in encouraging companies to mobilize. In the absence of more rigorous time-series polling, I asked corporate managers on the firm survey whether their companies were mobilizing more, less, or about the same amount as they did five years earlier, in 2010. (The exact question was "Compared to five years ago [2010], would you say that your firm's communications to its workers about politics and political information are more frequent, less frequent, or about the same frequency? Just give your best estimate.") Though not without its drawbacks, this question allows us to gain a better understanding of changes over time in mobilization within mobilizing companies. According to the firm survey, 66 percent of managers at mobilizing companies reported that their company was mobilizing about the same amount in 2015 as it had in 2010. But of those who reported changing their mobilization over this period, nearly twice as many managers reported that they had increased their mobilization compared to those who had decreased mobilization (21 percent versus 13 percent).

Two important implications of the account I have presented in this chapter are that the decision in *Citizens United* should have mattered most for companies engaged in explicitly partisan and electoral activities and that corporate affiliations with business associations, especially BIPAC, should have made managers more likely to take advantage of the newly favorable legal environment in the post–*Citizens United* world. The decision in *Citizens United* directly affects mobilization only during elections that involve endorsement or support for candidates, so we should see the largest effect on these modes of recruitment and smaller effects on mobilization related to either policy issues or more neutral get-out-the-vote efforts. These legal effects, moreover, should have been strongest for companies that had partnerships with business associations like BIPAC, which played an important role in translating the legal implications of the case for government affairs managers.

Figure 5.8 examines the proportion of managers increasing their intensity of mobilization since 2010. Compared to all businesses, firms engaged in electoral mobilization are more likely to report increasing their mobilization since 2010. These are precisely the companies we would expect to have been most affected by *Citizens United*, and these managers were indeed 11 percentage points more

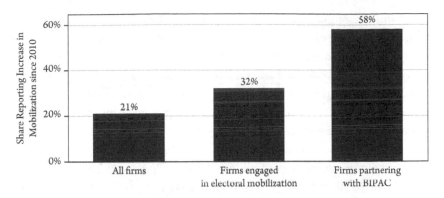

Figure 5.8 Changes in the intensity of employer mobilization since 2010. Data from 2015 firm survey. Denominator is all mobilizing firms, mobilizing firms reporting electoral mobilization, and mobilizing firms using the BIPAC Prosperity Project platform, respectively (sample sizes: 249, 86, 24).

likely to report increasing their activities since 2010. Companies that reported partnering with BIPAC were even more likely to increase their mobilization since 2010; over half (58 percent) of these managers reported increasing their activities in the wake of *Citizens United*—37 percentage points higher than the rate for all managers.

Can we be sure that the effect of BIPAC on the increasing intensity of mobilization really reflects the information and resources that the organization was providing to businesses? One way of answering this question is to examine the BIPAC effect while accounting for a variety of other firm characteristics, including size, ownership, union presence, and industry, which might explain *both* companies' decisions to mobilize *and* executives' choices about working with BIPAC. Even taking into account other business characteristics, however, I find that a business with no ties to BIPAC had only a 16 percent probability of increasing mobilization of its workers from 2010 to 2015, while a company with a BIPAC partnership had a 60 percent probability of mobilizing more over this period.[100] Affiliation with BIPAC clearly appears to matter, above and beyond other business characteristics, as executives were deciding whether to ramp up political mobilization in the wake of *Citizens United*.

Employer Mobilization: More of the Same Grassroots?

It is worth drawing a distinction between the conclusions I have reached in this chapter so far and the work of sociologist Edward Walker, who has carefully traced the rise of public affairs consultants who help companies mobilize the public around policy issues.[101] Walker points to a rise in corporate-led grassroots efforts beginning in the 1970s and 1980s, in response to the development of muscular public interest and labor movements in the 1960s and 1970s. While employer mobilization is closely related to these grassroots efforts, and many of the corporate managers who now help companies to mobilize their workers have experience with grassroots engagement, the historical development of employer mobilization is distinct from that of the corporate grassroots movement. Employer mobilization took off in the early to mid-2000s, and not as much in the 1970s and 1980s, even if there were numerous calls for employers to start mobilizing workers during that period.[102] No more than a handful of the largest and most prominent companies in the country—those represented on the Business Roundtable—had active employee engagement programs in 1978.[103] As one group of public relations experts reported in 1995, "employees and shareholders are rarely informed about how elected representatives stand on issues important to their company. . . . Many companies seem not to stress the importance of their employees' being engaged in political activity or invite such participation."[104] Even as late as the 2000s one labor law expert expressed doubt that "overt politicking to employees" happened much, writing to a journalist that he was "not aware of it happening with many employers."[105] One close observer of campaign finance wrote in an article tracing the rise of employer mobilization in 2004, "After growing slowly in the two previous election cycles . . . employer activism has entered the mainstream in 2004. Companies that do not communicate with workers about political issues have become the exception, amounting to a quiet revolution in the way business conducts itself in the political world."[106]

A second difference between employer mobilization and the more general rise of corporate grassroots activity is that while the grassroots mobilization movement was aided by private-sector consultancies, employer mobilization of workers tended to be led much more by business associations, especially BIPAC. A key reason for the delay between the development of the corporate grassroots movement and worker mobilization efforts is likely the thornier legal issues facing firms when they seek to communicate with their workers as compared to the general public—a point we saw repeated in the interview evidence from trade associations. As the group of public relations experts I quoted earlier explained, hesitation by companies to mobilize their workers through the 1980s and early 1990s likely resulted from "ethical concerns, doubt about the feasibility, or cost effectiveness of employee constituency efforts."[107] Managers needed more convincing to overcome their inherent risk aversion and engage their own workers in politics than they needed to mobilize the mass public in similar ways. The development and diffusion of employer mobilization of workers as a corporate political strategy, then, was different from that of grassroots corporate involvement more generally.

Finally, and most centrally for my own theory of employer mobilization, rooted in differences in economic power, the nature of corporate-led grassroots mobilization done outside of companies is very different from mobilization of workers inside a business. When companies mobilize their own workers, managers have extra leverage in making recruitment requests because of the economic power managers hold over workers. That same power imbalance is absent when companies recruit into politics ordinary citizens with no employment or economic ties to the business. (The political recruitment of contractors, suppliers, or retirees, which Walker also describes in his book, falls somewhere in between these extremes since these actors have some degree of economic dependence on businesses.) For instance, when Walmart organizes citizens to lobby city governments to permit the opening of a new store, the store cannot use the same implicit or explicit leverage of employment or wage changes to boost participation.

This difference matters practically, as we might well expect that employer mobilization of workers would be more effective than employer recruitment of other individuals, especially when companies have a great deal of economic power over their workers (as we saw in chapter 3). And from an ethical perspective, we might be more concerned about the potential for political coercion when employers are recruiting workers inside their business rather than citizens with fewer or no economic ties to the company. That same concern about coercion is much less relevant when citizens decide to participate in grassroots corporate activities free from any direct economic considerations.

The Interplay between Business Associations and Companies

In this chapter I have explored the return to employer mobilization as a corporate political strategy, illustrating how the broad shifts in the economy, technology, and law have made employer mobilization into a viable political tactic for managers to deploy once again, echoing the strategies that Reagan and Boulware pioneered at General Electric decades ago. But we have also seen that these broad changes, on their own, were insufficient for businesses to start mobilizing. For managers to fully grasp the feasibility and importance of this strategy, they needed to be sold on it by trusted sources in the business community. Here associations, especially BIPAC, played a central role in convincing managers of the usefulness—and legality—of mobilization.

This insight, that associations can change corporate behavior, has important implications for the study of business lobbying and practices more generally. Standard accounts of business mobilization in American politics portray business associations as being the political tools of corporate managers.[108] In these accounts business associations are created and supported to aid companies' efforts at changing public policy. For instance, according to these scholars, the Business Roundtable was created by managers concerned about the role of the federal government and an overly powerful labor movement in generating rampant inflation and economic stagnation.[109] The Roundtable, CEOs hoped, would provide a forum through which executives could stymie labor-friendly legislation and burdensome regulations. But absent from this traditional narrative is an appreciation of the ways that, once created, associations can, in turn, shape the behavior of their corporate members.

Though less well recognized in work on American business-government relations, a perspective on corporate managers' behaviors as being affected by social ties resonates with other work in comparative politics and sociology. For instance, comparative political economist Cathie Jo Martin has argued that American managers take their cues about public policy from their government affairs staffers, who in turn rely on their ties to business associations to shape their perceptions of the costs and benefits of particular government actions.[110] Similarly sociologists have found evidence that business managers develop their perceptions of the world based in part on their participation in corporate social networks.[111] My findings complement the conclusions of this work, showing that associations, even those motivated by narrow interests of organizational survival, can have powerful effects on corporate behavior through their close interactions with top managers. Associations can teach businesses what laws mean for political strategy and how managers can take advantage of new changes in the economy and society.

Now that we have seen what employer mobilization looks like from the perspective of managers (chapter 3) and workers (chapter 4) and traced how mobilization has developed over time (this chapter), we are ready to consider the difference employer mobilization makes in American politics and public policy. The next three chapters show the effects that mobilization has on how workers think about politics and participate in the political process (chapter 6), how mobilization has changed the contours of public policy debates (chapter 7), and the ways mobilization has shifted election outcomes (chapter 8).

PART II

WHAT DIFFERENCE DOES EMPLOYER MOBILIZATION MAKE?

6

Employer Mobilization and Worker Political Participation

In making the pitch to businesses about why they should mobilize their workers into politics, BIPAC's newly installed head argued to his fellow executives in 2016, "Too many times corporations are unwilling or are afraid to confront their employees with [political] issues and to communicate to them how public policy affects business for a fear of offending their talent. That is a huge mistake." This association leader stressed that "employees may not vote their business interest. They may have other cultural interests or identity interests that frankly might conflict with their business interest." As a result, he concluded, "employers have a duty to inform employees on how [political] issues may affect their livelihood in the long term."[1] If done right, BIPAC's head explained, workers would begin voting in their business interests—and not their other identities.

We have seen that in recent years a number of companies have taken up BIPAC's call and now regularly inform their employees about the implications of political issues and candidates for their companies' bottom line. When asked about it themselves, a number of workers say these messages shaped their political behavior and attitudes, including a substantial share of workers who said they changed how they thought about politics as a result of employer communications. But are these workers right in their self-assessment of the effect of employer messages? Does employer mobilization actually change how workers think about political issues—and their behavior too?

This chapter moves from considering workers' self-reports of the effects of employer messages to more definitive evidence of the causal weight of employer mobilization on worker political participation—whether or not workers end up thinking and voting in their "business interest," as BIPAC put it. Because tracking changes in individuals' political attitudes and practices is no easy task, I review several different types of evidence. A survey experiment of workers permits me to isolate the specific effect of messages that workers think come from their bosses on workers' policy views and their likelihood of engaging in political activity. The advantage of this approach is that we can be sure that any change in political views observed in the survey experiment can be attributed to the employer messages. The downside is that the messages I use are, by necessity, fictional (even though the text comes from real-world examples of mobilization). To get at the effect of actual employer mobilization efforts, I turn back to survey data to see whether workers who reported receiving messages from their managers in recent years possess systematically different outlooks on politics and patterns of reported political behavior compared to workers who did not receive such messages. Where possible, I also benchmark the effects of employer messages against those more commonly recognized in politics, like outreach from political parties and unions.

The upshot across these different sources of evidence is that employer messages, whether imagined by respondents in a survey experiment or actually fielded in practice, can reshape workers' preferences and actions just as much as, if not more than, messages from other political sources. Equally important, I find evidence in both the experiments and the surveys that economic power strongly affects workers' responses to employer messages. When workers are less secure in their jobs, they are more likely to shift their attitudes and behaviors in response to what their employers tell them. Similarly, when workers perceive the threat of retaliation from their bosses they are much more likely to report changing their behavior and attitudes in response to the employer messages they receive. A final dimension I explore in this chapter is whether workers who believe their employer can monitor their political preferences and behaviors are more likely to respond to their bosses' political requests. I find that the answer is a resounding yes: workers who thought (correctly or not) that their employer could track their political participation were substantially more likely to respond to their managers' messages and requests.

The Causal Effect of Employer Messages on Worker Attitudes and Behaviors

About half of all workers who have been contacted by their employer about politics reported responding to those messages in some way, including changing their attitudes about policy issues, turning out to vote, and contacting lawmakers. An important limitation to those survey results, however, is that they depended on workers' own recollections of their experiences with employer mobilization. It might be the case that the workers who did not change their attitudes or behavior in response to employer messages did not remember receiving such messages in the first place. Workers might also overstate the effects the messages had. Can employer messages actually shape workers' attitudes and behavior, and is there something distinctive about employer messages as opposed to generic information employees might receive from other sources?

To address these questions, I fielded an online survey experiment on 1,214 American workers (including 1,014 private-sector employees), recruited through the Internet polling company SSI, Inc. Although not a national probability sample like my worker survey, SSI recruited respondents so that they would be generally representative of the overall population of American workers on age, race and ethnicity, gender, and region. (Readers interested in the complete methodology for the survey can return to chapter 2 for more details.) The idea behind this experiment was to have workers read a series of messages, imagining that some were sent from their employers. I would then see if messages that workers believed came from their bosses led them to change their political beliefs and behavior. If the experiment was successful, it would provide evidence that the sort of messages that employers send to workers can indeed change workers' political behavior and attitudes. The experimental setup also permits me to see whether workers who expressed more concern about losing their jobs were more affected by employer messages than those who were less concerned about job loss, which would offer evidence in support of the relationships I proposed in chapter 1.

Obviously the experience of reading these hypothetical employer messages is different from actually experiencing such messages in practice. But in some ways this gap between the experience in the survey and in practice makes the survey an especially hard test of employer mobilization: if I can show that these fleeting hypothetical managerial messages can affect workers' political choices and actions, even stripped of the context of the workplace, then it seems more likely that such messages can actually have an effect when delivered on the job by managers and supervisors responsible for the economic fate of workers and their families. The other distinct advantage of this survey experiment is that by randomly assigning workers to receive either a hypothetical message or no message at all, I can be certain that any difference in the political attitudes and behaviors of the workers I observe is due to the receipt of the employer message and not other characteristics of the workers, such as their educational attainment or occupation.

I look at the experimental effect of employer messages on two different sets of outcomes: workers' attitudes toward increasing the minimum wage and their likelihood of contacting their member of Congress about a pending policy debate related to the Affordable Care Act. Both of these outcomes, as we have seen, are topics that employers discuss with their workers on a regular basis. Many employers, for instance, talk about the negative consequences of labor regulations, including the minimum wage, with their employees. Managers, moreover, often ask their employees to weigh in on policy debates that affect their company by contacting their members of Congress. For both outcomes, I examine the effect of workers receiving several different kinds of messages, again closely resembling the sort of appeals that we have seen in practice throughout the book. I summarize each of these messages that workers were randomly assigned to receive in Table 6.1, as well as each of the outcomes I study for those messages. I focus on the private-sector workers in the survey sample, given that this is the population of employees most relevant for differences in employer messages, as we saw in chapter 5.

Employer Messages and Preferences for the Minimum Wage

Responding to new grassroots worker activism, especially among fast-food and retail workers, a number of cities and states across the country have introduced and enacted measures to increase their minimum wages. Following suit, congressional Democrats have also introduced legislation to raise the federal minimum wage—the floor for all states to follow—to $15 an hour to match the "Fight for $15" campaign's demands, though as of 2017 the measure has been stalled by Republican control of Congress and the presidency. Nevertheless most Americans remain strongly supportive of raising the federal minimum wage. One poll from 2015 found that 75 percent of Americans supported an increase to $12.50 an hour, and 63 percent supported the even larger hike to $15 an hour.[2] Some, if not all, of the cost of a higher minimum wage would fall on employers, however, and as a result many businesses employing large numbers of low-wage employees have fiercely resisted such proposals. These businesses have argued that a minimum wage increase would force them to lay off low-wage workers in response to their higher labor costs. In a publication responding to Washington's proposed $15-an-hour minimum wage, the Job Creators Network asserted, "When governments mandate ultra-high minimum wages, it can have an unintended and deleterious impact on job opportunities for those younger people looking for entry to the job market."[3] Similarly the CEO of fast-food giants Carl's Jr. and Hardee's has publicly opposed measures to raise the minimum wage, arguing, "Does it really matter if Sally makes $3 more an hour if Suzie has no job?"[4] Can these arguments from employers to workers change workers' support for the otherwise very popular measure to raise the minimum wage?

I find strong evidence to suggest employer messages can indeed reduce worker support for the minimum wage, especially when employers make threats of job loss linked to minimum wage hikes. I first randomly assigned workers to receive one of three different conditions (see Table 6.1). Some workers simply received no message at all; this was the baseline condition. Another set of workers received the following excerpt, taken from the Employment Policies

Table 6.1. **Experiments for Studying the Effect of Employer Messages on Worker Attitudes and Behaviors**

Outcomes	Messages
Minimum wage preferences • Preferences for a $15-an-hour minimum wage ("strongly favor" or "somewhat favor" versus "neither favor nor oppose," "somewhat oppose," or "strongly oppose")	• No message • Summary of arguments against raising minimum wage • Summary of arguments against raising minimum wage from employer, including threat of layoffs if minimum wage is increased
Contacting Congress about the health insurance tax • Likelihood of contacting Congress about health insurance tax ("very likely" or "somewhat likely" versus "neither likely nor unlikely," "somewhat unlikely," or "very unlikely")	• No message • Summary of arguments against health insurance tax in the Affordable Care Act • Summary of arguments against health insurance tax in the Affordable Care Act from employer, plus employer threat of cuts in health benefits

Institute, an advocacy group that supports pro-business positions on labor mar-ket policies and is commonly cited by business representatives arguing against minimum wage increases:[5]

> There are a number of politicians who are currently calling for an increase in the federal minimum wage. Those politicians argue that an increase would help lift workers out of poverty. Please read the following information about increasing the federal minimum wage: According to a recent review by economists at the Federal Reserve Board and the University of California, Irvine, most economic research shows that a higher minimum wage reduces employment for the youngest and least-skilled workers, thus hurting many of the same workers that it is supposed to help. This is supported by research from economists from American and Cornell University who studied the states that raised their minimum wages between 2003 and 2007 and found no associated reduction in poverty.

A third set of workers received the Employment Policy Institute message but were told to imagine that the text came from their top managers at work. That letter also included language intended to replicate the sort of threats that employers sometimes include with their political communications that we have seen throughout the book. The text for this condition was as follows:

Dear valued co-worker,

There are a number of politicians who are currently calling for an increase in the federal minimum wage. Those politicians argue that an increase would help lift workers out of poverty. Unfortunately, the academic evidence paints a very different picture.

According to a recent review by economists at the Federal Reserve Board and the University of California, Irvine, most economic research shows that a higher minimum wage reduces employment for the youngest and least-skilled workers, thus hurting many of the same workers that it is supposed to help. This is supported by research from economists from American and Cornell University who studied the states that raised their minimum wages between 2003 and 2007 and found no associated reduction in poverty.

Your top managers here are also agreed that if the federal government were to raise the federal minimum wage, it would hurt our sales and force us to lay off a number of workers. Your job—and the jobs of your coworkers—might be at risk.

Workers who received the employer letter with the threat about layoffs were substantially less likely to support a $15/hour minimum wage. After reminding workers that the "federal minimum wage is currently $7.25 per hour," I asked, "Do you favor or oppose raising the federal minimum wage to $15 per hour?" and gave respondents five possible options, ranging from "strongly favor" to "strongly oppose." (Respondents could also answer that they did not have an opinion one way or the other.) Fifty-nine percent of respondents who saw no message (the baseline condition) reported that they either strongly favored or somewhat favored a $15/hour federal minimum wage (total sample: 237 private-sector workers). But for workers who received the employer message containing the threat of job loss, only 52 percent favored the $15/hour minimum wage (total sample: 269 private-sector workers), a decline of about 12 percent. Workers who read the generic arguments against raising the minimum wage fell somewhere in between, with about 56 percent reporting that they favored a $15/hour minimum wage (total sample: 250 private-sector workers).[6] These results suggest that information from employers that emphasizes layoffs—something employers are positioned to act on quite credibly—can move workers' preferences for an otherwise very popular policy.

Examining the ability of employer messages to shift workers' attitudes is only half of what I was hoping to test with the survey experiment, however. In chapter 1, I made the case that workers who are especially fearful of losing their jobs should be much more likely to respond to employer messages because they are more willing to do whatever it takes to keep their jobs. To test this prediction in the survey experiment, I asked participants to indicate their level of job security with the following question: "About how easy or difficult would it be for you to find a job with another employer with approximately the same income and benefits you have now?" Workers had five possible responses, ranging from "extremely easy" to "extremely difficult." If the argument about employment insecurity were true, we would anticipate that workers who reported that it would be difficult to find a new job with the same income and benefits would have been especially likely to change their attitude in response to the letter about the minimum wage. (Importantly, I asked about workers' perceptions of their job security *before* delivering the employer message, otherwise the employer message could have shaped workers' answers to the job security question.)[7]

Figure 6.1 reviews the evidence for this prediction, plotting the proportion of workers in support of raising the minimum wage to $15/hour by whether or not workers read the employer letter or no letter at all, and their self-reported employment security. To ease the presentation of these results, I grouped together respondents who indicated that it would be either "extremely difficult" or "somewhat difficult" to find a new job, and those who said it would be "neither easy nor difficult," "somewhat easy," or "extremely easy." The figure shows that the mock employer letter had a much larger effect on the attitudes of workers who were concerned about their job prospects (left panel); letters were estimated to reduce support for a $15/hour minimum wage from about 54 percent to nearly 33 percent (a decline of about 20 percentage points). In contrast, letters had no effect on workers who felt secure in their job prospects (right panel).[8] There was

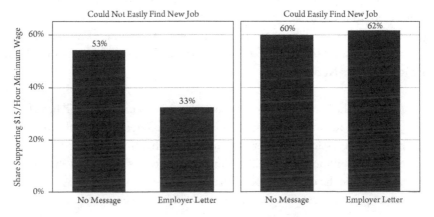

Figure 6.1 The effect of employer messages on workers' preferences for the federal minimum wage, by workers' employment prospects. Data from 2016 SSI survey experiment (sample sizes: 157 and 349, respectively).

no similar interaction with workers' employment prospects for the generic message that contained the arguments against the minimum wage but was not sent from an employer, reinforcing the unique relationship between employers and employees (see appendix).

Employer Messages and Congressional Contact

Employer messages can change worker attitudes about the minimum wage, but can they spur the actions that employers want their workers to carry out in order to change policy? The second experiment on the survey examined this question, probing whether an employer message could motivate workers to contact their members of Congress about an important policy debate: the tax on high-cost health insurance plans that was included in the 2010 health care reform law. In an effort to dampen the rapidly mounting costs of health insurance in the United States, congressional reformers included a tax targeting "really fancy [health insurance] plans that end up driving up costs," in the words of President Obama.[9] Though the 40 percent tax on high-cost health insurance plans is legally paid by insurers, most analysts anticipate that those insurers will pass on part or all of the tax to employers, who will pass it on to workers.[10] Although supported by health economists hoping to control medical costs, the tax has been panned by unions and businesses alike, which strongly oppose the taxation of health benefits. As a result Congress has taken several symbolic votes on repealing the health insurance tax, and at the end of 2015 voted to delay the implementation of the new levy by two years.[11]

The excise tax on high-cost health insurance plans is thus a real-world issue on which some employers have been contacting their workers, making it an ideal test for examining the mobilizing effects of employer messages. To conduct this experiment I randomly assigned workers to one of three groups. As before, one group received no message at all. The second group of workers saw the following text, arguing against the health insurance tax using language directly copied from the Job Creators Network:

> As part of the health reform law enacted in 2010, employers will have to pay a new sales tax on health insurance plans offered through the workplace. Congressional budget estimates show that this tax will represent over $101 billion between 2013 and 2022. Research suggests that this tax will raise the costs of health insurance for everyone, and may reduce future private sector employment by 125,000 workers.

The third group of workers received the following prompt from their employer, which included the same information from the Job Creators Network, a description of how the tax might hurt the ability of the employer to offer competitive benefits and wages, and an appeal to workers to contact their members of Congress to repeal the tax:

> Dear valued co-worker,
> As part of the health reform law enacted in 2010, employers will have to pay a new sales tax on health insurance plans offered through the workplace. Congressional budget estimates show that this tax will represent over $101 billion between 2013 and 2022. Research suggests that this tax will raise the costs of health insurance for everyone, and may reduce future private sector employment by 125,000 workers.
>
> Your top managers here are agreed that the health insurance tax will raise our costs of doing business, and make it harder to offer competitive wages and benefits to our workers.
>
> Congress is currently discussing a bill that would cut the health insurance tax, and we urge you to contact your Member of Congress to support the bill. Calling or emailing your Member of Congress will help your management continue to offer competitive wages and benefits.

After seeing one of these three messages, workers indicated how likely they were to contact their member of Congress about the health insurance tax, responding to the question "Congress is currently debating legislation that would cut a new sales tax on health insurance plans offered through the workplace. How likely are you to contact your Member of Congress about this issue?" Respondents could indicate how likely they would be to respond on a 1–5 scale, ranging from "very likely" to "very unlikely."

In all, about 40 percent of workers who saw no message about the health insurance tax indicated that they would be either "very likely" or "somewhat likely" to contact their member of Congress to advocate repeal of the health insurance tax (total sample: 253 private-sector workers). The proportion of workers who received the more generic information that was not identified as coming from an employer had a very similar likelihood of contacting Congress; about 42 percent (total sample: 253 private-sector workers). But the story was very different for workers who had received the letter from their employer: over half—55 percent—said they would be likely to contact Congress on this issue (total sample: 236 private-sector workers), a 13-percentage point difference with the generic messages and 15-percentage point difference with workers who received no message at all.[12]

Figure 6.2 summarizes these striking differences between workers by the message they received. As is clear, employer messages made workers substantially more likely to say they would engage in precisely the sort of behaviors

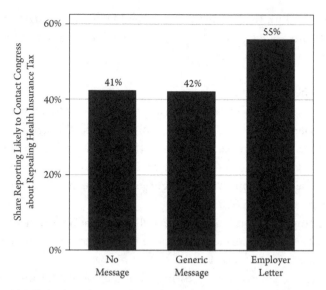

Figure 6.2 The effect of employer and generic messages on likelihood of contacting Congress about health insurance tax. Data from 2016 SSI survey experiment (sample sizes: 253, 253, and 236 workers, respectively).

that employers seek to encourage in their workforce around policy debates, above and beyond the effect of even generic information with the same policy arguments that employers use. Just as with the minimum wage experiment, employer messages that tie public policy to specific warnings of changes in employment, wages, and benefits are especially effective at spurring changes in workers' political orientation and, in this case, behaviors.

Do we observe the same sort of interaction between employment prospects and employer letters as we did with the minimum wage experiment? Figure 6.3 answers this question, showing, as before, the differential effect of employer letters depending on workers' assessment of their employment prospects. For both relatively secure and insecure workers, employer letters were estimated to increase the likelihood of contacting Congress about repealing the health insurance tax. But the effect of employer letters was much larger for more insecure workers—nearly a 30-percentage point increase—compared to the more secure workers.[13] Summed up simply, workers who felt more insecure in their jobs were more likely to respond to the employer letter about the health insurance tax than those who were less worried about finding new work. As before, there was no interactive effect between the generic messages about the health insurance tax and workers' employment prospects: such messages not from employers had little effect on workers regardless of whether they felt insecure in their jobs.

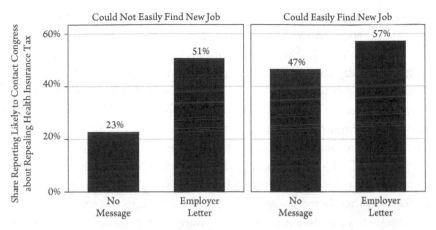

Figure 6.3 The effect of employer messages on likelihood of contacting Congress about health insurance tax, by workers' employment prospects. Data from 2016 SSI survey experiment (sample sizes: 143 and 346, respectively).

These survey experiments together provide concrete causal evidence that employer messages can shape workers' political attitudes and behaviors, even in a context where we hold everything else constant through random assignment. Messages from employers, especially those that incorporate threats of wage cuts or layoffs, can change the way workers think about the consequences of costly labor market regulations, like the minimum wage. Similarly, appeals from managers can greatly increase the likelihood that workers will plan on contacting Congress to lobby on behalf of their employer. And economic power—as measured by workers' employment prospects—shapes workers' responses to employer letters, even in this context where workers were merely imagining the receipt of employer messages.

The Effect of Employer Messages on Worker Political Attitudes and Knowledge

Workers change their minds on political issues based on fictional employer messages, but is it possible to discern whether actual employer messages have a systematic effect on worker attitudes about major economic policy issues? Although the 2015 worker survey I fielded asked about employer mobilization, it did not include questions about policy or issue stances. The 2016 Cooperative Congressional Election Study did ask extensive questions about employer mobilization, employer preferences, and worker policy attitudes. Those questions permit us to see if workers who were exposed to employer messages had different perspectives from those workers who did not receive such communications, after accounting for other possible explanations for workers' policy attitudes, such as education, partisanship, and ideology.

Of course a test like this one cannot pin down the exact effect of employer political contact, as there might well be other reasons that workers contacted by their bosses espouse different attitudes, opinions, and knowledge compared to those who were not contacted at work.[14] Nevertheless this correlational analysis does offer an important test of the effects of employer mobilization, especially when judged in concert with the experimental findings I just presented.

The 2016 CCES permits us to assess the effects of two types of employer messages on workers' specific policy attitudes. For each of these policies, I asked workers whether their employer had expressed an opinion on that issue and how workers themselves thought about those issues. Workers could indicate whether they supported or opposed these positions, and also whether they thought their managers supported or opposed these policies based on the communications they had received from their employer. (Note that there was a long series of survey questions between the items that asked workers for their own opinions and those of their managers to reduce the possibility that workers would be thinking about their previous response when answering one or the other.) The two policy areas, along with exact survey question text, include the following:

- Support for renewable energy standards. Question text: "Require a minimum amount of renewable fuels (wind, solar, and hydroelectric) in the generation of electricity even if electricity prices increase somewhat."
- Support for raising the federal minimum wage. Question text: "Raise the federal minimum wage to $12/hr by 2020."

Together these policies implicate two very different issues that employers regularly communicate to their workers, as we saw in chapters 3 and 4. If these employer messages are indeed persuasive, then we should expect that workers would be more likely to support these policies if their employer supports them and oppose them when their employer opposes them. Figure 6.4 evaluates this question, showing the proportion of workers agreeing with each policy depending on whether they reported that their managers also supported or opposed those policies. (Workers also had the option of indicating that they did not know their managers' positions if, for instance, workers did not receive any political communications from managers and supervisors.)

Figure 6.4 indicates that for each of the two policy issues, worker support fell along the lines predicted by their managers' positions. When their managers supported a policy, workers were substantially more likely to support that policy, compared to workers who did not know their managers' positions. We see the same story for managerial opposition: workers were more likely to oppose the

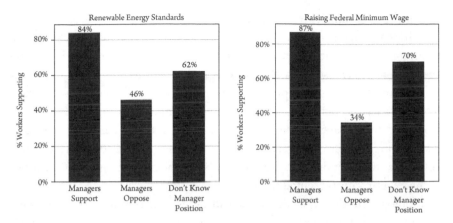

Figure 6.4 Worker opinions on policy and managers' policy stances: renewable energy standards and the federal minimum wage. Data from 2016 CCES (sample sizes: 370 and 371, respectively).

policies when their managers opposed the policies, compared to workers who did not receive employer messages on these issues.

In the case of renewable energy standards, workers whose employers supported new standards were 22 percentage points more likely to support those standards themselves compared to workers whose managers did not take a stand. Workers whose employers opposed renewable energy standards were about 16 percentage points less likely to support requiring the use of renewable energy sources. The differences were roughly the same size for raising the minimum wage: workers whose managers supported raising the federal minimum wage were about 17 percentage points more likely than workers whose managers did not communicate on that issue to support boosting the federal minimum wage. In contrast, workers whose employers opposed the federal minimum wage hike were 36 percentage points more likely to oppose the policy compared to workers whose employers did not take a stand.

Figure 6.4 thus makes it seem as though workers are taking cues from their employers when developing their attitudes about environmental and economic policies. Yet readers might wonder whether these findings really reflect causal relationships. Do liberal workers simply work for liberal employers, for instance? To get closer to a causal estimate, I use managers' stances on these two issues as the predictor of worker stances, after controlling for workers' gender, race, ethnicity, education, family income, age, political ideology, partisanship, industry, and employer ideology. (Full results appear in the appendix.) Even after accounting for these diverse factors, however, managerial stances remain a powerful predictor of workers' own preferences on the minimum wage and renewable energy standards.[15]

For the minimum wage, for instance, net of other factors 89 percent of workers whose managers support a boost in the federal minimum wage are predicted to support a boost themselves, compared to 69 percent of workers whose managers did not take a stand (a 20-percentage point difference). In contrast, only 42 percent of workers were predicted to support a federal minimum wage hike if their managers oppose it—a 27-percentage point drop in support from those workers whose managers did not take a stand. I found similarly consistent results for renewable energy standards. This analysis helps us to see that employees appear to adopt their employers' stands on policy issues, just as I identified in the experiments presented earlier.

Employer messages may shift worker attitudes on important economic issues, but do employer messages also increase workers' knowledge of American politics? To answer this question, we can consider whether the receipt of employer messages makes workers more knowledgeable about the basic attributes of their political system. The 2016 CCES asked respondents a variety of questions about their awareness of the party affiliation of their governor, representative, and two senators, as well as the partisan control of the House, Senate, state lower legislative chamber, and state upper legislative chamber. Together these eight items provide a baseline of knowledge about politics that is arguably essential for a minimum level of participation and representation: before citizens can hold their elected officials accountable, they need to know which party is in charge at various levels of government. And while there might be any number of other attributes about elected officials and facts that citizens need to know to hold officials accountable (such as knowledge about policy outcomes and the condition of the economy), partisan affiliation seems an especially basic and fundamental one.

Consistent with a large literature on the study of political knowledge and facts, I find that most Americans do not know much about which parties are in charge of different levels of government, nor even the partisan affiliation of their individual elected officials.[16] On average the typical American scored only a five out of a possible eight, and 46 percent of respondents scored less than five (12 percent could not answer any of the items correctly). Americans were especially bad at listing the partisan control of state offices (fewer than half could correctly name the partisan control of their state legislative chambers, for instance).

Did the receipt of employer messages improve the distribution of basic political knowledge? Analysis of the CCES data reveals that employer mobilization barely moved the average levels of political knowledge indicated by survey respondents. Recipients of employer political messages were no more likely to correctly report the partisan affiliations of their federal and state elected officials or which parties controlled different levels of government compared to individuals who did not receive political messages from their employers. The picture remained similar regardless of whether or not I controlled for other salient individual-level characteristics, such as those I described above.[17]

These survey results indicate that employer mobilization may systematically change the policy preferences of workers yet do not necessarily help workers hold their politicians more accountable. Next we will see how employer mobilization can change political participation and how employer mobilization stacks up against recruitment efforts from other groups, including the political parties.

Employer Mobilization and Worker Political Participation

In addition to showing how employer messages may change workers' political attitudes and knowledge, the analysis of the CCES poll offers an opportunity to look at the effect of employer messages on political action. The CCES poll asked respondents whether they had participated in five civic activities from 2015 to 2016: voting in the 2016 election, attending a political meeting, putting up a political sign or wearing a button, making donations to political causes, and volunteering for campaigns or candidates. In all, 70 percent of workers reported performing at least one of these civic acts, and the average number of acts was one. If employer messages were indeed spurring workers to greater political action, then we ought to see that workers who had received employer contact would have reported more political acts compared to those workers who had not received employer contacts, net of other individual characteristics. Since the CCES asked about political contact from the parties or political campaigns as well as labor unions, we can also compare the effects of employer messages against those types of recruitment in a head-to-head matchup.

Table 6.2 summarizes the effects of each of these kinds of contact on the 0–5 index of civic participation using an OLS regression (full results in the appendix). The first column shows the effect of each of these three types of contact—employer, union, or political party—without taking into account any of the characteristics of the individuals themselves. All three types of contact are related to higher participation, but especially party and campaign outreach.

The picture changes somewhat once I take into account the demographic characteristics of the individuals contacted by these three different actors, including their education, race, ethnicity, interest in politics, age, gender, ideology, income, strength of partisan identification, church attendance, union membership, and past participation in the 2012 election. Now we see that employer, union, and party contact offer roughly similar increases in civic participation. These results remain similar accounting for the geographic context in which the

Table 6.2. **Comparing the Effects of Employer, Union, and Party Mobilization on Participation, 2015–2016**

Type of Contact	Change in Civic Participation Index (0–5), No Controls	Change in Civic Participation Index (0–5), Individual Controls	Change in Civic Participation Index (0–5), Individual and Geographic Controls
Employer mobilization	+ 0.15 acts	+ 0.22 acts	+ 0.24 acts
Union mobilization	+ 0.52 acts	+ 0.38 acts	+ 0.31 acts
Party mobilization	+ 0.70 acts	+ 0.37 acts	+ 0.36 acts

Source: Data from 2016 CCES survey. Sample size is 823 for model with no controls; 720 for model with individual controls; 720 for model with individual and geographic controls. Individual controls include education, race, ethnicity, political interest, strength of partisanship, union membership, church attendance, income, age, age squared, gender, ideology, and voted in 2012 indicator. Geographic controls include district competitiveness (absolute value of Cook Partisan Voting Index) and state fixed effects.

contact is occurring by controlling for the competitiveness of the U.S. House district in which an individual resides, as well as taking into account the characteristics of the states. (The competitiveness measure captured the relative closeness of the 2008 and 2012 presidential elections.)[18] This most comprehensive set of results reveals that employer appeals may be just as effective as party or campaign messages.[19] Employer contacts raised civic participation by about 0.24 acts on the five-act scale and party contact and union contact by 0.36 and 0.31 acts, respectively. Employer messages were most effective at spurring participation by wearing buttons or posting signs and encouraging attendance at political meetings or events. In contrast, party contact had the largest effect on donating to campaigns or candidates. Union contact was most likely to foster button-wearing or sign-posting, as with employer messages.

Table 6.2 helps us to see that employer contacts are generally just as likely to spur employee political participation as more conventional forms of mobilization. But are particular kinds of workers more likely to respond to these messages by increasing their civic participation? In previous chapters we have seen the importance of employer monitoring of workers for effective mobilization campaigns. Chapter 3 showed that employers were more likely to report mobilizing their workers into politics, and to consider that mobilization as being more effective, if they were closely tracking employee participation in recruitment drives. And in chapter 5 we saw that the creation of new software platforms that could track workers' participation in workplace political activities—like writing to lawmakers, posting to social media, or donating to political campaigns—facilitated the spread of mobilization more generally across the corporate community.

Are workers who perceive (correctly or not) that their employer is tracking their political participation more likely to respond to political messages? We might well think that if workers believe their manager can see whether or not they voted, they will be concerned about the potential for retaliation if they did not follow through on their managers' requests. The CCES lets me test this prediction directly. Recall that in chapter 4, I found that 17 percent of workers participating in the 2016 CCES survey responded affirmatively to the question "How likely is it that your employer can track your political behaviors and attitudes, such as keeping track of whether you voted or which candidates you support?" Another 18 percent of workers said they were "not sure," bringing the total group of workers who think that monitoring is plausible to 35 percent. If perceptions of monitoring matter for how workers respond to employer political requests, then workers who thought that their employers could track their political behavior ought to be more likely to increase their participation after receiving a request from their bosses.

Figure 6.5 assesses this idea, showing the average number of political acts (on the 0–5 scale of acts) for workers who reported employer mobilization and those who did not. I further divide workers by whether they perceived the potential for employer monitoring of their political attitudes and behavior. The first thing to note is that workers who experienced employer mobilization reported higher

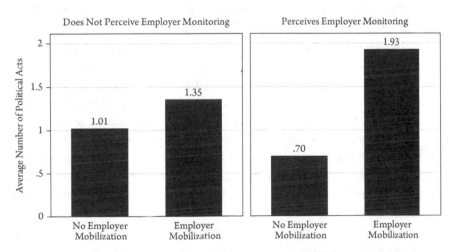

Figure 6.5 Worker political action, employer mobilization, and perceptions of employer political monitoring, 2015–16. Data from 2016 CCES. Political activity measured on 0–5 scale, including voting in 2016 election, wearing or posting political signs or buttons, attending political meetings or events, donating to political campaigns, or volunteering for political campaigns (sample sizes: 296 and 161, respectively).

political activity, on average, than workers who did not receive employer messages. This was true regardless of whether workers perceived employer monitoring (right-hand plot) or not (left-hand plot).

Yet the difference between mobilized and nonmobilized workers is quite striking between the right- and left-hand plots. The difference between mobilized and nonmobilized workers was substantially larger for workers who doubted their political privacy at work. In the right-hand plot—consisting of those workers who perceived the potential for employer monitoring—workers who received employer messages reported performing over 1.21 additional civic acts, on average, compared to workers who did not receive employer messages. That difference was just 0.33 acts for workers who did not perceive the potential for employer monitoring, as shown in the left-hand plot. Workers clearly appear more responsive to employer messages when they think their bosses might be tracking their political activities and beliefs.

Cautious readers might wonder if the effect of monitoring simply reflects other worker characteristics. Could it be the case that more poorly educated workers, for instance, are more likely to perceive monitoring and also to respond to employer messages? To address such concerns, I next control for a range of individual-level characteristics relevant for political participation, including education, race, ethnicity, interest in politics, age, gender, ideology, income, strength of partisan identification, church attendance, union membership, and past participation in the 2012 election (see appendix). Even after controlling for these varied characteristics, however, I continue to find that perceptions of employer monitoring strongly reinforce employer recruitment requests. The effect of employer messages on civic participation tripled for workers who felt that their employer might be closely tracking their political choices.[20] Combined with the evidence from the previous chapters, it is clear that monitoring matters just as much for workers as for employers in workplace mobilization campaigns. (Note that I did not find the positive interaction between perceptions of employer monitoring for either union or campaign mobilization, a reassuring result, indicating that perceptions of employer monitoring matter only for employer mobilization.)

The other factor that might matter for how workers respond to employer messages and requests are employee fears of political retaliation. Recall that in chapter 4 I found that over a quarter (28 percent) of employees expressed concern that employer retaliation might be possible. If these workers were indeed concerned about the possibility of their managers punishing them in some way for going against the company's political line, then they might feel a strong need to follow through on employer requests. The 2016 CCES polling strongly suggests that employee fears of political retribution mediates the effect of employer messages on worker civic participation—just like employee perceptions of monitoring.

Figure 6.6 shows the average number of civic acts reported for mobilized and nonmobilized employees, this time separating out workers by whether they perceived the potential for political retaliation from managers. As before, workers who reported receiving employer messages were substantially more likely to report civic action, regardless of whether or not they perceived the threat of political retribution from their bosses. But similar to the results we just saw, the difference between mobilized and nonmobilized workers was substantially larger for workers who worried about the potential for employer political retaliation.

On average, workers who perceived the potential for political retribution at their workplace reported performing one additional civic act if they received employer messages, compared to their counterparts who did not receive such messages. The difference for workers who did not perceive the potential for political retaliation was half that size (0.50 acts on the five-act scale). The results continue to hold accounting for other individual demographic and political characteristics that we might think would explain both perceptions of employer retribution and civic participation. I find the effect of employer messages doubles for workers who worried about employers punishing them in some way for their political views or actions.[21] (Reassuringly, I did not find the positive interaction with perceptions of employer retaliation for either union or campaign mobilization; such perceptions matter only for employer recruitment.)

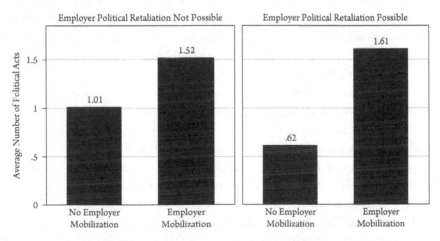

Figure 6.6 Worker political action, employer mobilization, and perceptions of the potential for employer political retaliation, 2015–16. Data from 2016 CCES. Political activity measured on 0–5 scale, including voting in 2016 election, wearing or posting political signs or buttons, attending political meetings or events, donating to political campaigns, or volunteering for political campaigns (sample sizes: 335 and 123, respectively).

One objection to this analysis is that I am assessing only workers' *percep-tions* of employer political monitoring and the potential for managers to with-hold opportunities for advancement based on workers' political choices and actions—not whether employers were actually tracking workers' political par-ticipation or making concrete threats of retaliation. Yet it is ultimately workers' perceptions of these practices that will dictate their reactions to employer mes-sages. Regardless of whether an employer is actually tracking employee political participation, for instance, employees who believe that their managers are moni-toring them will likely behave very differently from workers who believe in their political privacy at work—and that is exactly what we have seen.

Getting Employees to Think—and Act—in Their "Business Interest"

The BIPAC executive I introduced at the beginning of this chapter said that it was a "big mistake" for employers not to get their employees to think and vote on their "business interests." Combining the results of an original experiment of workers with surveys of workers who actually received employer messages, this chapter has shown that managers can indeed convince workers to shift their thinking about politics toward those business interests. The experiments demonstrated that messages about policy that workers thought came from their managers shifted their attitudes about policy—above and beyond the effects of more generic messages with information about public policies. We saw these same effects when shifting from the experiments to surveys of actual employees.

Yet despite conveying information about public policy to workers, there was no indication that employer messages changed workers' underlying levels of political knowledge. Workers who received employer messages scored no better on basic questions about American politics, such as which party controlled state and federal government or the party to which their elected officials belonged, compared to workers who had not received workplace messages. The lack of an increase in political knowledge, coupled with the finding that it was insecure workers and those who perceived employer monitoring who were most respon-sive to employer messages, raises serious questions about the place of employer mobilization in American politics. If managers are successfully changing the political attitudes and behaviors of workers not because workers fundamentally agree with their managers but because workers are fearful of losing their jobs and economic livelihood, then there is a serious concern about political coer-cion. I will return to this thorny issue in the concluding chapters. For now, I will trace the effects of employer mobilization on two other outcomes: public policy battles and elections.

7

Employer Mobilization and Public Policy

In chapter 4 we heard from a government affairs officer at an extractive resource manufacturing company that made extensive use of mobilization during elections and, equally important, during policy battles. That manager said he kept close track of worker participation in requests to attend town halls, write to lawmakers, and participate in the regulatory rule-making process because that way he could "keep track of who is a champion, who has responded to every single request or letter." He said that these champions were a critical part of how the company responded to potential policy threats. Reiterating Representative Tip O'Neill's old adage that "all politics is local," this government affairs officer explained that his company had employees and direct suppliers in 41 states, making it possible to "get local" with state and congressional politicians from each of those constituencies. When "legislative proposals or regulatory proposals . . . create political exposure, risk, [or] opportunity," this manager could thus activate the workers or suppliers who lived in the states and districts of relevant lawmakers, getting those workers to bombard an elected official with calls, letters, emails, and even appearances at local town halls.

He talked about a recent congressional showdown over reauthorization of the U.S. Export-Import Bank as an example of how his employee base could pressure wavering politicians to toe the company's legislative line. Created by President Franklin Roosevelt in 1934, the Export-Import Bank provides financial backing for foreign purchases of U.S.-manufactured goods. The bank is intended to support American companies making overseas sales that might otherwise be too risky without a government backstop. For years Congress easily reauthorized the bank's operations with votes from both parties. In recent years, however, the libertarian far-right wing of the Republican Party has taken aim at the bank as a prime case of "crony capitalism."[1] Newly elected Tea Party lawmakers in 2012 and again in 2015 threatened to hold up the bank's reauthorization as part of their fight against big government.

The manufacturer I interviewed depended heavily on the bank's loans to sell its extractive resource equipment overseas and so was deeply concerned about the prospect that Congress might block the bank's renewal in 2015. Accordingly the manufacturer began "educating our workers on the Ex-Im [Export-Import] Bank and its importance" to the company's bottom line. In emails, Internet material, and mailings, the company explained to workers that if the bank "is not reauthorized, the people working on the line making equipment would lose their jobs because that equipment would not be sold."

The government affairs division at the manufacturer then identified the key GOP members of Congress who might be swayed by pressure from their constituents and sent action alerts to the employees in those states and districts to contact their senators and representatives. As the executive explained to me, once workers got the action alert about the Export-Import Bank reauthorization, "they can click it and send a letter [to their member], [which] makes a difference." The hope, he explained, was that "the member of Congress will go to their staff, the poor young guy or girl who is answering the phone and reading emails and making tally marks for or against the [Export-Import Bank] bill," and the member would see the overwhelming support "from the grassroots in their constituency" for reauthorization of the bank. It was especially effective, the manager mentioned, for employees to convey the potential economic consequences of failing to reauthorize the bank to Congress. Ultimately the government affairs officer credited his company's employee mobilization with "moving the needle" on a number of wavering Republicans. The Export-Import Bank was indeed eventually reauthorized by Congress at the end of 2015.[2]

This company, like many of the ones whose executives and employees I interviewed, made employee mobilization a central piece of its political recruitment efforts. According to the company's internal mobilization website, the employee recruitment program "brings together the hard-working people of [the company] to ensure your voice is heard by our nation's policymakers. . . . Together we can help shape policies that strengthen America's energy future, protect our jobs and enable us to provide the energy America needs."

Zooming out from the specific example of the Export-Import Bank skirmish, how effective are employer mobilization strategies, like the ones mentioned by the manufacturer, at actually shaping congressional decision-making and policy? Certainly corporate managers in my interviews and survey data indicate that they feel employer mobilization can shape the decisions legislators ultimately make. But while managerial perceptions are persuasive, identifying concrete evidence that greater mobilization changed the course of policy debates would help us to see whether or not workplace recruitment has a substantive effect on American politics. That is the question I tackle in this chapter.

I first review the results of a new survey of senior legislative staff to show how employer-initiated employee messages to Congress shape how congressional offices view their constituents' preferences and ultimately make policy. The survey indicates that the top aides in congressional offices take employee messages very seriously—in many cases even more seriously than comparable correspondence from ordinary constituents or interest groups because of the potential job losses threatened by employee letters.

Next I review the results of two case studies that indicate the potential reach of employer mobilization into the policymaking process. The first case focuses on how Alaskan oil producers used mobilization of their workers to retain large corporate tax breaks even in the face of public support for a tax hike on oil companies. The second case study looks at employer messages about the Affordable Care Act during the health care reform law's early years. Employer messages, I show, helped to sow early skepticism about the law. The case studies and congressional survey together show that the accounts I received from corporate managers were generally accurate: employer-initiated recruitment of workers can indeed "move the needle" on public policy across a wide range of issues.

How Employer Mobilization Can Shape Congressional Decision-Making

As the interviews and survey evidence revealed, many companies deploy mobilization to shape policymaking in Congress. Companies report, for instance, having their workers write to or call their member of Congress to support bills that companies favor. In a guide for contacting legislators, International Paper, a major pulp and paper products manufacturer, explained to its workers that if the company is against a piece of legislation, workers should tell their member of Congress that they oppose the bill "because it would have serious economic disadvantages and could result in layoffs at our facilities."[3]

One example of the sort of letter companies might ask workers to send to their member of Congress follows. This alert comes from an extractive resource manufacturing company and was intended to oppose Obama administration efforts to offset reductions in the corporate tax rate through new taxes on the oil and gas sector. As is typical for these letters, the information is prepopulated based on information the company has on its workers, though each employee is encouraged to customize the letter by adding their own personal touches.

The Honorable [Representative Last Name]
U.S. House of Representatives
1230 Longworth House Office Building
Washington, DC 20515

Dear Representative [Last Name],

As your constituent, I'm writing today to tell you about an issue that is important to me and to the company I work for.

As a citizen who is proud to work in the oil and natural gas industry, I'm concerned about President Obama's call to raise taxes on the industry. My hard work, and that of my colleagues, helps to ensure that Americans have the fuel they need to power their everyday lives.

During this year's State of the Union Address, President Obama discussed the importance of job growth. I agree. Americans need all the jobs they can get. With the uncertain economy and continued high unemployment rates, our country cannot afford to pass measures that stifle the growth of America's oil and natural gas industry—an industry that supports over 9 million jobs.

Raising taxes on a crucial source of energy is not a long-term solution to our nation's challenges. Instead, it's one that will threaten our country's energy security and place millions of jobs at risk. With the right policies, America's oil and natural gas industry can create more jobs and provide more revenue for the federal government.

[Company] is known for its leading innovation in [Areas of Innovation].

We have an opportunity to chart a new course that leads to economic and energy security. With your support and the support of your colleagues in Congress, we can get our country back on the right path!

Sincerely,
[Employee Name]
[Employee Address]

In having their employees contact members of Congress, such employers are following an increasingly common playbook that many other interest groups use in attempting to influence legislation. Indeed congressional offices report that the volume of constituent mail they receive has increased nearly 300 percent from 2002 to 2010 (and over 500 percent in the U.S. Senate).[4]

Despite the mounting volume of communications, congressional staff—the front-line aides responsible for reviewing constituent messages and presenting summaries and recommendations for policy action to their members—report that they still make an effort to respond to each and every letter, email, fax, and phone call they receive. "Constituents who take the time to contact our office directly . . . about their concerns are given priority treatment. Their comments are recorded, and the data is shared with the entire staff for immediate action," explained one House legislative director in an anonymous survey.[5] Congressional staff indicate that personal contact from constituents also has a significant effect on legislators' decision-making. According to one 2015 survey conducted by the Congressional Management Foundation, a nonpartisan, non-profit organization that studies best practices for congressional offices, about 90 percent of legislative staff said that individualized postal letters or emails would have "a lot of positive influence" or at least "some influence" on the decisions of their member of Congress if the member had not already made up his or her mind.[6] The only two categories of contact that staff reported to be more effective were in-person visits from constituents and contact from community leaders who represented groups of other constituents. In fact letters and emails were reported to be more effective than visits from lobbyists or endorsements of the news media.

The Congressional Management Foundation survey indicates a mechanism through which employer mobilization could be shaping congressional decisions. But that study did not compare the effectiveness of employer-initiated messages with letters generated by other interest groups or individual constituents. How do staff perceive employer-initiated employee contact with Congress? And are employer-initiated employee messages to Congress taken as seriously as letters from ordinary citizens or non-profit citizens' associations? To answer this question, I—along with two of my political science colleagues, Matto Mildenberger and Leah Stokes—conducted a survey of top staff in U.S. Senate and House offices during the fall of 2016. (See chapter 2 for the full methodology.) In all, 101 of these top staff, generally chiefs of staff or legislative directors, completed our online questionnaire.

One way of getting at legislative staff perceptions of employer mobilization is simply to ask them how useful it is for businesses to recruit employees to contact their offices about pending legislation. To do this my collaborators and I first gave staff the following prompt: "Businesses often contact Congressional offices to support or oppose policy proposals. Thinking about the ways that businesses have contacted your office about policy proposals in the past year, which strategies have been most useful to your office as you deliberate over legislation?" We then asked staff to rate how useful different business strategies had been for their offices, including "Having their employees write to your office with their opinions about policy," "Offering research and assistance drafting legislation, including model bill language," "Offering political advice, such as talking points and polling data," and "Having their employees support your member's electoral campaign."

I have summarized the staff ratings of these different strategies in Table 7.1. Research and assistance in drafting legislation was reported to be the most useful thing that businesses could do to help top congressional aides, with 49 percent

Table 7.1.   **Legislative Staff Rank Business Strategies for Shaping Legislation**

Business Strategy	Extremely or Very Useful (%)	Moderately or Slightly Useful (%)	Not at All Useful (%)
Having employees write to office	30	61	9
Having employees support campaign	11	51	39
Offering assistance with legislation	49	44	7
Offering political advice	28	56	16

Source: Data from 2016 legislative staff survey. Sample sizes are as follows: having employees write to office (88), having employees support campaign (85), offering assistance with legislation (87), and offering political advice (87).

of staff reporting that such a strategy was "extremely" or "very" useful; this is consistent with past work that identifies this sort of informational lobbying as being very important for harried, busy staff who do not have enough time or resources themselves to conduct the research needed for writing bills.[7] One mode of employer mobilization—having employees write to Congress with their opinions about pending bills—came in second, at 30 percent of staff, followed closely by companies offering political advice, including talking points and polling. Staff were, on average, least likely to report that businesses encouraging employees to support the election campaign of their member was helpful. These initial results suggest that top legislative staff find employer mobilization helpful, especially when it involves having employees express their support for or opposition to particular policy proposals.[8]

Not all offices responded to the questions about business strategies in the same way, however. In particular, there were two important factors that shaped legislative staff's perceptions of employer mobilization: partisanship and attention to election challenges, especially primary challenges. Disaggregating the survey results by party, Republicans tended to rate corporate lobbying strategies as being more useful than did Democrats. The biggest difference was in employee support of a member's electoral campaign: 72 percent of Republicans ranked this as being useful, compared to only 53 percent of Democrats. This makes sense given that employer electoral drives tend to favor Republican over Democratic candidates. The second major difference across congressional staff was for those offices reporting that concerns about "primary opponents" were either "extremely" or "very" important when we asked staff "What shaped your thinking on whether your member should support or oppose . . . policies?" Staff in offices that reported they were concerned about primary challengers were also substantially more likely to report that electoral employer mobilization was useful to them. A full 92 percent of these offices reported that having businesses mobilize workers to support members' electoral campaigns was useful. This also makes sense to the extent that employer mobilization can help vulnerable candidates win competitive primary races.

These results from the legislative staff survey indicate that employer mobilization can be an important tool for congressional offices in tight races and as their members deliberate over public policy decisions. Yet the self-reports by staff do not capture whether employer-initiated employee communications or contact with Congress are more or less effective than other types of communications that congressional offices might receive. To answer this question, we can look to an experiment embedded in the legislative staff survey. In that experiment my collaborators and I asked staff to imagine that they had received constituent communication on a bill pending in Congress— something like the message from the extractive resource manufacturer I described above. Staff were randomly assigned to receive different descriptions of the constituent communications, with the variations indicated in brackets as follows: "Imagine your office is considering a bill that is under debate in Congress. Your office receives [2, 20, 200] letters from constituents [supporting, opposing] this bill. The letters have very [similar, different] wording to one another. The letter writers identify themselves as [employees of a large company based in your constituency, constituents, members of a non-profit citizens group]."

The survey then asked staff three questions about the effect of those letters on their deliberations over the bill in question: "How likely are you to mention these letters to your Member?"; "How significant would these letters be in your advice to your Member about their position on the bill?"; and "How representative do you think these letters are of your constituents' opinions?" Staff responded to each of these questions on a 1–4 scale: "not at all," "not very," "somewhat," and "very."

By randomly assigning staff to read some combination of the details of the hypothetical letters, I can estimate the causal effect of a staffer receiving messages coordinated through an employer's mobilization drive—as compared to letters sent from ordinary citizens or a non-profit advocacy group. To be sure, this experiment is stripped of the important political context that accompanies debates over congressional legislation. But the advantage is that it can reveal the exact effect of employee messages on staff thinking about legislation.

Figure 7.1 reviews the findings from the communications experiment, plotting how staff responded to the three questions if they thought the letters had

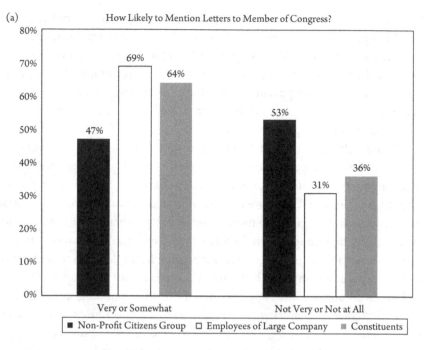

(a) How Likely to Mention Letters to Member of Congress?

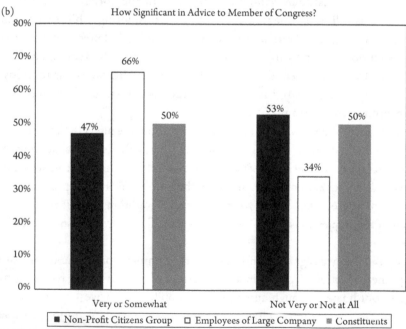

(b) How Significant in Advice to Member of Congress?

Figure 7.1 Top congressional staff perceptions of constituent messages from employees, individuals, and advocacy group members. Data from 2016 legislative staff survey. Sample sizes for each of the treatment groups: 17 staff saw "non-profit citizens group" condition; 29 staff saw "employees of a large company" condition; and 36 staff saw "constituents" condition.

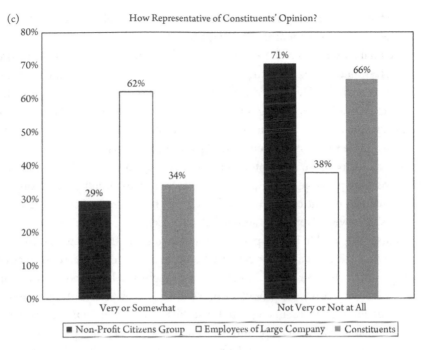

Figure 7.1 Continued

come from employees, ordinary constituents, or members of an advocacy group. Looking first at whether or not staff would mention the letters to their bosses, we see that more staff said they would be "very likely" or "somewhat likely" to report employee letters to their member of Congress, but the difference with the other two categories of authors was not large. In general the authorship of the letters did not matter much in whether staff would brief their member on those communications. That finding is consistent with the fact that many offices have policies in place to review all constituent correspondence, regardless of its source.[9]

The picture changes, however, when we asked staff how significant the letters would be in their advice to their member of Congress on whether to support or oppose the hypothetical bill. No staffer reported that letters from non-profit citizens' groups would be "very" significant in his or her advice, compared to 8 percent of staff who thought the letters were from ordinary constituents, and 14 percent of staff who thought the letters were from employees. In all, over 65 percent of staff who thought the letters were from employees said the letters would be "very" or "somewhat" significant as they considered how to brief their member, compared to 50 percent for constituent-written letters and 47 percent for the non-profit advocacy group letter-writers.[10] Employer-initiated letters from workers, then, have the potential to carry extra weight in the minds of staff when staff and members are considering legislation—well above and beyond the effects of letters from ordinary citizens or other interest groups.

The final plot in Figure 7.1 shows how top legislative staff interpret constituent correspondence as reflecting (or not) the public opinion of their state or district as a whole. This is perhaps the most consequential effect of constituent communication, as messages not only inform lawmakers about the position of the specific letter-writer but also shape legislators' perceptions of their constituents' preferences more generally. As the plot reveals, employee messages are substantially more relevant as staff form perceptions of their constituents' opinions than messages from either individual citizens or advocacy groups. A whopping 62 percent of staff who saw messages from employees reported that the messages were "very" or "somewhat" representative of their constituents' opinions, compared to just 34 percent of staff who thought the letters were from ordinary constituents and 29 percent who thought the letters were from advocacy groups.[11] Over 33 percent of staff who thought the letters were from nonprofit advocacy groups and about 11 percent who received hypothetical letters from individual constituents reported that those letters were *not at all representative* of their constituents' opinions. A significant portion of top congressional staff, then, were ready to dismiss the representativeness of letters from ordinary citizens or advocacy groups but not letter-writers who identified themselves as being employees at a large business.

One common concern for any organization mobilizing citizens to contact elected officials is that those officials may discount the opinion of a large number of letters that come from the same organization; that is, there are diminishing returns to having additional mobilized citizens contact a member's office. The staff survey, however, revealed no evidence of such diminishing returns for employers: regardless of whether staff thought that there were 20 or 200 letters coming from the same employer, they were just as likely to think that employee letters were more significant and representative compared to constituent or advocacy group communications.

In a similar vein, although staff were less likely to evaluate letters that were "very similar" in their wording positively—only 2 percent of staff thought that such letters would be "very significant" for their member's decision-making— employee letters were not disproportionately penalized by staff for being carbon copies of one another. Staff discounted near-identical letters from employees in the same way as they did letters from advocacy groups or ordinary citizens. Thus the downside of employers mobilizing employees to contact Congress—at least as captured on this legislative survey—is no greater than the downside for other groups.

While troubling for the representation of ordinary citizens in the legislative process, this simple experiment reveals a powerful mechanism by which employers can shape the thinking of top legislative aides and, through them, members of Congress. Top legislative staff have a strong bias in favor of correspondence from private-sector employees, above and beyond ordinary constituents, which creates the possibility for employers to influence how members vote on legislation and perceive public opinion more generally.

Why is it that members are so attuned to correspondence from mobilized employees and not other interests? One explanation is that certain offices view businesses as being a more important part of their political constituency than other offices. If that is the case, we should expect that congressional offices that report relying on business more frequently for legislative help would be more attuned to employee letters over letters from other sources.

One item on the staff survey lets me test this possibility. That item asked top congressional staff to indicate how important a variety of information sources had been for their thinking about legislation, and one of those sources was "information from businesses." In all, 42 percent of senior legislative staff said that information from businesses was either "extremely important" or "very important" in their thinking and recommendations to their bosses.

Were these staff more attuned to the hypothetical employee letters we presented to them? I found little evidence for this prediction. In fact staff who reported that they were *less* reliant on businesses for information about legislation were actually *more likely* to say that they would report the employee letters to their bosses than staff who said that they were *more* reliant on business.[12] What are we to make of this surprising finding? One plausible reason is that offices that rely more heavily on businesses already have strong relationships with executives representing employees in their districts and states. As a result those offices might find employee letters less surprising or relevant. In contrast, offices that have weaker ties to business might find employee letters more unusual or useful when they do receive them.

If not ties to businesses, what else can explain the deference staff give to employer-initiated employee messages over letters from ordinary constituents and interest groups? Another explanation is that staff are more attuned to employee letters because of concerns about job loss in their district or state. Since employee correspondence often reflects the threat of greater unemployment—as the examples from International Paper and the extractive resource manufacturer indicate—then legislators from districts and states facing higher joblessness should be more attuned to those letters from businesses than messages from other constituents. Warnings from many employees working at the same business saying that their employer might need to make layoffs if a lawmaker votes one way might carry more weight when that lawmaker is already facing the prospect of high joblessness among his or her constituents.

I can test this explanation by seeing whether staff representing states and districts with high unemployment were more responsive to the employee condition in the survey experiment. I use data on average unemployment by congressional district and state over a five-year period, from 2011 to 2015. While this relatively lengthy period is dictated by the available data from the U.S. Census Bureau, it also has the benefit of smoothing out shorter-term ups and downs in labor market conditions. This unemployment rate should thus reflect districts and states with persistently high unemployment in recent years—exactly the congressional offices that might be most attuned to business decisions.

Staff from above average-unemployment constituencies were no more likely to say they would mention employee letters to their bosses (the first outcome). But I do find very strong evidence that staff from above average-unemployment areas were more likely to say that employee letters (as opposed to constituent or citizens group letters) would be significant in their advice to their member of Congress. Figure 7.2 shows how staff responded to the hypothetical employee letters differently depending on the unemployment rate in their district or state. I have divided staff into two groups: those from districts and states with above- and below-average unemployment. (The average unemployment rate from 2011 to 2015 was 7.8 percent.) Staff representing districts or states with below-average unemployment responded to employee letters about the same way as they did to letters purportedly from individual constituents or citizens groups. Nearly 55 percent of staff who thought the letters were from employees at the same

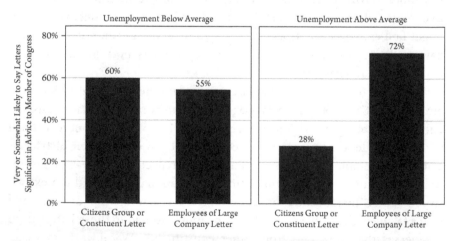

Figure 7.2 District and state unemployment and share of top congressional staff saying that letters would be "very or somewhat significant" in their recommendations to their members of Congress. Data from 2016 legislative staff survey and the American Community Survey (2011–15 file). Average unemployment rate: 7.8 percent. Sample sizes: 43, 14, 22, and 22, respectively.

large company said the letters would be "very or somewhat significant" in their advice to their member of Congress. That is not all that different from the 60 percent of staff who saw the citizens group or ordinary constituent letters condition and said the same thing.[13]

The picture looks very different when we turn to the staff from districts and states with above-average unemployment. Here there was a 44-percentage point difference between how staff responded to the citizens group and individual constituent letters and the employee letters. Fewer than 30 percent of these staff said that citizens group or individual constituent letters would be "very or somewhat significant" in their advice to their member of Congress. By contrast, over 70 percent said the same thing when they thought the letters came from employees. Staff from high-unemployment districts and states were much more attuned to letters from employees when thinking about their recommendations to their bosses.

Staff from constituencies with higher joblessness also were more likely to think that employee letters were representative of their constituency as a whole, as shown in Figure 7.3.[14] As before, there was not much difference in how staff representing below-average unemployment districts and states responded to employee letters, as opposed to letters from citizens groups or individual constituents: 38 percent said that citizens group or constituent letters were "very or somewhat representative" of their constituency as a whole, compared to 45 percent who saw the employee letters.

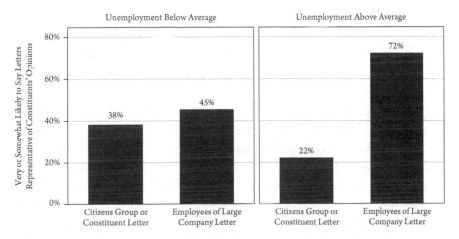

Figure 7.3 District and state unemployment and share of top congressional staff saying that letters would be "very or somewhat representative" of public opinion in their constituency. Data from 2016 legislative staff survey and the American Community Survey (2011–15 file). Average unemployment rate: 7.8 percent. Sample sizes: 43, 14, 22, and 22, respectively.

There was an entirely different response among high-unemployment congressional offices. Only 22 percent of staff from these districts and states said that letters from citizens groups and individual constituents were "very or somewhat representative" of their member's district or state. There was a 50-percentage point difference with staff who saw the hypothetical employee letters: 72 percent of staff in the employee letters condition said that these letters were "very or somewhat representative" of their constituents as a whole.

In sum, the congressional staff survey shows results highly consistent with descriptions from my managerial interviews that discuss how employee communications to politicians carry the threat of potential repercussions in a way that other communications to Congress may not. Employee letters indicate that a well-mobilized group of citizens (and potential voters) in a member's constituency care deeply about an issue—and might be willing to vote against the member should he or she not follow through on their demands.[15] Just as important, these employee letters also signify the threat of unemployment more generally, as employees channel corporate warnings about layoffs if legislators do not follow the company's recommendations, echoing the descriptions of structural business power from Charles Lindblom that I reviewed in chapter 1.[16] Those warnings of joblessness resonate especially loudly for congressional offices that are more attuned to the poor economic conditions in their local communities. But Congress is not the only institutional arena in which employer messages can carry significant heft. Employer recruitment efforts shape state policy decisions too.

Mobilizing for Tax Cuts on Oil Production in Alaska

As governor of Alaska, Sarah Palin, the former 2008 GOP vice presidential nominee, had overseen a sharp increase in taxes on the state's oil producers.[17] When fuel prices soared across the country, Palin wanted to make sure that her state got its share of the oil industry's record profits. She ultimately succeeded in passing controversial legislation that amounted to a $1.6 billion tax hike on oil companies such as BP, ConocoPhillips, and Exxon Mobil. Unsurprisingly the measure was opposed by those businesses, and after the law passed, the president of BP Alaska expressed hope that "once the impact of this legislation is clear, the administration and the legislature will revisit the issue."[18]

Six years later newly elected GOP governor Sean Parnell announced his support for a measure to repeal Palin's tax, replacing the state's graduated tax rates on oil companies with a flat rate. Proponents of SB21, which included the major oil companies operating in the state, argued that a lower tax rate was necessary to spur greater investment and recover from the Palin tax hike. A consultant for the oil industry explained, "If you look at worldwide investment levels over the last few years, they've risen tremendously [but under the Palin plan] we've stayed flat. In fact, we've declined some. SB21 is a response to that, to try and increase the amount of investment that's coming in the state."[19] Defenders of the old progressive tax system countered that SB21 would mean that "oil companies get the biggest share, a much larger share of that [profit]" flowing from oil production.[20] Repealing Palin's tax hike also meant much less revenue for the state, including the generous dividends the state offers residents. Ultimately the oil companies won the legislative debate, and on a mostly party-line vote SB21 passed the Republican-controlled Alaskan legislature in April 2013.[21]

Alaskan affiliates of BIPAC's Prosperity Project played an important role in mobilizing voters to contact their legislators to support SB21.[22] As the chairman of BIPAC's Alaskan chapter put it, "This victory is huge. . . . Even more exciting is that the Prosperity Project tools were a central part of the effort. . . . As a result, over 12,400 letters to legislators were generated on the oil tax issue alone. In this state, that is a LOT!"[23] The chairman declared that "industry is pretty pleased" with the fruits of their mobilization campaign.[24] His enthusiasm was well founded: 12,400 letters to the legislature amounts to over 200 letters per member of the Alaska statehouse and represents correspondence from about 2 percent of the entire adult population in the state.

Proponents of more progressive taxes on the oil producers were not ready to concede defeat, however, and immediately announced that they would be challenging SB21 with a voter referendum in the upcoming primary election. A "yes" vote on Ballot Measure 1 would repeal SB21 and restore the Palin-era progressive tax rate structure, while a "no" vote would leave in place the current tax regime, with its lower rates on oil producers. An intense political campaign ensued. Supporters of the referendum emphasized the unfairness of SB21 for Alaskans, the negative effects of SB21 on state finances, and the need for ordinary citizens to have a say in the control of their state's natural resources. Organized interests supportive of the repeal of SB21 included two major unions in Alaska (the State Employees Association and the International Brotherhood of Electrical Workers), which were supported by donations from several wealthy individuals.[25] Palin herself even campaigned for the repeal vote.[26] In all, repeal proponents spent a little over half a million dollars.[27]

Opponents of the ballot drive included many state Republican organizations, business groups, several labor organizations (most prominently the Teamsters), and the major oil companies with a presence in Alaska.[28] Their campaign emphasized the need for lower taxes on oil production to spur investment and job creation. Individual companies—especially the oil companies—poured millions of dollars into the campaign. BP and ExxonMobil, for instance, each contributed more than $3.6 million to the effort.[29] The opposition campaign could thus count on over $14 million to spend on ads and voter outreach, or more than 28 times the amount held by proponents of the old tax system.[30]

Despite the fact that proponents of the ballot initiative were so badly outspent, polling conducted during the campaign suggested a dead heat between the two sides, with a sizable contingent of undecided Alaskans.[31] In an effort to persuade that group and shore up support for their lower tax rates, oil companies launched an aggressive workplace mobilization campaign to contact their employees and convince them to vote against the ballot measure.

Prosperity Alaska, BIPAC's affiliate in the state, created a website for employers to show their workers that included a variety of arguments against the referendum. "It's about attracting investment to boost production," the site argued, stating that the reasons to support SB21 were simple: it created a "business-friendly tax structure that will compel oil companies to fund high-cost Alaska projects, ultimately resulting in more oil production . . . and increased revenue to the state."[32] Prosperity Alaska also suggested a number of creative activities for employers to encourage greater turnout opposing the ballot measure. Employers could urge their employees to post selfies with their ballots on social media, hold turnout contests in different divisions within companies and between different firms, and place bets on how high turnout would be at a particular workplace.[33] Another priority of Prosperity Alaska was to encourage employees to cast early ballots, if possible, so that their votes would be locked up in advance of the election. "Vote Early, Vote Today!" implored the Prosperity Project.[34]

Some oil producers went even further in their mobilization efforts. One investigative journalist discovered that ConocoPhillips workers at the Alaskan oilfields were called into a "safety stand-down" meeting in January 2014, an event typically used only after a major workplace accident.[35] But rather than hearing from managers about safety standards, workers were given a presentation on why they should vote against the upcoming ballot measure, which included a warning that if the measure passed, ConocoPhillips might have to make significant layoffs. There was no room for workers to question the company's position. "The feeling was that if we didn't stay quiet we could get blackballed," explained one construction worker. All throughout the summer ConocoPhillips had "distributed signs, buttons, branded pens, and magnets urging workers to vote against the tax break repeal," warning that the company might "re-evaluate" its planned investment in the region if the measure passed and the tax cuts were revoked. The other two major oil companies operating in Alaska—ExxonMobil and BP—also engaged in similar practices. BP barraged its workers with emails, town halls, and other messages through the year. Said one BP worker, "They let it be known that if SB 21 was repealed that there would be layoffs. . . . It was clear how they wanted us to vote."

Did the oil producers' efforts affect the referendum, which ultimately failed, with 52.7 percent of Alaskans voting to retain the tax cuts on oil companies? An ideal research design would compare the votes cast by otherwise similar Alaska workers who did and did not receive employer messages. Unfortunately no such survey exists. The next best approach might examine the turnout and vote choices of Alaskans in areas with higher and lower levels of mobilization by the oil companies. Again no such records exist. As an alternative, however, we can use a measure of the concentration of employment in the oil and gas sector as a rough proxy for the prevalence of employer mobilization, since this was the industry engaged in the most extensive mobilization during the debate over tax cuts. We would expect that areas where Alaskans were more heavily reliant on employment in the oil and gas sector would have been more likely to oppose the referendum in light of extensive employer mobilization.

Using data at the level of Alaska state legislative districts (the smallest geographic level with available data), we see precisely this pattern, as demonstrated by Figure 7.4. Areas where more workers were employed in the extractive

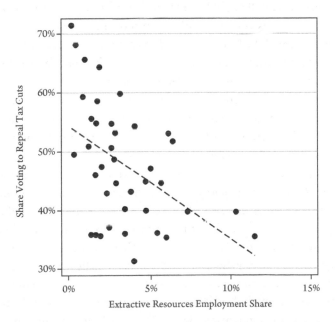

Figure 7.4 Employment in extractive resources sector and support for Alaska tax cuts on oil production. Unit of analysis is the state lower chamber legislative district. Extractive resources employment data from the American Community Survey (2009–13 file). Ballot Measure 1 data from the Alaska Division of Elections.

resources sector were much more likely to vote no on the referendum, supporting the status quo tax system with big breaks for oil producers. A 5-percentage
point increase in the share of workers employed in the extractive resources sector is predicted to have reduced support for the ballot measure by about 10 percentage points.[36]

We might be concerned, however, that the relationship in Figure 7.4 is picking up on the underlying liberalism of particular geographic areas and not necessarily the deployment of employer messages. Perhaps areas where there is
greater employment in the extractive resources sector are simply more conservative and supportive of business interests in general. To account for this factor,
we can use President Obama's vote share in the 2012 election as a measure of
political ideology within each district. However, even taking into account past
support for President Obama, we continue to see a relationship between the
share of workers in the extractive industries and support for the referendum.
A 5-percentage point increase in the share of workers employed in the extractive
resources sector of the economy is predicted to have reduced support for the
ballot measure by about 8 percentage points, after accounting for Obama's past
electoral performance.[37]

While providing initial evidence in support of employer mobilization, the
relationship identified in Figure 7.4 does not test the specific mechanism of
employer recruitment. It might be the case that oil and gas sector workers would
have supported the tax cuts even without employer messages. To dig deeper, we
can take advantage of the fact that oil and gas companies were encouraging their
workers not only to vote against the ballot measure but also to cast absentee and
early ballots rather than vote in person on Election Day. As BIPAC has argued
in its materials to employers, "In today's mobile workplace, absentee voting is
vitally important—and many people forget they have that option. Let's not lose
even one vote!" Accordingly BIPAC has recommended that employers begin
absentee and early voting ballot drives months before an election.[38]

We can thus examine not only the *overall level of support for the ballot measure* but the *difference in support for the ballot measure between absentee or early
voters and regular voters*. In areas of more intensive employer mobilization, we
would expect that there would be a larger gap in support for the ballot measure
between absentee and regular voters, given that mobilized workers would be
casting absentee or early ballots—and those early ballots would be disproportionately in favor of retaining the tax cuts. This analysis is especially compelling
because factors that might lead some areas to support or oppose the ballot measure (such as underlying political ideology) are no longer a concern.

Table 7.2 tests the relationship between the extractive resource workforce
and the gap in support for the tax cuts between regular and early/absentee voters. For districts in the lowest fourth of extractive resource employment (or

Table 7.2. **Difference between Support for Alaskan Ballot Measure 1 between Early/Absentee and Regular Voters, by Extractive Resources Employment**

	Extractive Resource Employment Quartile			
	Low			*High*
Difference in Support for Tax Cuts between Regular and Early/Absentee Voters	0.4 pp	1.9 pp	3.7 pp	4.7 pp

Unit of analysis is the state lower chamber legislative district (39 districts). Extractive resources employment data from the American Community Survey, 2009–13 sample. Ballot Measure 1 data from the Alaska Division of Elections. Ballot Measure 1 would have repealed the tax cuts on oil production.

about 1 percent of workers employed in gas and mineral extraction), there was a gap of only 0.4 percentage points in the level of support for Ballot Measure 1 between regular and early/absentee voters. But shifting to a district with the highest concentration of extractive resource employment (or about 7 percent of workers employed in extraction) increases the gap between early/absentee and regular voters to about 5 percentage points.[39] This analysis thus shows that there was a bigger gap between the choices of regular voters and early/absentee voters in areas of higher employment in the extractive resource industry—precisely what we would expect if more intensive employer mobilization campaigns were convincing extractive resources employees to cast early and absentee ballots in favor of retaining the tax cuts.

Another way of testing the mobilization pathway in Alaska is to see whether employer mobilization encouraged greater early and absentee voting in general. To do this, we can compare the changes in the early and absentee vote in the previous off-cycle election (2010) and in 2014, the year when the oil production tax cuts were on the ballot. If oil and gas companies were indeed encouraging their workers to cast early ballots for the tax cuts, then we should see the biggest increases in early and absentee voting between 2010 and 2014 in the districts with a greater concentration of employment in the extractive industries. This analysis is appealing because it focuses on change in early voting over time *within* electoral districts, holding constant fixed characteristics of the districts that might otherwise explain why some areas saw higher rates of early voting in 2014 compared to others.

Figure 7.5 probes this relationship and shows that all geographic areas saw increases in the rate of absentee and early voting on Alaska ballot measures from 2010 to 2014. But the largest increases in early and absentee voting were

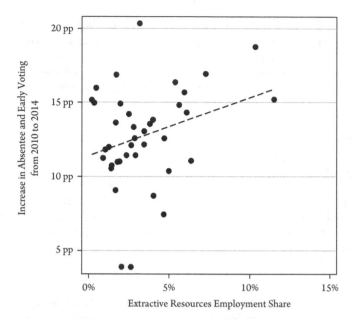

Figure 7.5 Change in ballot measure early and absentee voting from 2010 to 2014 by extractive resources employment. Unit of analysis is the state lower chamber legislative district. Extractive resources employment data from the American Community Survey (2009–13 file). Ballot Measure 1 data from the Alaska Division of Elections.

concentrated in areas dominated by the extractive resources industry, indicated by the upward-sloping trend line. Each percentage point increase in the concentration of employment in the extractive resources sector is predicted to have increased the rate of early and absentee voting from 2010 to 2014 by about 0.4 percentage points—a modest but substantively relevant effect.[40] This plot is consistent with extractive resources companies encouraging their workers to cast early and absentee ballots in advance of the election.

To be sure, this analysis is not airtight. It may well be the case that oil and gas sector workers were simply more likely to support the tax cuts and to file absentee or early ballots than other types of voters, regardless of the employer messages they received. (Alternatively, workers in these areas might have been responding to other sources of information about the ballot measure outside of work.) Still, considering the analysis of the difference between absentee/early voters and regular voters in their support for the tax cuts, the difference in absentee/early voting rates between 2010 and 2014, and the qualitative evidence of the intensive mobilization campaign launched by the oil companies and Prosperity Alaska, this case study offers a sizable body of evidence that mobilization played a role in winning an important victory for Alaska oil producers. We will see the consequences of employer mobilization for another prominent policy debate in the following section.

Employer Mobilization against
the Affordable Care Act

If you were an employee of Cintas, a major provider of office uniforms and other workplace supplies, in the fall of 2012, you would have received a rather ominous series of communications from your company's CEO in the run-up to that year's elections. As we saw in chapter 4, one letter cautioned workers about the negative impact that the new national health care reform program would have on the company's bottom line.[41] Cintas's CEO wrote that "the new health care law amounts to the single largest tax on Americans and business in history," and he estimated "that our health care costs will increase by over $50 million."[42] With those costs in mind, the CEO warned about the effect of the law on the company's "ability to run our business effectively and efficiently, on our ability to attract and retain customers and on our ability to provide the level of benefits, opportunities, and development we believe our partners want, need and deserve."[43] The message to workers was clear: Obamacare would be very bad for Cintas's operations.

Cintas was not the only company sending pessimistic messages about the effect of Obamacare on its workforce. The CEO and founder of Papa John's, the national pizza delivery chain, announced that the health care reform program was going to cost his business between $5 million and $8 million annually and speculated that franchise owners were going to have to slash employee hours to avoid the new requirements on providing minimum health insurance coverage for their full-time workers.[44] Although John Schnatter, the company's CEO, said that he was not "pro or against" the reform law, he compared Obamacare to the federal postal service, arguing that "the worst entity in the world for running the thing [Obamacare] is the government."[45] The CEO of restaurant chain Applebee's in New York, Zane Tankel, gave a television interview to announce that the health care reform program would prevent him from hiring new workers or building new restaurants in the region.[46] "We've calculated it will be some millions of dollars across our system. So what does that say—that says we won't build more restaurants. We won't hire more people—exactly the opposite of what the President says," argued Terkel.[47] Even small businesses joined the chorus. One evangelist for employer mobilization relayed a powerful account of how a restaurant owner in Wisconsin communicated the dangers of Obamacare to his employees. According to that champion for mobilization, the restaurant owner

> heard his employees talking about the benefits of Obamacare. And he thought, they have no idea that this might put them out of a job. What will I do? And so he gathered all of his employees together, and put 100 pennies on the table. . . . These 25 pennies are what I use to pay for

the food in this restaurant. . . . These 20 some pennies are the lights, the air conditioning, the utilities. These over here are the ones that pay your wages and benefits. Here's the taxes. And he had like three pennies left, and he said, this is what I take. But since Obamacare, he took money out of his pocket, put it on the table, and said, I don't take home any more. That means that some of you might not be working here soon. And those of you who are might be serving fewer chips and salsa. And you know, simple things like that can wake up . . . people who still haven't understood that our free enterprise system is something we need to protect.[48]

In short, a range of employers were communicating with their workers about the Affordable Care Act soon after it had passed to warn of the negative consequences that businesses would face as a direct result of the law. Did these messages ultimately affect worker attitudes and perceptions of the health reform program? Answering this question is important because the public's skepticism of the program in its early years made it difficult for Democrats to propose important and necessary changes to the law. It also made it more appealing for Republicans, including President Donald Trump, to run against the health care reform law in recent elections.[49]

As we learned in chapter 4, about 10 percent of employees reported that they had ever heard from their employers about issues related to health care or health policy. But the worker survey did not ask respondents whether they had received messages specifically about the health care reform program, nor did it inquire into their attitudes toward the ACA. That makes it difficult to use the worker survey to establish a relationship between the receipt of employer messages about the ACA and worker attitudes about the ACA. Fortunately another poll, fielded by the well-respected, nonpartisan Kaiser Family Foundation, provides just such information.

Since the passage of the Affordable Care Act in 2010, Kaiser has commissioned a monthly nationally representative telephone poll of American adults asking respondents their perceptions of and experiences with the national health care reform law. One of those tracking polls, fielded more than a year after the passage of the ACA in December 2011, asked Americans to list the sources from which they had received information about health care reform. That list included employers as an option. The Kaiser survey, fielded on a national sample of 1,212 adults, thus provides a perfect opportunity to study the effect of employer information on perceptions of the ACA.

Figure 7.6 summarizes the share of workers reporting relying on different information sources about national health care reform. Workers were most likely to report relying on newspapers (68 percent), conversations with friends and

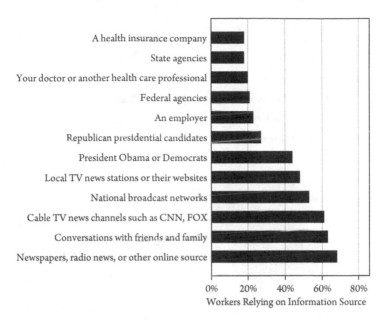

Figure 7.6 Sources of information about the Affordable Care Act. Data from 2011 Kaiser survey. Employed respondents only (sample size: 438).

families (63 percent), and cable news networks (61 percent) in 2011. But a significant share of workers—23 percent—reported that they relied on information from their employers during this early period of the ACA's implementation. Workers were about as likely to turn to employers as they were to rely on Republican presidential candidates, federal agencies (including the Department of Health and Human Services, the main federal agency administering the law), and their doctors or other health care professionals for information about the ACA.

Were employers neutral providers of information about the law, or did they have a slant favoring or opposing the ACA? The Kaiser survey asked respondents who ranked a particular information source as being their "most important source" whether the outlet was mostly positive or negative in its orientation toward the ACA. Using the responses to that question, we can generate a composite measure of how positive or negative a particular source was toward the ACA by subtracting the share of respondents indicating that a source was mostly negative from the share of respondents reporting that a source was mostly positive. Figure 7.7 summarizes the ideological slant of the sources listed in Figure 7.6. Values above zero indicate that more respondents ranked a source as being positive toward the ACA than ranked the source as being negative toward the ACA; values below zero indicate the opposite.

Figure 7.7 shows, unsurprisingly, that information from President Obama or other Democrats tended to be disproportionately positive toward the ACA.

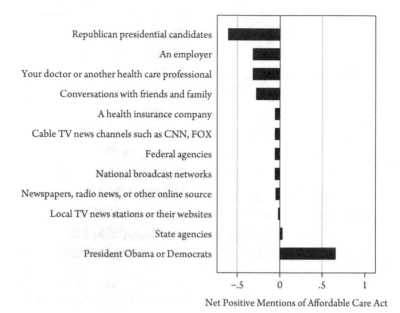

Figure 7.7 Slant of information sources toward the Affordable Care Act. Data from 2011 Kaiser survey. Employed respondents only (sample size: 438).

Information from state agencies, local TV stations, and newspapers tended to be more evenly divided, without much of a slant one way or another. Information from families and friends, doctors and other health care professionals, and employers, on the other hand, all tended to be heavily skewed against the ACA. Reassuringly for the validity of this survey question, respondents indicated that information from Republican presidential candidates for the 2012 race was the most negative toward the ACA—a finding that certainly resonates with the tone of the campaign.[50] Though not as extreme as GOP presidential contenders, employers were also overwhelmingly negative toward the ACA in their communications with workers: 42 percent of respondents indicated that employers gave them negative information about the ACA, while only 10 percent reported receiving positive information. The Kaiser survey fits with the results from my own worker survey, which indicated that employer messages about health care tended to be disproportionately conservative in tone.

Did the information that workers received from their employers influence how workers viewed the ACA at the end of 2011? To answer this question, we can examine another survey question that assesses respondents' perceptions of the health care reform law. The question asked about the effects of the ACA on respondents and their families, as well as on the country as a whole: "Do you think (you and your family/the country as a whole) will be better off or worse off under the health reform law, or don't you think it will make much difference?"

If conservative employer messages were affecting these outcomes, we would expect that workers who had received messages from their employers about the ACA would be less likely to report that the ACA made them better off compared to workers who did not receive such pessimistic messages from their bosses. Figure 7.8 provides initial evidence of just such an effect. Individuals responding to the Kaiser survey who relied on employer-provided information about the ACA were less likely to say they felt the ACA left the whole country, as well as themselves and their families, better off. Just over 40 percent of respondents who did not rely on employer information felt the ACA left the whole country better off, but that share fell by 7 percentage points for respondents who reported relying on employer information about the law (right plot). Similarly respondents relying on employer information were 5 percentage points less likely to say they thought the ACA left themselves and their families better off (left plot).

Figure 7.8 does not account for other factors that might explain the relationship between attitudes toward the ACA and employer information, however. To more accurately measure the effect of employer information on these two outcomes, we can conduct an analysis controlling for the other sources of information a respondent reported relying upon (such as from newspapers or from political candidates), as well as a range of other important respondent characteristics. These characteristics include any other factors that might plausibly lead some respondents to be exposed to employer information *and* to hold particular views about the ACA. Accordingly I account for education, race and ethnicity, political ideology, partisan identification, self-reported health, household income, age, gender, self-reported knowledge about the ACA, and insurance status. (Refer to the appendix to this chapter for full variable information, as well as complete regression results.)

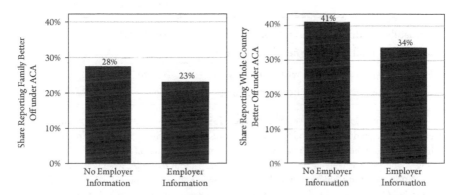

Figure 7.8 Attitudes toward the Affordable Care Act and reliance on employer information. Data from 2011 Kaiser survey (sample size for both plots: 593).

Table 7.3 summarizes how the receipt of employer messages shaped respondent perceptions of the ACA by comparing workers who did and did not receive employer messages about the ACA, controlling for other factors. Respondents who received employer messages about the ACA were about 9 percentage points less likely to believe they and their families were better off under the ACA compared to respondents who did not receive employer messages, other factors held constant.[51] There were similar differences in attitudes between contacted and noncontacted workers on perceptions of the effect of health care reform on the country as a whole. Respondents reporting employers as a source of information about health care reform were 7 percentage points less likely to believe the country was better off under the ACA compared to respondents who did not receive employer messages, other factors held constant.[52]

How persuasive was the information given by employers to their workers about the ACA? The Kaiser survey permits me to answer this question by assessing whether or not respondents changed their opposition to components of the ACA after hearing pro-ACA arguments delivered by the survey administrators. Respondents who said they opposed the individual mandate—the requirement that nearly all Americans buy health insurance or pay a fine—were randomly assigned to receive messages in support of that provision on the survey.[53] Initially 65 percent of workers indicated they did not favor the mandate.[54] Of these employed respondents who started out opposed, 45 percent reversed their position after being exposed to pro-ACA messages; the remaining respondents said they were still opposed despite the pro-ACA messages they had just heard.[55]

Table 7.3. **Employer Information and Attitudes about the Affordable Care Act, 2011**

Outcome	Effect of Relying on Employer Information
Probability of thinking you and your family will be better off under the health reform law	26% to 17%
Probability of thinking the whole country will be better off under the health reform law	40% to 34%

Data from 2011 Kaiser survey. Sample sizes: 739 and 726, respectively. Table shows the change in the predicted probability that a survey respondent believes he or she is personally better off under the ACA (top row) or the whole country is better off under the ACA (bottom row) associated with relying on employer information about the ACA. Results account for education, race and ethnicity, political ideology, partisan identification, self-reported health, household income, age, gender, self-reported knowledge about the ACA, and insurance status, as well as other sources of information. See appendix and text for more details.

If employer information was especially persuasive to Americans, then we might expect that those individuals who received their ACA information from employers would be less likely to be persuaded by the survey's pro-ACA messages than those respondents who received their information from other sources. Alternatively, if employer information was generally unconvincing, we might expect that respondents who received their information from employers would be more likely to shift their stance on the mandate after receiving pro-ACA messages from the survey administrators. A third possibility is that, on net, employer messages were neither persuasive nor unconvincing, making recipients of corporate communications about the ACA no more or less likely to change their stance toward the individual mandate.

To judge these alternatives, I examine whether recipients of employer information were more likely to start favoring the individual mandate, after accounting for the same set of worker characteristics I described above, as well as the other possible sources of health care reform information. Recipients of employer information who initially disagreed with the individual mandate were about 14 percentage points less likely to come around to supporting that provision of the ACA than were individuals who received their information about health care reform from other sources.[56] Put differently, nearly half of the respondents who did not receive employer information were persuaded to temper their opposition to the ACA, compared to about 34 percent of respondents who relied on their managers for information about the law. Employer messages about the ACA thus appear to produce skeptical attitudes that are more durable than messages from other information sources.

A final advantage of the Kaiser survey is that it permits me to test an important question about employer mobilization: To what extent are employers communicating to their workers about issues on which employers are deeply knowledgeable and where workers might benefit from employer information—and to what extent are employers simply conveying a political or ideological position? The ACA provides a good case for evaluating this question because employers are, plausibly, one of the most important sources of information about health care policy for the majority of workers who receive their health insurance coverage through the workplace.[57] For these workers covered by employer-based health plans, it makes good sense to listen to what top managers and supervisors say about the effects of the Affordable Care Act. If employer messages about health care reform were mostly nonpolitical and technical, referring to the effects of the law on workplace health plans, we would expect that workers covered by employer-sponsored health insurance plans would be more likely than non-workplace-covered workers to receive information about the ACA from their employers. We might also anticipate that employer-insured workers would be more likely to shift their attitudes in response to information about the law from managers and supervisors.

As I show in the appendix to this chapter, neither of these propositions held up in the survey. Workers who did not receive health insurance coverage from their employers were just as likely to report receiving information from their employers about the health reform law as were workers who did depend on employment-based health insurance. In addition workers tended to become more pessimistic about the health reform law regardless of whether they got their coverage through the workplace. This evidence from the Kaiser survey strongly suggests that employers were not simply communicating the technical effects of the Affordable Care Act to their insured workers who might be affected by the law's changes, but rather were communicating political or ideological positions opposing the law.

Employer Mobilization and Public Policy

"Send a letter to your legislators, urge them to stop the unnecessary overreach!" implored one action alert to the employees of a large manufacturing company whose manager I interviewed for this book. "It is critical that you are part of the policy discussions occurring at the federal and state levels that impact how our industry does business." This chapter has examined what happens when companies, like this manufacturer, make their employees part of policy discussions in federal and state government. It showed that employer efforts to engage workers in the legislative and regulatory process can indeed produce big returns for companies' bottom lines.

The legislative staff survey showed that aides report taking employer-initiated employee letters to Congress very seriously. In fact staff may even take those employee letters more seriously than similar correspondence from ordinary citizens and even other advocacy groups. The correspondence experiment indicated that top congressional aides thought employee letters would be both more significant in their recommendations to their bosses and more representative of their constituents' opinion as a whole than letters from individual constituents and citizens groups. I further showed that employee letters are especially persuasive for congressional offices that are more sensitive to economic conditions in their districts and states, demonstrating that employee letters may carry the economic threat of job loss. That backs up assessments made by former members of Congress. One past GOP representative from Virginia, Tom Davis, noted that when he was in Congress and "a company would come into my office that had 100, 200, or 1,000 citizens that lived in my district—and the issue that they wanted to discuss would impact them [as employees of a company]—that was the most important thing to me as a legislator."[58]

Beyond Congress, the case study of the Affordable Care Act demonstrated that employer communications can sway workers' opinions and preferences about important public policies. Using an unusually rich set of survey data, I was able to trace how employer messages led workers to become more durably skeptical of the ACA in the law's early years. That case study was especially important because it allowed me to adjudicate whether employer messages carry more heft when they focus on areas where employers conceivably have economic or practical expertise they can share with workers. As I documented, it was not the case that employers were more likely to communicate negative messages about the Affordable Care Act to workers who were receiving workplace sponsored health insurance. That means employers were expressing skepticism about the law even in cases where the employer and employee might not have been directly affected by the program. Instead, confirming the results from chapter 4, employer messages about the law tended to be more ideological.

The effect of employer mobilization on public policy extended well beyond the federal government. In the case of the Alaska ballot initiative, we saw evidence that managers may have convinced their workers to change how they were voting (casting early or absentee ballots), as well as changing their support for taxes on oil producers. A concerted employer recruitment drive of employees in the oil production industry in that state helped to retain a business-friendly tax cut, even in the face of significant public opposition.

Between managers' perceptions of the effectiveness of employer-led mobilization presented in chapter 3 and the results from this chapter, there is good reason to think that mobilization does matter in determining the policies that elected officials in the United States ultimately enact. And they affirm that employer mobilization has a conservative, pro-market bent, helping companies to advance their bottom lines by defeating regulations, lowering taxes, and dismantling social programs. We will see further evidence for this tilt of employer messages in the following chapter, which shows how employer mobilization efforts in recent years have helped to elect Republican politicians to office.

Employer Mobilization and Elections

David Siegel is now perhaps most famous as the star of the 2012 documentary *The Queen of Versailles*, which tracked the timeshare mogul's quest, along with his wife, to build the largest private home in the United States (named Versailles). Siegel's wealth, built on highly leveraged real estate transactions, collapsed during the filming of the movie in the wake of the 2007 financial crisis.[1] The movie thus makes for an enlightening take on wealth, housing policy, and inequality in America. The documentary also reveals— unexpectedly—insights about Siegel's own activities with employer mobilization. In a very brief moment taped during an interview for the movie, Siegel claims that he was personally responsible for the election of George W. Bush in 2000. "The biggest impact [I had] on the world was getting George W. Bush elected," Siegel states quite matter-of-factly. "I got him 2,000 votes in Florida." When the filmmakers ask him to expand on that claim, Siegel says only that what he did "was legal."[2]

In a later interview with a reporter from Bloomberg *Business Week*, Siegel elaborated in more detail about his electoral involvement in the 2000 race: "Whenever I saw a negative article about [Democratic presidential candidate Al] Gore, I put it in with the paychecks of my 8,000 employees." But Siegel did not simply stop there. "I had my managers do a survey on every employee. If they liked Bush, we made them register to vote. But not if they liked Gore. The week before [the election] we made 80,000 phone calls through my call center—they were robocalls. On Election Day, we made sure everyone who was voting for Bush got to the polls. I didn't know he would win by 527 votes. Afterward, we did a survey among the employees to find out who voted who wouldn't have otherwise. One thousand of them said so"—a total twice as large as Bush's margin of victory.[3] In 2012 Siegel was at it again. A month before the presidential contest between GOP candidate Mitt Romney and Democratic incumbent Barack Obama, he sent a message to his employees arguing that despite what they had heard, "the economy doesn't currently pose a threat to your job. What does threaten your job however, is another 4 years of the same Presidential administration."[4]

Can employer efforts like Siegel's really move election outcomes? In chapters 6 and 7 I offered evidence that employer messages do indeed change workers' attitudes and behaviors—for instance, making workers more skeptical of policies employers oppose and more likely to contact members of Congress. But we might well think that shaping workers' electoral participation, and through it, electoral results, is much more challenging given all of the other factors that affect elections. Partisan identification, the quality of candidates, and their coverage in the media are potentially competing factors that might swamp the effect of employer political messages and requests. This chapter delves into the 2014 elections to show how employer efforts to elect business-friendly GOP candidates did in fact result in more votes and dollars for those candidates. Though the evidence in this chapter is more tentative than in chapters 6 and 7, it still indicates that employers are playing a role in both voting and campaign contributions.

Electoral Consequences of Employer Mobilization in 2014

Does mobilization matter for who wins and who loses in elections? Certainly the results I presented in chapter 4 suggest that it should; nearly one out of every six workers contacted by their bosses reported that they changed their vote choice as a result of employer messages, and managers reported that they had successfully used mobilization to elect favored candidates to a range of political offices.

BIPAC, the group aiding businesses in mobilizing their workers, also describes its electoral campaigns as being very successful. Writing after the 2014 elections, BIPAC noted that turnout was about 6 percentage points higher in states with an extensive BIPAC-led employer mobilization presence, and 80 percent of their favored candidates ultimately won.[5] BIPAC further claimed that in many close congressional races, the number of workers using their online platform "accounted for more than the overall margin of victory."[6] Were BIPAC and its employer mobilization drive really that successful in the 2014 midterm elections?

We can assess the effect of BIPAC-led employer mobilization more rigorously in 2014 thanks to internal data from the organization tracking the intensity of recruitment efforts across states. The data I have obtained measure the volume of get-out-the-vote messages employers and business associations sent to workers in the run-up to the 2014 election—the sort of messages at the heart of employer mobilization efforts. By standardizing this count by the number of employees in each state, I can produce an index of employer mobilization intensity that is comparable across states with different sizes of labor forces. The index of employer mobilization registers highest for Delaware, North Dakota, and Oklahoma, and lowest for Vermont, Massachusetts, and Maine, as Figure 8.1 indicates. Of course BIPAC's efforts in Figure 8.1 do not represent the totality of employer mobilization that occurred in the 2014 election. As we saw in chapter 3, many companies and associations go at it alone, without BIPAC's help, or through another trade association. But BIPAC does represent one of the largest individual worker recruitment campaigns in the business community, reaching about a fifth of the private-sector workforce at last tally. For the narrower purposes of my analysis, moreover, BIPAC is an appealing case study because I have precise estimates of the intensity of its employer outreach by state.

Did more intensive employer mobilization campaigns result in more votes for BIPAC-favored candidates, who were overwhelmingly Republican?[7] The left panel of Figure 8.2 plots the intensity of employer mobilization efforts against the vote share received by Democratic candidates for the Senate in the 2014 elections; the right panel does the same for Democratic gubernatorial candidates. There is a strikingly negative relationship between employer mobilization and the performance of Democratic candidates for both offices. States with more intensive employer mobilization coordinated by BIPAC, like Oklahoma, Iowa, Ohio, South Dakota, Nebraska, and Wyoming, were also the states where Democratic candidates fared worse.

But it would be a mistake to jump to the conclusion that the relationships in Figure 8.2 necessarily represent the direct effect of employer mobilization

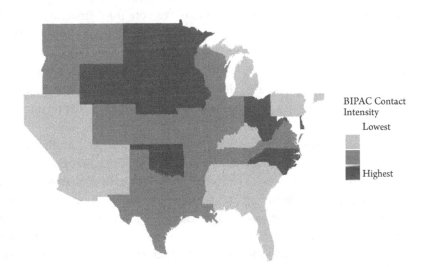

Figure 8.1 BIPAC employer mobilization intensity in the 2014 electoral cycle. Darker shades indicate more intensive BIPAC contact during the 2014 election cycle scaled by total state employment (in quartiles). Total state employment data from the Bureau of Labor Statistics.

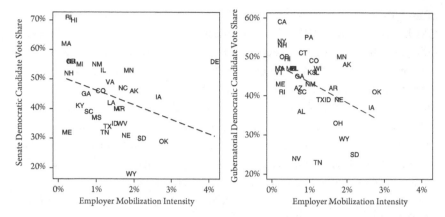

Figure 8.2 Employer mobilization intensity and 2014 Senate and gubernatorial races. Left plot shows the bivariate relationship between Senate Democratic candidate vote share and employer mobilization intensity; right plot shows the bivariate relationship between state gubernatorial candidate vote share and employer mobilization intensity. Two-party vote share data from the U.S. Election Atlas.

on election outcomes. Assuming that BIPAC was acting strategically, it would have mobilized employees in states in which it was most likely to make a difference in electing Republican candidates. Similarly perhaps more employers were active in BIPAC's campaign in states that had more conservative electorates to begin with.

We can get closer to the effect of BIPAC mobilization on voter behavior by examining whether workers were less likely to vote for Democrats in states with more intensive BIPAC mobilization after accounting for a host of other demographic and electoral factors. For that information we can turn to the 2014 Cooperative Congressional Election Study, which polled close to 50,000 adult Americans across the country after that year's elections. That wave of the CCES provides a range of information about respondents, including their turnout and vote choices in the 2014 elections.

My approach is to examine the effect of state-level BIPAC mobilization on the probability of an individual worker voting for Democratic candidates for Senate and gubernatorial races, net of other important individual demographic and contextual features, including union membership, education, gender, family income, race and ethnicity, partisan affiliation, and ideological orientation, as well as Democrats' past performance in the state. If we observe that these employee voters were less likely to vote for Democrats in states with more intensive BIPAC-led mobilization campaigns, even net of other factors, it would present strong circumstantial evidence that BIPAC mobilization matters for individual vote choices.

Once I account for the composition of voters in each state and their political preferences and behaviors, there is no relationship between BIPAC mobilization and employee voting behavior in the 2014 senatorial races. BIPAC mobilization did not appear to matter for the votes that citizens cast for the Senate, at least in 2014. There is, however, a very strong relationship between BIPAC mobilization and gubernatorial vote choices. Employee voters in states with the most intensive BIPAC mobilization campaigns were about 11 percentage points less likely to vote for Democratic gubernatorial candidates than were employee voters in states with the least intensive mobilization drives.[8] To put the BIPAC effect in context, union voters were about 5 percentage points more likely to vote for Democratic gubernatorial candidates than voters without such a tie to the labor movement, net of other voter and state characteristics.

That comparison implies that the full effect of BIPAC mobilization was just as large as—if not larger than—the effect of union affiliation in 2014. In a way, that is a big victory for BIPAC on its own. As I mentioned in chapter 5, the organization set about to match the grassroots organizing strength of the labor movement—and by this account, they have. Business now has its own electoral ground game that can counter labor.

Employer Mobilization and Campaign Contributions

The worker survey results from chapter 4 suggest that employers' electoral appeals also occasionally include requests for political donations, though these contribution requests were the least common of all the reported managerial messages. Nevertheless we might wonder if these requests make a difference as political candidates raise money for their campaigns. As I was completing this book, a team of economists working out of Arizona State University, Bocconi University, and the Swiss Finance Institute produced a preliminary analysis that let us assess precisely this question.[9] Examining federal campaign contribution data from 1999 to 2014, the researchers looked to see if employees in the 1,500 largest publicly traded corporations were more likely to contribute to the same candidates as their CEOs—a sign that CEOs might be nudging (or pushing) their employees to donate to particular candidates.

The authors found that employees gave over $1,000 more to political candidates if their CEO had also donated to the same candidate. Figure 8.3 summarizes the striking relationship between employee and CEO contributions to the same candidates, using data generously provided by the authors of the study. I have grouped CEO contributions into four equal-size categories (quartiles)

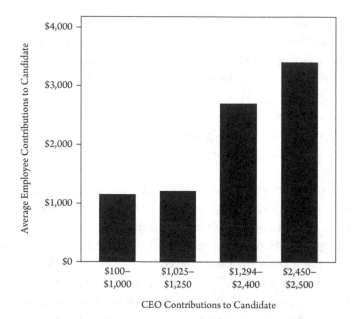

Figure 8.3 Employee and CEO contributions to same candidates, 1999–2014. Figure shows the average contributions made by employees to the same candidates their CEOs supported, by quartiles of CEO contributions (only among CEOs who made contributions). Data provided by Viktar Fedaseyeu, Ilona Babenko, and Song Zhang.

and estimated the average contributions made by employees at the companies directed by those CEOs for each of the categories. The more money that CEOs donated to a particular candidate's campaign, the more their employees also gave to that same candidate. If a CEO gave between $100 and $1,000 to a candidate, for example, their employees gave $1,150, on average, to the same candidate. And if a CEO gave even more—say, $2,500—to a candidate's campaign, their employees gave, on average, over $3,000 to that same candidate.

It might well be the case, however, that employees and CEOs independently recognized the same politicians who were good for their companies. To evaluate this hypothesis, the authors examined variation in employee political giving within the same companies over time, focusing on moments when CEOs were replaced or the same CEO changed his or her political giving. In both cases employees continued to give more to the same candidates as their top management, meaning that the relationship cannot simply be explained by company- or executive-specific characteristics that would lead CEOs and employees to support the same candidates. In one of the most convincing analyses of their paper, the trio of economists showed that the relationship between employee and CEO giving held up when looking at cases where CEOs died or retired due to old age—moments of executive turnover that are most likely unrelated to the departing CEO's politics. The relationship between employee and CEO donations was especially strong, moreover, when companies reported spending more money on political communications to their workers, evidence of the relationship being a result of deliberate efforts by companies to encourage workers to donate to the company's preferred candidates. Importantly—and quite consistent with my own argument about economic power—the authors also found that the relationship between employee and CEO giving was stronger in areas of higher unemployment, where employees might be more concerned about their standing in the labor market.

My own analysis of federal donation data reinforces the conclusion that employee political contributions are closely tied to the mobilization efforts of managers. Looking at the candidates BIPAC endorsed in 2014, for instance, I found that employees who worked at the companies affiliated with BIPAC's board of directors or the steering committee of the Prosperity Project—companies that were mobilizing their workers into politics using BIPAC's platform and supporting the same candidates as BIPAC—gave substantially more to the 44 U.S. House and Senate candidates BIPAC had endorsed. Employees at BIPAC-affiliated companies gave only about $82, on average, to non-BIPAC-endorsed candidates during the 2014 elections but gave $757, on average, to the politicians that BIPAC endorsed.[10] The left plot of Figure 8.4 summarizes this striking difference between employee contributions at BIPAC-affiliated companies for candidates endorsed and not endorsed by BIPAC in 2014.

Just as in the economists' analysis of contributions, however, it might be the case that employees at BIPAC-affiliated companies would have given to those candidates that BIPAC endorsed regardless of the endorsement. For instance, these candidates might have been well known to be friendly to business causes, and employees at BIPAC firms would have known that regardless of the BIPAC endorsement. To deal with this concern, we can look at the contributions made by employees to BIPAC-endorsed candidates before and after the endorsement was made. If employees would have given to these candidates regardless of the endorsement, then there should be little difference before and after the BIPAC endorsement was made. If, however, the endorsement was important in motivating employee giving—say, because of explicit employer messages—then we should expect an increase in giving to BIPAC-favored candidates after BIPAC made its endorsements.

The right plot in Figure 8.4 assesses this question and shows a big increase in giving to BIPAC-endorsed candidates after the group's endorsements were made. Employees at BIPAC-affiliated companies gave just under $400 to BIPAC-endorsed candidates before BIPAC's endorsement and more than twice as much to those same candidates after endorsements were released. This relationship holds up even when I look at variation in electoral giving within

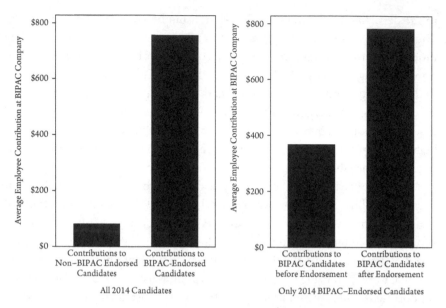

Figure 8.4 Donations from employees at BIPAC-affiliated companies to candidates in 2014. Left plot shows the average donations made by employees at BIPAC-affiliated companies (on BIPAC's board of directors or the Prosperity Project steering committee) to candidates that were and were not endorsed by BIPAC's Prosperity Project. Right plot shows the average donations made by employees at BIPAC-affiliated companies to BIPAC-endorsed candidates before and after the BIPAC endorsement. There were 34 BIPAC-endorsed candidates identified in the donation data and 261 employees who gave to those BIPAC-endorsed candidates at 35 companies. Donation data from Database on Ideology, Money in Politics, and Elections.

candidates and companies over time (see appendix for full results). This analysis of the Prosperity Project's endorsements and employee giving at BIPAC-affiliated companies provides further evidence that managers can strongly affect the political giving patterns of their employees—not only to corporate PACs but also directly to politicians' campaign coffers.

Elections and Employer Mobilization

"Alone, your [political involvement in elections] may seem insignificant. But when you join with other Company leaders . . . you can make a difference to [our company's] future." So proclaimed an appeal from one of the companies I interviewed asking workers to vote for and contribute their wages to "local, state and federal political candidates who support pro-business initiatives." In this chapter we have seen that the appeal is indeed right: when companies like this manufacturer rally behind candidates for state and federal races, their workers tend to support those candidates too—and together they can make a difference in who is ultimately elected to office. The results from the 2014 election provided evidence that BIPAC's electoral campaign worsened the fate of Democratic gubernatorial candidates. And campaign contribution records show that employees are substantially more likely to give to the candidates backed by their executives in ways that resemble the mobilization appeals I have documented elsewhere in the book.

I have shown that mobilization can powerfully shape how workers think about politics, decide to engage in politics (or not), the policies that Congress and the states consider, and the candidates who win electoral races. At the same time, there is a systematic bias in the policies, causes, and candidates favored in employer mobilization drives: when employers recruit their workers into politics, it tends to be for cutting taxes and regulations and supporting generally Republican politicians. As we will see in chapter 9, the disproportionate benefits that mobilization affords to one narrow set of interests—especially those associated with a conservative business perspective—are just one reason to be concerned about the growth of employer mobilization and to prioritize research into the consequences of employer mobilization for American democracy.

What Employer Mobilization Means
for the Study of American Politics

Americans receive political communications and messages from a variety of sources in their daily lives. Some talk with friends, family members, or fellow participants in civic associations; others listen to the radio or watch television; and still others receive messages about politics in the pews or in union halls. Throughout this book I have made the case that we need to add the workplace to that list of political spaces, and more specifically, we need to recognize that employers are communicating with their workers about politics. Some 25 percent of American workers report that their employer has ever provided them with a political message, and nearly 50 percent of all managers I surveyed reported doing something to engage their workers in politics. The total share of employees receiving messages may have even increased to some 30 to 40 percent of the workforce as of the 2016 election. Employer mobilization, as I have dubbed this practice, is *prevalent* across the American labor force.

Employer messages come in a variety of forms. In some cases employers are simply reminding their workers to register or turn out to vote. In other cases employers are trying to achieve specific objectives, such as electing certain parties or candidates or changing public policy. In general, employers report more explicitly political contact with their workers, sending messages about candidates or policies rather than simply reminders about turning out to vote. In both cases information from employers to employees has also become increasingly *personalized*, with managers using the information they have gathered about their workers to customize recruitment requests and messages by employees' rank in the company, their work routines, the location of their business, and their past political activities, especially voting. And employer messages sometimes involve *pressure*, as employers issue warnings of job loss, wage cuts, or plant closures in an effort to spur political participation or to change employees' preferences and attitudes. Over a third of employees reported being fearful of repercussions for their political views and actions at work or had actually seen political retaliation in their workplace.

Last, employer messages are *persuasive*, encouraging workers to change their political behavior and attitudes to match the preferences of their employers. We saw evidence for this in the worker survey, with about half of all employees reporting that they responded in some way to their employers' political messages. This conclusion was further underscored with both the experimental and case study evidence from chapters 6 through 8, which showed that messages from employers reshape workers' political behavior and attitudes, and ultimately policy and electoral outcomes. Those analyses are consistent with the firm survey evidence and the interviews I conducted with top corporate managers, both of which indicated that managers see mobilization as a highly effective means of changing American politics.

Of course, as I illustrated in chapters 3, 4, and 5, not all employers engage in mobilization, and not all workers are equally persuaded by their bosses' messages. Companies were especially likely to mobilize when presented with a concrete threat from public policy, when they were already highly active in politics, when managers had more economic power relative to their workers, and when managers were in a good position to closely monitor workers' political attitudes and activities.

In a similar vein, looking across workers, those who were especially fearful of losing their jobs were most likely to respond to employer messages. These workers, when contacted by their bosses, were more likely to change their minds on policy issues, such as the minimum wage, and to change their political behavior, for instance contacting members of Congress. Similar to the findings for corporate managers, perceptions of monitoring mattered for workers' responses to their employers. Employees were much more likely to respond to requests for political participation when they perceived that their managers could track their political attitudes and follow up on their political behaviors, including voting. And perhaps most troubling, workers were more likely to respond to employer messages when they feared political retaliation from their bosses.

These results invite scholars to consider employers as important political recruiters of citizens and open up a number of avenues for future research. Much more can be learned about the ways that employers are similar to or different from other political recruiters that are more typically studied by political scientists, including parties, unions, civic groups, and churches. One obvious place to start answering these questions is to focus on the nature of the relationship between workers and employers and how it differs from other organizations. Unlike when a voluntary association or political party tries to mobilize citizens, an employer already has a great deal of information about each of its potential recruits—including their salaries, work routines, and contact information—without workers ever needing to volunteer any of those details. Most mobilizing businesses—over three-quarters of firms that reported engaging their workers into politics—reported that they targeted specific workers to receive political information, drawing on the information that companies had gathered on their workers.

Further work on employer mobilization might thus examine in more detail how employers can take advantage of this information to more effectively motivate employee participation. For instance, future work might examine whether appeals from employers that are customized by different worker characteristics are more or less effective than more general employer messages or messages from other political actors. It might be the case, for example, that customizing messages on the basis of workers' occupations or job routines is an especially powerful means of targeting—but only when such appeals are made through the workplace as opposed to in other settings, like in civic groups.

Future research might also investigate the extent to which employers are going beyond basic demographic and political information to target political appeals to workers that include more sophisticated measures of worker sentiment and behavior. For instance, do employers ever condition political recruitment based on personality assessments of their workers? Most job-seekers (perhaps some 60 to 70 percent of workers) will take a personality test as part of the employment application process.[1] Although these tests have come under legal and academic scrutiny for their possibly discriminatory nature, some of the biggest retail and hospitality employers continue to deploy them when hiring front-line workers. (The Yahoo! Answers Forum, for instance, has hundreds of posts with titles such as "Anyone know the answers to the walmart personality test [sic]?") If such personality test performance data are stored with an individual's human resources files, they could conceivably be used as part of a mobilization drive.

Beyond personality scores, companies are also using text analysis software to assess the "sentiments" of workers through their email, chat, and Internet correspondence. When combined with social network analysis, these tools can be used to predict employee behavior, as at one Fortune 1,000 firm. A *Harvard Business Review* case study explained about that large employer, "Semantic analysis identified a small team of salespeople in the middle of negotiating their defection to a competitor. The sentiment analytics software had identified both atypical frequency and vocabulary between the sales people and—more provocatively— radically different exchanges between the sales people and key accounts. The story doesn't have a happy ending."[2] Will employers merge this kind of advanced monitoring with their political recruitment efforts to see if employees are generally supporting the same candidates and causes as their bosses, or if employees have ideologies or beliefs that run contrary to their businesses?

Switching from the employer to the employee perspective, it would also be helpful to examine whether workers understand the full range of information that employers can and do collect on employees. How do employees view their privacy rights on the job, and how does that compare to what employers can do in practice? Under what conditions are employees more or less likely to support monitoring by managers and its deployment in political campaigns in the workplace?

The distinctive capacities that employers possess for political recruitment go beyond monitoring and data collection. Equally unique to employers is the fact that managerial requests for political participation are coming from someone citizens depend on for their economic livelihood and with whom they interact on a daily basis. I have argued that this should make workers just as attuned to political messages they receive from their managers as from other recruiters, if not more attuned, especially when workers are worried about their jobs. More could be done, however, to understand exactly how economic threats from employers motivate workers to comply with employer requests, especially the specific nature of the threats that employers might deploy. At what level of threat do employees feel compelled to comply with employer messages? How often do employers need to follow through on their threats for such warnings to remain credible? Closely linked, does the repeated use of threats reinforce or undermine their effectiveness? How frequently do employers blame politics or policy for specific layoff or wage cut decisions? And how often and under what conditions do workers believe these justifications for layoffs or wage cuts?

The implicit or explicit threats that employers can pose to workers make employers relatively distinct as political recruiters. But it also makes employer mobilization potentially ethically problematic—an issue I explore in more detail in the conclusion. Setting these concerns with coercion aside for now, it would be useful for researchers to study the process of employer mobilization within particular companies to understand if it is possible for managers to deliver messages to workers in ways that workers would be less likely to find intimidating or coercive. That is, can employers design recruitment campaigns that take advantage of the positive aspects of the workplace without exploiting the power they possess to intimidate workers into complying with requests and messages with which workers might disagree? Moreover, following the distinction I developed in chapter 1, are there conditions under which employers can move from being mere mobilizers, asking workers to participate in discrete political tasks, to organizers that instill a greater civic spirit in their employees?[3] Research designs that combine experimental approaches—say, partnering with a company willing to vary the messages it delivers to its workers—with in-depth interviews with employees would be an especially helpful approach to understand how employees interpret and process different kinds of recruitment messages that employers might deploy.

A final feature of the workplace that makes it relatively special as a context for political communications and recruitment is that discussion of politics is not the central reason for companies' existence; it is generally secondary to a business's core activities of producing particular goods and services. That means even at a company that is mobilizing its workers into politics, most of the contact and communications that managers have with workers and that workers have with one another are unconnected to politics. Closely related, the workplace provides an opportunity for reaching Americans who might not otherwise be engaged in politics, since workers have typically not chosen a company based on their interest in politics. These characteristics together make the workplace an interesting place for testing theories of political persuasion, since workers are not expecting to receive political communications—a situation very much unlike, say, the meeting of a political organization or a television program about politics. Future research might investigate the specific ways that employers can take advantage of this context of the workplace to reach Americans who might not otherwise participate in the political process, encouraging them to build the skills and habits necessary to engage in politics.

Apart from its implications for the study of individual political behavior, employer mobilization invites a range of new research in the area of interest group politics and business-government relations. If employers are indeed mobilizing their workers into politics to promote political causes and candidates, as I have suggested, we should add mobilization to the list of strategies that are already extensively studied by scholars of interest group influence, like hiring lobbyists and participating in business associations.

Building on the case studies I presented in chapters 6 through 8, future work might investigate the conditions under which mobilization is especially effective at changing politics and how it interacts with the other political strategies a business might deploy. While I have studied the perceptions of corporate managers and legislative staffers in this book, other scholars might turn to politicians to understand how mobilization shapes the political process. Through interviews or elite surveys, researchers could see how aspiring or current officeholders view employer mobilization, and in particular which types of mobilization are most effective at achieving different political ends. How important are plant or office visits for politicians running for office, especially in comparison with other tactics a company might use to build relationships with politicians? Which sorts of candidates are most likely to take advantage of these relationships with businesses? What kind of employer-initiated employee messages to legislatures (including threats of layoffs) are most likely to inspire action? Attention to the potential electoral effects of employer recruitment would be especially helpful since my findings in this area were the most tentative.

Further studies might also attempt to uncover in more detail the economic costs of mobilization campaigns that have gone wrong. Consumers appear very willing to avoid companies that donate to political causes and candidates with which they disagree.[4] Might consumers retaliate against companies that engage in overly partisan or coercive mobilization? In a similar vein, at what point do employees start to resent or protest their employers' political recruitment drives? When do such employees decide to leave their employers, or perhaps reduce their work effort? Under what circumstances do employers need to pay workers more to compensate for the costs of more partisan endorsement or recruitment? Other models of employer market power emphasize that employers might pay their workers above-market wages ("efficiency wages") in order to increase the costs of unemployment so employees have a stronger incentive to follow employer demands. Might we expect a similar dynamic for companies engaging in especially partisan or coercive mobilization? These are all questions that would help us to understand how employer mobilization changes the structure of American labor markets.

Finally, while scholars have begun to study employer political recruitment in other developing democracies, we know little about whether employer mobilization occurs in other advanced democracies in the present day.[5] Understanding whether employer mobilization is happening in those countries and, if so, what form it is taking is likely to be an especially useful line of research, as it could illuminate the economic and political factors that shape corporate managers' incentives to recruit their employees into politics. For example, how do party and electoral systems affect businesses' incentives to mobilize their employees? Unfortunately, as with the study of employer mobilization within the United States, no cross-national survey that I have encountered asks about employer political recruitment. Yet there are signs that employer mobilization might exist in other advanced democracies. For instance, during the 2016 referendum on whether the United Kingdom should stay in the European Union, the Airbus Group, one of the world's largest aerospace manufacturers, wrote to all of its 15,000 British employees explaining that it makes "good economic sense" to cast a ballot in favor of continued European Union membership.[6] In short, my hope is that this book will spur greater interest in understanding employer mobilization not only within the United States but also in other countries.

Conclusion

Employer Mobilization and American Democracy

Employer mobilization opens up a range of fascinating research questions for scholars of public opinion, political behavior, interest group lobbying, and business-government relations. But it also raises some serious issues that should be troubling to citizens and politicians from all political backgrounds.

Looking across the history of the United States we have seen that employers have long used their relationship with employees to promote the election of favored political candidates and the passage of valuable public policies. While the most recent efforts by American employers to engage their workers in politics are distinct from earlier examples in the United States, these efforts still retain important—and troubling—continuities.

No U.S. corporate managers are marching their employees to the voting booth and carefully monitoring the ballots cast, as they once did in the era before secret voting. Yet at the same time, American employers have developed tools for electronically tracking many other political activities that they might ask employees to do, such as contacting lawmakers and contributing to campaigns. And there is strong evidence that even with the secret ballot, employers now possess the means of discerning the political attitudes of their workers. Many workers feel, and even act, as if their ballots are not all that secret. So while employers may no longer have the same means of monitoring the vote as they once did, new technological advances have meant that they can still keep close track of a range of other behaviors—and possibly voting too.

Just as employers no longer have the ability to enter polling places to track employees' votes, managers cannot call in the National Guard or their own security forces to enforce political compliance, as they did in the past. The threat of violence against defiant employees is thus much less credible than it once was, and our democracy is certainly stronger because of those protections. But even without the threat of violence, American workers still feel a great deal of economic pressure to respond to managerial messages, and even more so today than in previous decades because of changes in economic power and labor and election laws. A surprisingly large proportion of workers—over a third— reports believing their employers might punish them for their political views and actions or have actually witnessed such retaliation against other employees at their workplace.

In short, it would be overly pessimistic to argue that current employer mobilization efforts are anything close to resembling those from developing democracies, or even before Progressive Era electoral reforms in the United States. But there are still traces of continuity in present-day mobilization, above all the threat to workers that failure to comply with employer messages will result in economic sanctions. Sometimes that threat is explicit, as with the workers who received warnings of plant closures, layoffs, or cuts to wages and hours, and sometimes the threat is merely implicit and a function of workers' own perceptions of their economic power relative to their bosses. In both cases, however, we might worry whether workers are being coerced into backing candidates and policies that they might not wish to support but feel they must in order to maintain their economic livelihood, as I documented in chapters 4 and 6.

In the remainder of the conclusion, I expand on these concerns associated with employer mobilization, describing why coercive mobilization poses a threat to individual workers' political rights and to American democracy more generally. I then propose a variety of reforms that could address coercive mobilization, paying close attention to the political and legal feasibility of different policy alternatives. I end by discussing how curbing coercive employer mobilization could help to address long-standing fears about the implications of corporate capitalism for American democracy.

The Virtues of a Political Workplace

Before discussing the risks of employer political coercion, it is worth reflecting on the benefits of political discussion in the workplace between coworkers and between employers and employees. Both kinds of political conversations can benefit workers, companies, and the country as a whole.

Important work from two political scientists, Diana Mutz and Jeffery Mondak, offers the most detailed picture of political discussions between coworkers that we have to date.[1] Those authors show the workplace is a site of vibrant political discussions, surpassing other locations of conversation—churches, homes, neighborhoods, schools—by wide margins. The workplace also produced more diverse political conversations than exchanges with other social acquaintances, with coworkers reporting that they were more likely to disagree with one another than with political discussion partners from churches or schools. Most strikingly, employees who were exposed to more political diversity at work were more likely to espouse a greater understanding of opposing political perspectives and increased political tolerance. Mutz and Mondak credit the workplace with these appealing features because it attracts individuals from a diverse range of backgrounds and beliefs. Unlike, say, the college or church that you choose to attend, you typically have far less control over the ideological makeup of the place where you work. The authors find that nearly 70 percent of workers said they had no choice in picking who their coworkers would be.[2] That means the workplace is one site where Americans spend a considerable amount of time on a regular basis and yet do not necessarily get to self-select into networks of individuals who share their ideological commitments.

Results from my own surveys of workers confirm some of the earlier conclusions reached by Mutz and Mondak. A full 83 percent of employees in my 2015 telephone survey reported that they knew the political orientation of their coworkers, suggesting that those workers had at least some political communication with their colleagues. And similar to the Mutz and Mondak findings on the diversity of perspectives in the workplace, 58 percent of employees in 2015 reported that their coworkers tended to have a different ideology from their own. These findings collectively give us strong reasons to support the workplace as a site of vibrant political discussion. At a time when pundits and political analysts bemoan the insularity of political life, the workplace offers the promise of an arena where Americans can think about politics in ways that promote exposure to, and perhaps even acceptance of, diverse beliefs and positions.[3]

If those are the reasons to support and protect political discussions between coworkers, what are the reasons we might have to celebrate political talk between workers and their bosses? At a basic level, employers are in a good position—some might argue the best position—to inform their workers about political issues that affect their industry and their business. When it comes to understanding how pending trade legislation in Congress might affect employment and wages at a particular manufacturing plant, for instance, the top management at that company are ideally suited to providing those details to workers. That company might already have a government affairs division staffed by experts on public policy who have combed through the relevant legislation in all its complexity, distilling the consequences of a bill in plain English for the company's workforce. That level of analysis and understanding of public policy is likely out of the reach of most workers, who often do not have the time or resources to closely track legislative debates and the content of public policy.[4] While unions might have once provided that role of a trusted "policy translator" for workers, clearly they are no longer in a position to do so for most of the labor force. Employers might provide such a replacement—at least on some issues.

Apart from democratizing access to policy information, we might also laud the ways that employer mobilization can encourage greater civic engagement, especially during elections. The United States has had one of the lowest rates of voter turnout throughout the twentieth century compared to other countries. Pooling data from 1945 to 2001, one international study found that the United States ranked a depressing 120th out of 169 countries in its average turnout rate.[5] We placed right below the Dominican Republic and just above Benin with an average of 66.5 percent of registered voters turning out to vote over this period. By contrast, many of our peer rich democracies averaged rates that topped 80 percent. Given these low rates of participation, employer mobilization might hold the promise of encouraging greater turnout at the polls, especially among workers of low socioeconomic status who are otherwise unlikely to participate, as we saw in chapter 4.

Assessing the workplace as a site for political discourse, then, it is fair to say that there are a variety of features we might want the legal system to preserve—and even to encourage. We might want to ensure, for instance, that coworkers feel comfortable engaging in frank and open conversations with one another about politics, regardless of their rank in a company or their own opinions, the ideologies of their coworkers, or those of their employers. And managers ought to have the opportunity to share information about how pending policy changes will affect their companies and workers and to engage in civic recruitment campaigns to help their workers register and turn out to vote. Yet even as there are a variety of benefits associated with employer political recruitment, so too are there important concerns.

Reasons for Concern about Coercive Employer Mobilization

Most workers reported being either untroubled or even supportive of the messages they received from their employers. But at the same time a significant minority reported fearing missing out on advancement in their jobs because of their political actions and views or had seen political retaliation toward other employees. Troublingly, lower-income workers were substantially more likely than higher-income workers to report these fears. Fifty percent of workers in the lowest fifth of the income distribution reported such fears, compared to only 26 percent of workers in the highest fifth of the income distribution and 34 percent of workers overall. Employer mobilization in a context where workers fear political retribution is the sort of employer political messaging that especially concerns me—and that I believe ought to trouble politicians and all Americans as well.

When employers make political requests of workers to support a particular bill, candidate, or issue in ways that make workers fear for their economic livelihood, I worry that workers may feel unduly pressured to support their employers' positions. There is strong evidence to back up this concern: as we saw in chapter 6, workers were substantially more likely to respond to their employers when they were more fearful of losing their jobs and when they feared retribution from their bosses. This kind of mobilization creates a serious threat to the right of workers, as citizens, to arrive at their political preferences and decisions free from the undue influence of others. Coercive mobilization also violates individual workers' rights to free speech, as they are pressured into making political statements they may not believe but feel are necessary to appease their employers. This kind of mobilization is, in essence, forced or compelled political speech, which the U.S. Supreme Court has found to be an unconstitutional violation of workers' First Amendment rights in other contexts.[6]

Beyond its troubling implications for workers' rights, coercive mobilization could have a strong chilling effect on workplace political discussions between coworkers—conversations that we saw are often highly beneficial for workers and society in general. While I did not ask about political conversations between coworkers in my 2015 telephone survey of workers, one online poll of workers I conducted in 2014 suggested that employees who indicated they were uncomfortable with their employers' political messages were about 15 times more likely to say that they were uncomfortable discussing politics with their coworkers compared to respondents who reported that they were comfortable with their employers' political outreach.[7] It is not difficult to imagine why this relationship might emerge: when employers create an atmosphere in which employees feel strongly pressured to toe the company line, it is hard for coworkers to have the sort of open discussions about their political beliefs with one another envisioned by proponents of a civic workplace.

Quite apart from the concerns about its effects on individual political speech and expression, employer mobilization also poses serious threats to the quality of democratic representation because it is occurring against a backdrop of mounting economic and political inequality. Organized business interests and wealthy Americans are substantially more likely to have their preferences for policy change expressed by politicians than are ordinary Americans, and employer mobilization affords one additional tool that businesses and managers can use to advance their policy goals—potentially at the expense of the representation of workers and less affluent citizens.[8] The workplace offers a valuable political resource to those who can mobilize employees, and in previous decades both labor and employers were well positioned to deploy that resource. These days, however, it is only business—not labor—that can take advantage of politics at work in any significant way.

Employer mobilization thus creates a new pathway through which concentrated economic power, and inequalities in that economic power, can seep into the political process. But as opposed to the traditional critique of corporate money in politics—that there is too much of it—employer mobilization puts the focus on the market power of businesses as being worrisome for the quality of American democracy. What is potentially problematic about employer political recruitment of workers is not that companies have lots of money to spend on such efforts from their corporate treasuries—many advocacy groups also have large budgets for grassroots mobilization—but rather the unequal distribution of market power at work between employers and employees.

This critique of businesses' market power resonates with growing rhetoric from scholars and political advocates around busting the "new trusts," or the massive corporate conglomerates that have emerged in seemingly every industry and are now accused of promoting inequality, stifling job growth, and fostering economic stagnation.[9] As Senator Elizabeth Warren has put it, the "problem is that concentrated markets create concentrated political power. . . . The larger and more economically powerful these companies get, the more resources they can bring to bear on lobbying government."[10] Coercive employer recruitment of employees would be problematic at any time, but it is especially worrying when corporate economic power is becoming ever more concentrated in a handful of large businesses. This not only implies that employers will be in a better position to direct pressure on workers to comply with employer political requests but also that the American workforce might be subjected to a smaller range of political perspectives in the workplace. Thus, to the extent that we worry about the outsized role of business interests in politics, we should worry about the development and spread of employer mobilization, especially in the contemporary era of mounting corporate consolidation.

What Can Be Done?

I believe that now is the appropriate moment to take action to curb the most coercive and troubling employer mobilization practices. To delay action will only increase the risk of having such practices spread further and become more intensive. To see what delay might bring, we need only examine how the process of private-sector labor organizing has evolved over the past few decades. According to the best research on these trends, it is now standard practice for workers to be "subjected to threats, interrogation, harassment, surveillance, and retaliation for union activity," facilitated by a large industry of consultants who specialize in helping employers avoid unionization.[11] From 1999 to 2003 employers threatened to close facilities in 57 percent of union elections, actually discharged workers in 34 percent of elections, and threatened to cut wages or benefits in 47 percent of elections. All evidence suggests that the intensity of these practices has increased over time.[12] Labor drives, in short, pit workers directly against employers, with the latter pursuing a "no holds barred" approach to stopping workers from voicing their support for unions. It is not a stretch to imagine that in our era of deeply polarized politics, the most intensive forms of employer mobilization might resemble something like a union drive if left unchecked.

Given the political risks that more coercive mobilization engenders, how might we curb such practices? One clear solution flows from the analysis I have presented throughout this book: if diminished worker economic power makes it easier for employers to pressure workers into responding to political messages and requests, we should take steps to strengthen workers' voice at work. If American employees were in a more secure position relative to their managers, then managers would have a much harder time making intimidating or coercive requests of their workers. Recalling the historical analysis in chapter 5, it is clear that there are some aspects of worker bargaining power that will be impossible to restore. Reformers seeking to bolster worker power cannot return to an era of diminished competition with lower-wage countries, nor can they easily reverse the financial pressure that managers face to generate strong short-term returns for shareholders. These are features of the economic landscape that are likely here to stay for the foreseeable future. However, there is one realistic step that advocates of greater worker economic power can take: making it easier for workers to organize and collectively bargain with their employers.

The possibilities for unions to curb coercive and intimidating mobilization occur both on the employer and the worker side. Unions can help workers to negotiate collective bargaining agreements that ban coercive employer recruitment efforts. Those same collective bargaining agreements could also include provisions that protect workers from being treated differently based on their political views or actions (and inactions). More indirectly, employers might be less likely to attempt intimidating mobilization in the first place were workers to have access to strong labor representation, knowing full well that workers might protest such recruitment to their union representative.

In the interest of equalizing political voices in the workplace, the government should thus make it easier for workers to organize and represent themselves formally in the workplace through a union or similar organization. Such a reform would not be easy; legislative proposals to lower the barriers to unionization have floundered even during recent periods when Democrats were in full control of Congress and the White House.[13] Yet survey evidence consistently finds that even as union density has fallen sharply over time, a majority of workers still want to join a union, or something resembling one.[14] In addition, nearly

three-quarters of Americans—74 percent—reported that they thought workers' "right to join a union" is "very" or "somewhat" important.[15] Reformers seeking to curb the most egregious and concerning aspects of mobilization, then,
should focus on measures that facilitate the process of forming a union.[16] For
instance, they could make it possible for a simple majority of workers to indicate their support for unions in their workplace without a lengthy and formal
election, increase the penalties levied against employers that violate labor laws,
and expand the structures that labor unions can take beyond those that dominated the manufacturing-era economy of midcentury into more recent "alt-
labor" forms that are better suited to the service-sector jobs of the twenty-first
century.[17]

To be sure, not all unions are equally democratizing for workers, and there
are many historical examples of unions that have applied coercive strategies of
their own to pressure workers into supporting particular union-backed candidates and policies. Yet it is hard to envision another actor in the contemporary
American economy that could buttress the economic standing of workers in the
workplace in the same way unions do. Through collectively bargained employment agreements, including rules on how managers can fire workers or change
workplace conditions and hours and wages, unions can directly provide protection for employees against politically motivated discipline and dismissals. These
provisions would take the bite out of more coercive employer messages, since
covered employees would recognize that they do not have to worry about retaliation for failing to respond to their bosses' messages.

Perhaps even more important, unions provide a democratic forum for employees to effectively express their collective voice to managers, including their preferences for more or less employer mobilization. Unions thus would give workers
the opportunity to convey to management whether they want political recruitment in the workplace and, if so, what that recruitment and mobilization should
look like. As labor economists Richard Freeman and James Medoff explain in
their seminal book, *What Do Unions Do?*, this democratic voice is important
because working conditions represent a collective action problem from the perspective of any given worker.

It may well be the case that a majority of workers would prefer a particular
change to the workplace, such as favoring less coercive employer political recruitment from their managers, but it is not in the interest of any particular worker
to take a stand against his or her boss. "Without a collective organization, the
incentive for the individual to take into account the effects of his or her actions
on others, or to express his or her preferences, or to invest time and money in
changing conditions, is likely to be too small to spur action," argue Freeman and
Medoff. "Why not 'let Harry do it' and enjoy the benefits at no cost?"[18] This
is especially likely to be true given the potential for employer retaliation: "The

danger of job loss makes expression of voice by an individual risky."[19] Employer mobilization is precisely the sort of workplace issue that unions would be well-equipped to address, helping workers to articulate their preferences for the volume and content of workplace political mobilization and then to ensure that management is responsive to those preferences.

Considered together, measures to increase worker bargaining power through greater workplace representation would reduce the prospects of intimidating or coercive mobilization, leveling the playing field between managers and employees. This proposal has the virtue of letting employees decide for themselves the level of workplace mobilization with which they are comfortable. This balance would likely differ from workplace to workplace. In companies in which workers and employers had closely shared policy interests, employees might be fine with managers sending endorsements of particular political candidates or urging workers to lobby on behalf of the company because the workers would feel that their interests are well represented by management. In other companies, however, employees might be less open to mobilization, seeing such efforts as going against their own preferences and economic interests. In these more divided workplaces, employees' improved bargaining power would permit them to voice their opposition to their managers' efforts without fear of retribution or retaliation.

Setting aside more political mobilization drives that involve elections or policy lobbying, a focus on worker bargaining power also permits employers to engage in more civic-oriented recruitment efforts, such as encouraging workers to register or turn out to vote or volunteer in politics in nonpartisan ways. These nonpartisan efforts, some of which I discuss in more detail later, are an important way that employers can help to address the problem of low civic engagement and participation in politics.

In short, increased worker bargaining power reduces the most problematic outcomes associated with coercive employer mobilization while leaving open the possibilities of using the workplace as a space in which managers can promote civic engagement and coworkers can discuss politics with one another. Focusing on building worker political and economic power through unions also has the advantage of being a self-enforcing strategy for restricting coercive employer mobilization. Unlike, say, a new law restricting the political strategies that employers can deploy in the workplace, building union power across the private sector will, in itself, discourage coercive mobilization going forward and does not necessarily rely on the government to monitor and enforce violations of the law.

Barring full Democratic control of the federal government, however, the odds of labor law reform seem nonexistent. Given that challenge, citizens, policy activists, and politicians worried about coercive employer mobilization should also consider new legislation in the interim that would either directly or indirectly restrict political intimidation of workers while still permitting employers to provide useful and relevant political information to their workforce. An ideal solution would focus on federal legislation that would reach all, or nearly all, private-sector employers immediately. I review the strengths and weaknesses of three separate proposals for such federal legislation while emphasizing that building worker bargaining power remains the first best alternative for curbing political coercion at work.

Extending Corporate PAC Restrictions to All Corporate Political Activities

To address the new opportunities for political employer coercion that managers now have, Congress could extend the legal restrictions already applied to corporate political action committees to companies themselves. As part of the legislation governing PAC activities, Congress has already ruled that companies and unions cannot collect contributions or anything else of value from workers through "physical force, job discrimination, financial reprisals, or the threat of force, job discrimination, or financial reprisal . . . or as a condition of employment."[20] Corporate PACs cannot, for instance, mandate employee contributions or participation in political events, even if workers are paid for their time. Lawmakers have even gone a step further and made a sharp distinction between PAC solicitations that are made of rank-and-file workers and those made of corporate executives or shareholders. Requests made of rank-and-file workers are subject to far more restrictions and scrutiny than are requests to corporate executives. The clear intent of these provisions was to protect ordinary employees from undue pressure by their managers.[21]

With a small change in the relevant statutory language, Congress could replace references in campaign finance legislation to PACs with corporations (and, by extension, unions), barring businesses and labor organizations from collecting contributions or expenditures through coercive means. Proponents of this approach note that violations could be enforceable through civil actions and that Congress could include reasonable exemptions for explicitly political employers (parties and interest groups), as well as employees whose main job involves politics (such as lobbyists).[22]

This approach is appealing in its simplicity, requiring only minor changes to the existing campaign finance framework. It also permits employers to continue to provide political information to their workers and even to make requests of workers' time and money, so long as they do not use coercive means of obtaining those contributions. One drawback to a PAC regulation-based strategy is that by building on existing campaign finance law, this proposal focuses on regulating only the most electorally oriented employer political communications and requests. The contributions and expenditures referred to within the statute are those related to political campaigns, meaning that political communications that are not electoral in nature, such as those about public policy, would be left unregulated. As we have seen, most employer mobilization efforts are not related to candidates or elections but are instead focused on legislation and policy. This proposal would thus still permit coercive mobilization that occurs around policy initiatives. The PAC restriction approach would even permit coercive mobilization around policy issues that borders on, but does not cross into electoral politics, such as when managers denounce the tax plan of a political candidate that a company opposes without making an endorsement. Another issue with the PAC restriction proposal is that it would depend on the existing set of campaign finance institutions for enforcement. As we have seen, however, the Federal Election Commission has struggled to even *investigate* charges of political coercion that would violate existing campaign finance law in the case of Murray Energy. While elegant, then, this proposal would still leave big holes in the protections offered to workers, both on paper and in practice.

Banning Political Captive Audience Meetings

An alternative approach to regulating employer mobilization is to focus on the ways employers are communicating to workers, regardless of whether those messages and requests are electoral in nature. One model in this vein has been pursued by Oregon and New Jersey, which have passed versions of the Worker Freedom Act. That law prohibits employers from firing or penalizing employees who decline to participate in mandatory employer-sponsored meetings about religious, labor, or political issues—what one legal scholar has dubbed "political captive audience meetings."[23] Under such a law, employers could still hold meetings to discuss politics, but managers could no longer compel workers to participate or to comply with political requests made at those meetings.

A captive audience approach is appealing because it applies to both electoral and policy-related communications alike, unlike the PAC restrictions proposal. And the inclusion of restrictions not just against mandatory political meetings but also religious gatherings at work has the advantage of creating a strong appeal to civil libertarians as well as progressives, a point I explore in more detail below. Still, the provisions of the Worker Freedom Act are mostly focused on employer-compelled meetings or other gatherings, which, as we have seen, are relatively rare. Far more common are employer political messages, typically in the form of emails, letters, or content posted on corporate websites. If political reformers were to seek federal legislation based on the Worker Freedom Act, such a bill ought to more centrally target these other means of communication.

Protecting Workers against Political Discrimination on the Job

An even more encompassing option for addressing coercive mobilization is to grant workers federal protection against political discrimination on the job, much like workers already have federal employment rights based on their sex, race, color, national origin, and religion. That would mean employers could not hire, fire, or change the working conditions of employees based on employees' political beliefs or actions. Such a change could be implemented by simply adding "political beliefs or actions" to the list of classes already protected by Title VII of the Civil Rights Act of 1964. By expanding the list of protected employee classes to include political beliefs and behaviors, the United States would join most other developed democracies.[24] Australia, Canada, and Japan, as well as all of the signatories to the European Convention on Human Rights, which includes European Union members, have provisions in place to protect employees from employer retaliation on the basis of politics. And closer to home, Washington, DC, and several states, including Montana and California, have laws that protect workers from employer actions made on the basis of political beliefs. One version of this proposal, which I have developed together with labor law scholar Paul Secunda, would delegate the responsibility for implementation of these protections to the Equal Employment Opportunity Commission, an agency already well equipped to handle the logistics of enforcing workplace antidiscrimination statutes.[25]

There are a number of advantages to pursuing the political discrimination provision, as opposed to bans on captive audience meetings or the PAC restriction approach. First, protecting workers against political discrimination would encompass both electoral and nonelectoral employer messages, preventing employers from retaliating against workers for either their opinions about parties and candidates or employee activities related to public policy and legislation. The political discrimination approach, moreover, does not try to delimit the specific activities that employers can and cannot engage in, as with the captive audience proposal, instead recognizing that political pressure may take very different forms. What is more, banning political discrimination would move enforcement of this protection away from the less effective realm of campaign finance (within the hamstrung Federal Election Commission) to the relatively more effective domain of employment discrimination. Last, and perhaps most important for the political fate of this proposal, adding political beliefs and actions to the list of protected classes would skirt the issue of the government regulating what employers can and cannot say to employees, which potentially runs afoul of a growing body of jurisprudence recognizing the free speech rights of employers, an issue I will revisit shortly.

Proponents of measures to curb coercive employer political mobilization will surely face the charge that such legislation would be relatively unprecedented in the United States. Reformers will thus need good examples of how restrictions could work. Campaign finance limits on corporate PACs provide one such case of the federal government successfully legislating how political resources can be collected and distributed by employers. But another, more sweeping example of regulation on political recruitment in the workplace comes from the Hatch Act.

The Hatch Act: An Important Precedent for Regulating Employer Political Coercion

Enacted in 1939, the Hatch Act set limits on how federal employees, as well as certain state and local employees, can participate in politics. It is worth examining the support the Hatch Act has attracted from all corners of the political landscape for a model of what kind of support restrictions on employer political recruitment could garner. Take, for instance, hearings that were held in Congress in 1993. In those proceedings, members of Congress and interest group representatives from across the political spectrum denounced the pressure that federal workers might feel to participate in politics as improper and morally wrong. Senator William Roth Jr., a Republican from Delaware, inveighed against any changes that might loosen the Hatch Act's restrictions out of fear of the intimidation that federal employees would face from their superiors or other groups. "What will be allowed will become expected, and as it is human nature to want to get ahead, employees will feel obligated to participate in partisan campaigns in order to gain a promotion or bonus," explained Senator Roth.[26] Similarly a representative from the American Civil Liberties Union stated plainly, "Employers cannot use their positions of trust to intimidate workers or the public to conform to their political judgment. This is the very antithesis of free and robust expression of First Amendment rights."[27] In a striking example of just how popular the law's restrictions had become, the president of the left-leaning watchdog group Common Cause appeared on a panel alongside the head of the conservative Right to Work Committee to implore Congress to address problems of "implicit coercion" that federal workers might face on the job.[28]

The bottom line during these hearings was that actors from a range of political positions felt that no federal workers should experience intimidation or pressure from their supervisors—or other groups—to participate in politics. Clearly there are important differences between the motivations for the enactment of the Hatch Act restrictions and proposals governing employer political recruitment in the private sector. Corruption and misuse of public resources are concerns that are not applicable in the same way to private-sector firms as they are in government (though there may be parallels when companies use shareholders' monies to engage in political coercion with which shareholders disagree).[29] But the logic of protecting subordinate employees from undue political coercion from their supervisors is one that ought to apply to all employees alike.

The Legality of Employer Mobilization Restrictions

New federal legislation to curb employer mobilization is likely to face significant legal challenges from the business community. While appropriate defenses will depend on the form that such legislation eventually takes, I can still sketch out the broad contours of why new restrictions on employer mobilization have sound backing in American law, focusing on two distinct lines of argument.[30]

Employer Speech versus Employer Conduct

Perhaps the most pressing issue concerning the legality of employer mobilization legislation involves the expanding free speech rights of companies. In a landmark decision in 1978, the Supreme Court struck down a Massachusetts statute prohibiting most corporate political contributions and expenditures intended to influence referendum and initiative proposals, arguing that there is "no support in the First or Fourteenth Amendment, or in this Court's decisions, for the proposition that such speech loses the protection otherwise afforded it by the First Amendment simply because its source is a corporation."[31] That decision heralded a new era for the Court, implying that companies had rights to free speech in the political process. Corporate free speech rights have only grown in the ensuing years, culminating in the *Citizens United* decision from 2010.[32] Since then the Supreme Court has also recognized the right of for-profit (but closely held) companies to opt out of regulations that challenge First Amendment rights to practice religion free from government intrusion (through the decision in *Burwell v. Hobby Lobby* in 2014), and corporations have also brought a range of new free speech cases against government regulations, increasingly successfully.

In light of this body of law recognizing a corporate right to free speech, could the federal government regulate how businesses can communicate with their workers? If framed as restrictions on employers' free speech, such a regulation seems unlikely to withstand judicial scrutiny. But if such a policy were framed as limiting employers' conduct with respect to their employees, there would be a much stronger case for its legality. American courts have long permitted the federal government to set rules on employment relationships. For instance, the federal government regulates how employers can hire and fire workers. (They cannot do it on the basis of race or sex, for example.) In addition, managers (and indeed all coworkers) are prohibited from sexually harassing their subordinates, even though such harassment might be construed as the exercise of free speech. In defending the ability of the government to regulate this kind of employer conduct, some legal scholars have noted that the workplace creates a unique situation of "economic and social dependence" between subordinates and their bosses, which necessitates greater worker protections against intimidation and harassment.[33]

An even closer analogy to employer mobilization limits might be the National Labor Relations Act, which sets restrictions—albeit loose and poorly enforced ones—on how employers can communicate with workers during union organizing drives.[34] A manager cannot explicitly threaten workers with job loss or reprisal if workers decide to support a union. In a similar vein, private-sector employers cannot make promises to reward workers with higher wages, better working conditions, or promotions should workers oppose unionization. Between each of the three legislative approaches I have outlined—extending PAC restrictions to companies themselves, banning captive audience meetings, and protecting employees from political discrimination—an approach based on addressing political discrimination seems most likely to escape claims of suppressing corporate free speech. Adding political beliefs and actions to the list of protected classes does not change the ability of employers to communicate with their workers.

The Freedom Not to Speak and to Not Support Objectionable Speech

A second set of reasons employer mobilization restrictions could be legal under present doctrine has to do with the First Amendment protections extended to employees in unionized workplaces. One concern with unions that the Supreme Court has recognized is that workers might be compelled to pay dues to a labor organization whose political activities workers oppose. Workers would thus be forced to subsidize political speech that they dislike, a violation of workers' First Amendment rights to choose which political causes they support. As a result the Supreme Court has ruled that in settings where unions collect mandatory dues from workers, unions can charge workers only for the costs associated with collective bargaining, worker representation, and grievance procedures but not political activities.[35] That way no worker is compelled to support potentially objectionable political speech. That same logic could be applied to employer mobilization. If employers are requiring that workers participate in politics, it could be construed as a violation of workers' rights to choose their own forms of political speech. Restrictions on the ability of employers to compel their work-ers to participate in politics would then be a very natural means of preserving workers' First Amendment free speech rights. This argument has the advantage of potentially appealing to conservatives who might otherwise be more likely to side with employers than with workers; if unions cannot force their members to participate in political speech, then neither should employers.

Still, comparisons between laws governing union dues collection and pro-posals to restrict employer political recruitment are strongest on rhetorical, not legal grounds. Legal arguments about the First Amendment free speech rights of workers require state action, which is absent in the case of private-sector politi-cal recruitment. Neither the federal nor state governments are directly involved when a private-sector employer decides to compel their workers to participate in politics. In contrast, the First Amendment rights of public workers protesting union dues are automatically at play because the government is their employer. Similarly the state is involved when private workers oppose union dues because of the federal legislation governing private-sector unions (the National Labor Relations Act). The absence of First Amendment considerations for private-sector employees helps to underscore that workers in the private sector lack constitutional rights to free speech.

Building Political Support in Favor of Regulating Employer Mobilization

New federal laws against intimidating political recruitment must attract suffi-cient political support to clear Congress and the executive, so it is worth reflect-ing on what a coalition in favor of workplace political protections might look like. One starting point is the 2016 CCES. The results from that poll reveal that broad majorities of American employees—stretching across party and ideologi-cal lines—support restrictions on the ability of employers to campaign in the workplace, retaliate against employees whose views clash with their managers, and reward workers whose political participation aligns with their business.

The 2016 CCES asked respondents about their opinions on six potential employer actions that represent a range of the varieties of mobilization I have examined. For each action, respondents were asked whether they thought the action "should be permitted by law" or "should be prohibited by law." (Respondents also could say they did not know.) The following list provides the exact survey text I used for each employer action:

- Firing rank-and-file workers for supporting a specific political candidate or party.

- Asking rank-and-file workers to support a specific political candidate or party.
- Asking rank-and-file workers to support bills in Congress or state governments.
- Firing rank-and-file workers for supporting specific political issues.
- Promoting rank-and-file workers for supporting a specific political candidate or party.
- Promoting rank-and-file workers for supporting specific political issues.

Figure C.1 summarizes the responses to these items and shows that in all cases broad majorities of Americans believed that each activity should be restricted by law. In no case did more than 20 percent of respondents believe that any of these activities should be permitted by law. The strongest support for legal restrictions was for firing and promoting workers for supporting particular candidates and parties—both generally legal in most states, as we saw in chapter 5. Americans were most divided about employers asking rank-and-file workers to support federal or state legislation: 19 percent said this ought to be permitted by law and another 22 percent said they did not know one way or another.

In sum, there appears to be a very strong appetite in the general population for curbing the most coercive aspects of employer mobilization, such as when employers might reward or punish workers for following up, or not, on political requests. While more divided about policy-based employer outreach, a significant majority of Americans still thought these more common types of contact ought to be illegal too. Interestingly there were not significant divisions in support for legal restrictions on employer mobilization by party or ideology. Large proportions of liberals, conservatives, Democrats, and Republicans alike all supported tighter limits on what employers could ask of their employees when it comes to politics and policy. Figure C.2 divides respondents by party and shows the striking degree of similarity in responses across Democrats and Republicans. Curbing employer mobilization—especially by putting limits on the possibilities of rewarding or punishing workers for their political views and activities—may thus be a rare issue that can attract mass support across the political and ideological spectrum.

Reformers seeking to pass new federal legislation can therefore count on broad support from the American public. This mass support for new legislation could be further bolstered by interest group advocates as well. Labor unions would be a natural ally of a movement to restrict employer political recruitment, as the historical force checking the power of companies and representing the interests of ordinary workers in politics. Organizations advocating for the protection and expansion of civil liberties, like the American Civil Liberties Union or People for the American Way, are another source of support, as this issue could be framed as workers' right to political speech. This sort of framing might also appeal to more traditionally conservative libertarians, who prioritize

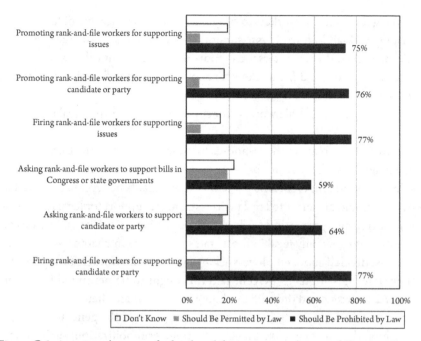

Figure C.1 Americans' support for legal prohibitions on employer mobilization. Data from 2016 CCES (sample sizes: 824–826 depending on item).

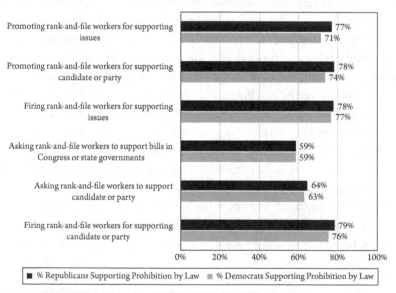

Figure C.2 Americans' support for legal prohibitions on employer mobilization, by partisan identification. Data from 2016 CCES (sample sizes: 335–337 for Democrats and 213–214 for Republicans depending on item).

the protection of individual rights against violations by powerful agents in the private and public sectors.

While a framing based on violations of workers' rights could make an employer mobilization campaign more appealing to unions and civil liberties–oriented groups, a focus on the disproportionate voice granted to employers through workplace mobilization could make this issue compelling to campaign finance reformers as well. Just as these reformers are concerned that *Citizens United* and other pieces of the campaign finance legal regime grant powerful economic interests an oversized role in the policymaking process, so too should these groups direct their attention to employer mobilization. The sort of campaign finance groups attracted to this issue could come from across the political spectrum, just as with mass supporters. A growing group of conservatives, for instance, has voiced concern that companies can secure favorable treatment from government, and many in the far-right Tea Party movement have directed as much of their anger on "crony capitalists" as on government.[36] Such conservative groups might thus support restrictions on employer mobilization as a means of limiting the rents companies can extract from public policy.[37]

Alternatives to National Legislation

At the time of this book's writing, it seems highly unlikely that the federal government will tackle coercive employer mobilization legislation given the Republican control of Congress and the White House. Notwithstanding the broad public support for new legislation restricting employer mobilization from conservatives and Republicans, it is hard to imagine a Republican-controlled Congress passing a law seen as restricting employers' prerogatives to hire, fire, and discipline their workers. Congressional Republicans have strongly opposed measures to deal with corporate political speech in the wake of the *Citizens United* decision and have also repeatedly stymied bills to buttress workplace protections for employees, such as raising the minimum wage, ensuring pay equity for women, and facilitating unionization.[38]

As a result, barring full control of the federal government by Democrats, new national legislation seems unlikely. But advocates of workplace political protections do not need to throw in the towel just because the federal legislative process is deadlocked. Although new federal legislation would be ideal, there are still other avenues for addressing coercive employer mobilization, and taking these initial steps might even build support over time for later congressional action.

Executive Action

A presidential administration sympathetic to workplace protections could make progress by using its leverage as an employer and a contractor to limit coercive mobilization. The Obama administration used a similar approach to address a range of labor market protections that it did not manage to pass through Congress. For instance, under the Obama presidency, the White House directed federal contractors to raise the minimum wage paid to their workers, implement paid sick leave, stop discrimination against LGBT workers, and increase their reporting of labor violations.[39] Another presidential administration could similarly issue regulations on the ways contractors recruit workers into politics. While these federal regulations would not reach the same number of workers as new federal legislation, they would reach a broad cross section of workers and set a benchmark for private-sector employers to follow.[40]

State Legislation

Individual states provide another opportunity for pursuing employment protection against coercive mobilization, and as we have already seen, two states, Oregon and New Jersey, have already taken action to stop coercive meetings about politics and religion at work. More states could follow suit in passing these measures or strengthening statutes related to the protection of political rights. The California Labor Code, for instance, forbids employers from controlling or directing the political activities and affiliations of their employees.[41] Other states could adopt similar measures or strengthen their existing provisions to match those of California. Of course favoring state over federal legislation cuts both ways for advocates of protections against employer political coercion. While some states might experiment with new initiatives to protect private-sector workers against political intimidation on the job, other states might move in the opposite direction, explicitly legalizing a greater scope of permissible employer recruitment.[42] And perhaps even more worrying, I found that existing state laws did not appear to either curb coercive employer mobilization or reduce the pressure workers felt to respond to employer messages when they feared for their jobs. (Recall the results from chapter 5.)

Private-Sector Initiatives

If the states and the federal government fail to act, it still might be possible to reduce coercive political mobilization in the workplace through outside social and economic pressures. Consumers, investors, and unions could help to convince managers to establish voluntary guidelines for how businesses would deal with political mobilization in the workplace. Those guidelines could then include a set of appropriate activities in which managers could engage, ranging from helping workers to register and turn out to vote to educating workers on important bills pending in Congress. The guidelines could also include explicit stipulations that employers could not threaten workers with economic retaliation for refusing to comply with corporate political requests, nor could managers discipline workers for political activities or beliefs.

Businesses might also pledge to place a disclaimer on all political communications to workers stating that nothing in the message should be construed by workers to be a requirement of their jobs and that managers will not reward or punish them based on their political participation (or lack of participation). Failure to comply with the new corporate code of conduct would result in public backlash from consumers, shareholders, and corporate watchdog groups.

The Bipartisan Policy Center recently partnered with two private-sector employers, the hotel giant Marriott International and the coffee chain Starbucks, to produce its own guidelines for nonpartisan employer mobilization in the run-up to the 2016 election.[43] Those guidelines are a very good start for a private-sector code of conduct. Recognizing that "enterprises of all shapes and sizes have an obligation to facilitate active citizenship by their employees and members," the guidelines also specify that enterprises must "adhere to a standard of complete nonpartisanship," which entails walling off their mobilization from any other political activities at the company, including PACs or the recruitment of executives. In addition the guidelines make clear that "employee or member participation in Initiative programs and best practices is purely voluntary"—and to back up that point the guidelines stress that "there would be no requirement that individuals participate in these programs," nor can participation (or nonparticipation) have an effect on employee job standing, compensation or benefits, or future prospects within the company.

To help with monitoring and to encourage a culture of reporting, companies could help to establish a hotline or website where workers could anonymously report violations of the code of conduct to an affiliated non-profit organization. One example of an online approach to monitoring is the website Coworker.org, which helps workers put pressure on their employers to change unfair labor practices through online petition campaigns. The advantage of this strategy is that it can be pursued at the same time as a legislative approach. The disadvantage of voluntary tactics is that they depend heavily on continued countervailing pressure from consumers, labor organizations, and investors to stay effective. Voluntary codes of conduct have also had only limited success in other areas of labor policy.[44]

Apart from joining voluntary codes of conduct, companies could ensure that their internal employee handbooks foster, or at the very least do not discourage, political discussions among coworkers. The survey of employers conducted by the Society for Human Resource Management that I described in chapter 3 indicates that 18 percent of the Society's members prohibit employees "from engaging in any form of political activity on the organization's premises." While companies have every right to keep employees from disrupting the workplace, they should permit employees to have the sort of political discussions that are so valuable for individuals and society as a whole. Companies have to comply with the existing law in this area too. The National Labor Relations Act protects the right of employees to engage in "concerted activity"—even outside of a labor union—that advances the mutual aid and protection of their fellow cowork-ers.[45] Such concerted activity includes the right of employees to discuss political issues if it relates to their well-being at work—a fairly expansive definition. These are protections that many large employers may be violating when they stipu-late that workers cannot discuss political issues on the job or ban workers from posting about their company on social media. For instance, the National Labor Relations Board recently ruled that Mexican fast-casual food chain Chipotle had violated labor law by banning "political/religious activity" at work, as well as barring employees from discussing their employer on social media.[46]

Some companies may choose to take these steps on their own, but others may not without outside pressure. One particularly promising avenue for generating such pressure involves leveraging the power of institutional investors, especially public-sector employee retirement funds. These funds control vast amounts of capital and therefore have a great deal of bargaining power to change company practices; the California Public Employees' Retirement System, for instance, controls nearly $300 billion in assets, and the New York State fund for public employees controls close to $200 billion.[47] Public employee retirement funds are increasingly using this heft to advance social and economic objectives, such as promoting environmental concerns and improving working conditions in the companies in which they invest.[48] By pledging not to support companies that engage in political intimidation or coercion and that facilitate employee political discussions at work, such institutional investors could promote new standards for publicly traded businesses.

Another complementary approach involves the economic, social, and gover-nance (ESG) ratings assigned to companies. There are now a number of consul-tancies that specialize in rating the ESG practices of publicly traded firms—for instance, evaluating companies' commitments to addressing climate change or avoiding doing business with governments that violate human rights. Adding corporate practices around employer mobilization and employee political rights to these ratings could encourage publicly traded companies to avoid coercive and intimidating recruitment or policies that chill employee political speech. These approaches would have the advantage of leveraging the potentially very powerful disciplining effects of investment markets to curb unwanted employer practices.

The Bottom Line: Addressing Coercive Employer Mobilization Requires Many Perspectives and Approaches

My objective in providing many different possibilities for addressing employer political intimidation is to show that failure to enact any one piece of legislation need not—and indeed should not—stop an effort to address this problem. Even though the scale of this practice may seem daunting, reformers have a variety of options that could make a difference—and they are measures that could be pursued concurrently with one another. Just as important, the broad scope of these proposals underscores the fact that employer mobilization is an issue that cuts across a number of disparate fields of practice, including labor and employment law, campaign finance, human resource management, unions, and free speech. In addressing the problem of coercive employer messaging and recruitment, then, there is a unique opportunity for reformers and impassioned individuals from each of these fields to communicate with others working in adjacent areas. This means, for instance, giving union advocates the chance to connect the work they do with reformers committed to expanding political speech rights, or for campaign finance activists to think more broadly about political power as it is exercised in the workplace. An overarching lesson that is likely to emerge from this collaboration is that the boundaries of what employers can and are doing with their workers—and in society more generally—has expanded into new areas that were previously limited by the state, unions, or consumers. A campaign to end political intimidation in the workplace could therefore help spur a productive dialogue at the intersection of all of these issues, which are tied together by a fundamental concern about the distribution of corporate and citizen voice and power.

Toward a More Democratic Workplace—and Society

Toward the end of his career, the esteemed political theorist Robert Dahl increasingly expressed concern about the relationship between what he termed "corporate capitalism"—the present-day economic system in which most resources and workers are located within large companies—and democracy. Two features of corporate capitalism especially troubled him. Corporate capitalism appeared to be increasingly concentrating economic resources in the hands of a small group of managers and owners. Those economic resources, Dahl worried, could be readily translated into political power that could overrun the democratic process. Second, "because the internal government of the corporation was not itself democratic but hierarchical and often despotic"—in the sense that owners were not democratically accountable to the workers at a company and could hire and fire at will—"the rapid expansion" of the corporate form "meant that an increasing proportion of the demos would live out their working lives, and most of their daily existence, not within a democratic system but instead within a hierarchical structure of subordination."[49]

Coercive employer mobilization is a clear manifestation of both of these prescient fears that Dahl expressed about the era of corporate capitalism. By generating a new political tool available only to employers, managerial mobilization of workers provides a new means for companies and the managers who direct them to advance their interests above and beyond other actors in politics. And the reason employer mobilization works so well is because of the high degree of control, perhaps even "despotic control," managers can exercise over their employees. When employees lack democratic rights at work, they are dependent on their managers for their economic livelihood—and the more dependent workers are on their managers, the more responsive they become to their employers' political requests.

Addressing coercive employer mobilization will thus help to remedy one important and growing symptom of the troubled relationship between democracy and corporate capitalism. There is no reason workers should need to renounce their freedom from political domination when they come into work every day.[50] My hope is that this book, and any ensuing attention to employer mobilization, can open a broader discussion about how to make the workplace— and therefore the American political system—more democratic.

Chapter 2 Appendix

SSRS Survey of Workers

SSRS Omnibus is a national, weekly, dual-frame bilingual telephone survey designed to meet standards of quality associated with custom research studies. Each weekly wave of the SSRS Omnibus consists of 1,000 interviews, of which 500 are obtained with respondents on their cell phones and approximately 35 interviews are completed in Spanish. All SSRS Omnibus data are weighted to represent the target population. The complete survey instrument that SSRS used follows:

EM-01.   Are you self employed?

    1   Yes   (SKIP TO NEXT INSERT)
    2   No
    9   (DO NOT READ)Don't know/no answer

EM-01a. Do you usually work the same schedule each week, or not?
         (READ LIST IF NECESSARY)

         (PROBE FOR CORRECT "NO" RESPONSE)

    1   Yes, you work the same schedule each week
    2   No, you do not work the same schedule each week—you set your work schedule
    3   No, you do not work the same schedule each week—your employer sets work schedule
    4   No, you do not work the same schedule each week—you and your employer set schedule, but you have more control

    5   No, you do not work the same schedule each week—you and your employer set schedule, but your employer has more control

    6   No, you do not work the same schedule each week—you and your employer set schedule with equal control

    9   (DO NOT READ) Don't know/no answer

EM-03.   Do you supervise anyone at your main job?

    1   Yes

    2   No

    9   (DO NOT READ) Don't know/no answer

EM-04.   To what extent, if at all, do you worry about the possibility of losing your main job?
           (READ LIST)

(ROTATE 1-4/4-1)

    1   Worry a great deal

    2   Worry some extent

    3   Worry a little

    4   Don't worry at all

    9   (DO NOT READ) Don't know/no answer

EM-05.   Are you a member of a union or teachers association?
           (IF NO) Have you ever been a member of a union or teachers association?

    1   Currently a member

    2   Once a member, but not now

    3   Never a member

    9   (DO NOT READ) Don't know/no answer

EM-07   About how many employees does your employer have across all locations that your employer operates?
           Just give your best estimate.

    1   1–49

    2   50–199

    3   200–499

    4   500 or more

    9   (DO NOT READ) Don't know/no answer

EM-10.   Thinking about the conversations you have with your co-workers, what are the political views of most of your co-workers?
           (READ LIST)

(ROTATE 1-5/5-1)

1   Extremely liberal

2   Somewhat liberal

3   Moderate

4   Somewhat conservative

5   Extremely conservative

9   (DO NOT READ) Don't know/no answer

EM-12.   Do the top managers in your main job make it clear which political candidates or party they prefer? (READ LIST)

1   Yes, very clear

2   Yes, somewhat clear

3   No

9   (DO NOT READ) Don't know/no answer

EM-13.   I am going to ask you about specific situations where your managers and supervisors may have contacted you about politics or political issues, such as contacting you about voting, political candidates, or public policies. Have you ever (INSERT ITEM)?

1   Yes

2   No

9   (DO NOT READ) Don't know/no answer

(SCRAMBLE A–I; J always last)

a.   Received an email from a manager or supervisor about politics

b.   Received a letter from a manager or supervisor about politics

c.   Received a phone call from a manager or supervisor about politics

d.   Seen a posting on a company website about politics

e.   Had a meeting with a manager or supervisor about politics

f.   Been asked to attend a political event by a manager or supervisor

g.   Been asked to volunteer for a political campaign by manager or supervisor

h.   Received message with your paycheck about politics

i.   Seen posters or flyers in your office about politics

j.   Had any other contact with manager or supervisor about politics (NOT SPECIFIED)

(IF EM-12=1 OR 2 or EM-13a–j=YES TO ANY)

EM-14.   How often has a manager or supervisor in your main job contacted you about politics or political issues? (READ LIST)

1   About once every week

2   About once every month

3   Several times per year
4   One time per year or less
9   (DO NOT READ) Don't know/no answer

(IF EM-12=1 OR 2 or EM-13a–j=YES TO ANY)
EM-16.   What did your manager or supervisor mention to you when they contacted you about politics or political issues?
Did your manager or supervisor mention (INSERT ITEM)?
1   Yes
2   No
9   (DO NOT READ) Don't know/no answer

(SCRAMBLE A–I; J always last)
a.   Information about registering to vote
b.   Information about turning out to vote on Election Day
c.   Information about a presidential candidate
d.   Information about a political candidate for the U.S. House of Representatives
e.   Information about a political candidate for the U.S. Senate
f.   Information about a political candidate for state government
g.   Information about a bill or a policy
h.   Information about contacting a lawmaker
i.   Information about donating to a political candidate
j.   Other kinds of political information (NOT SPECIFIED)

(IF EM-12=1 OR 2 or EM-13a–j=YES TO ANY)
EM-17.   What issues did your manager or supervisor mention to you when they contacted you about politics?
Did your manager or supervisor mention (INSERT ITEM)?
1   Yes
2   No
8   (DO NOT READ) Don't know/no answer

(SCRAMBLE A–H)
a.   The environment
b.   Taxes
c.   Regulation
d.   Trade and competing with other countries
e.   Health care
f.   Education and training
g.   Unions
h.   Employment and jobs
i.   Any other issue (NOT SPECIFIED)

(IF EM-12=1 OR 2 or EM-13a–j=YES TO ANY)

EM-19.   When your manager or supervisor contacted you about political issues, what were the political views of your manager or supervisor's message?
(READ LIST)

1   Extremely liberal
2   Somewhat liberal
3   Moderate
4   Somewhat conservative
5   Extremely conservative
9   (DO NOT READ) Don't know/no answer

(IF EM-12=1 OR 2 or EM-13a–j=YES TO ANY)
(ROTATE VERBIAGE IN PARENS)

EM-20.   How much did you (agree) or (disagree) with the messages that your manager or supervisor provided to you about politics or political issues?

1   Strongly agree
2   Somewhat agree
3   Neither agree nor disagree
4   Somewhat disagree
5   Strongly disagree
9   (DO NOT READ) Don't know/no answer

(IF EM-16c, d, e, f, h, i=YES TO ANY)
(ROTATE VERBIAGE IN PARENS)

EM-21.   Were the political candidates discussed by your manager or supervisor mostly (Democrats), mostly (Republicans), or were the political candidates evenly divided between the two parties?
(READ LIST)

1   All Democrats
2   Mostly Democrats
3   Evenly split between the parties
4   Mostly Republicans
5   All Republicans
9   (DO NOT READ) Don't know/no answer

(IF EM-12=1 OR 2 or EM-13a–j=YES TO ANY)

EM-22.   Did the political information you received from your manager or supervisor change your mind about politics or voting? Did the information (INSERT LIST)?
(READ LIST)

1   Yes
2   No
9   (DO NOT READ) Don't know/no answer

(SCRAMBLE A–G; H always last)
  a.   Make you more likely to register to vote
  b.   Make you more likely to turn out to vote on election day
  c.   Make you more likely to vote for a particular candidate
  d.   Make you more likely to volunteer for a political campaign
  e.   Make you more likely to change your mind about a particular issue
  f.   Make you more likely to contact a lawmaker about an issue
  g.   Make you more likely to donate to a political candidate
  h.   Information had other effect (NOT SPECIFIED)

(ASK IF EM-22c, d, f, g=YES TO ANY)
(ROTATE VERBIAGE IN PARENS)
EM-23.   Did your manager or supervisor's information make you (more) or
         (less) likely to support your manager or supervisor's preferred politi-
         cal candidates? Would that be much (more/less) likely or somewhat
         (more/less) likely?
  1   Much more likely
  2   Somewhat more likely
  3   Somewhat less likely
  4   Much less likely
  9   (DO NOT READ) Don't know/no answer

(IF EM-12=1 OR 2 or EM-13a-j=YES TO ANY)
EM-24.   How comfortable or uncomfortable are you with the contact you had
         with your manager or supervisor about politics and political issues?
         (ROTATE 1-5/5-1)
  1   Very comfortable
  2   Somewhat comfortable
  3   Neither comfortable nor uncomfortable
  4   Somewhat uncomfortable
  5   Very uncomfortable
  9   (DO NOT READ) Don't know/no answer

(IF EM-12=1 OR 2 or EM-13a-j=YES TO ANY)
EM-25.   When your manager or supervisor discussed politics or political issues
         with you, did your manager or supervisor ever (INSERT ITEM)?

1   Yes
2   No
9   (DO NOT READ) Don't know/no answer

(SCRAMBLE, ROTATE)
- a.   Mention changing or cutting worker hours because of politics
- b.   Mention changing or cutting jobs because of politics
- c.   Mention closing offices or plants because of politics

(IF EM-12=1 OR 2 or EM-13a-j=YES TO ANY)

EM-26.   In your own words, please tell me anything you remember about the messages about politics or political issues you received from your managers or supervisors. For instance, do you remember how you received the message, what issues the message discussed, or which political candidates your managers and supervisors mentioned?
(PROBE ALL RESPONSES FOR CLARITY AND TO THE NEGATIVE)
(WHAT DO YOU REMEMBER ABOUT THAT? WHAT ELSE DO YOU RECALL, ETC.)

1   Answer given
9   (DO NOT READ) Don't know/no answer

(IF EM-05=1 OR 2)

EM-27.   Has a union ever contacted you about politics or political issues, such as voting, political candidates, or legislation? Have you ever (INSERT ITEM)?

1   Yes
2   No
9   (DO NOT READ) Don't know/no answer

(SCRAMBLE A–H)
- a.   Received an email from a union about politics
- b.   Received a letter from a union about politics
- c.   Received a phone call from a union about politics
- d.   Seen a posting on a union website about politics
- e.   Had a meeting with a union about politics
- f.   Been asked to attend a political event by a union
- g.   Been asked to volunteer for a political campaign by a union
- h.   Seen posters or flyers from a union about politics
- i.   Had any other contact with a union about politics (NOT SPECIFIED)

(IF EM-27=YES TO ANY)

EM-29.   What issues did the union mention to you when they contacted you
         about politics? Did they mention (INSERT ITEM)?
   1   Yes
   2   No
   9   (DO NOT READ) Don't know/no answer

(SCRAMBLE A–H)
   a.   The environment
   b.   Taxes
   c.   Regulation
   d.   Trade and competing with other countries
   e.   Health care
   f.   Education and training
   g.   Unions
   h.   Employment and jobs
   i.   Any other issue (NOT SPECIFIED)

(IF EM-27=YES TO ANY)

EM-32.   Did the political information you received from the union change
         your mind about politics or voting? Did the (INSERT ITEM)?
   1   Yes
   2   No
   9   (DO NOT READ) Don't know/no answer

(SCRAMBLE A–G)
   a.   Information make you more likely to register to vote
   b.   Information make you more likely to turn out to vote on election day
   c.   Information make you more likely to vote for a particular candidate
   d.   Information make you more likely to volunteer for a political
        campaign
   e.   Information make you more likely to change your mind about a
        particular issue
   f.   Information make you more likely to contact a lawmaker about
        an issue
   g.   Information make you more likely to donate to a political candidate
   h.   Information have any other effect (NOT SPECIFIED)

EM-33.   In which INDUSTRY is your main job?
         (READ LIST ONLY IF NECESSARY: Pick a category that best
         matches your employer's products or services.)

01 Construction
02 Education
03 Financial activities, insurance, or real estate
04 Health care
05 Information technology
06 Leisure and hospitality, including arts, entertainment, and recreation
07 Manufacturing
08 Natural resources and mining (such as agriculture and forestry)
09 Professional, scientific, technical services, and management
10 Public administration, including federal, state, and local government
11 Transportation and warehouses
12 Utilities
13 Wholesale or retail
96 Other industry (NOT SPECIFIED)
99 (DO NOT READ) Don't know/no answer

EM-34. In which OCCUPATION is your main job?
(READ LIST ONLY IF NECESSARY: Pick a category that best matches the kind of work you do in your main job.)
01 Architecture and engineering
02 Arts, design, entertainment, sports, and the media
03 Business and financial operations
04 Building and grounds cleaning and maintenance
05 Community and social services
06 Computers and mathematical
07 Construction and mining
08 Education, training, and libraries
09 Farming, fishing and forestry
10 Food preparation and serving
11 Health care practitioners, such as doctors or nurses
12 Health care support staff
13 Installation, maintenance, and repair
14 Legal services
15 Life, physical, and social sciences
16 Management
17 Military
18 Office and administrative support
19 Personal care and service
20 Protective services
21 Sales and related to sales
22 Production

23   Transportation and material moving
96   Other occupation (NOT SPECIFIED)
99   (DO NOT READ) Don't know/no answer

EM-35.   In which state do you work in your main job? If you work in multiple
states, please give the state in which you spend the most time.
(INSERT STATE LIST)

(IF EM-12=3 OR 9 AND EM-13a–j=NO TO ALL)
EM-36.   Imagine that the managers and supervisors at your main job encouraged you to vote for particular political candidates. How likely or
unlikely would you be to support the candidates that the managers
and supervisors at your job had endorsed?
(READ LIST)
1   Very likely
2   Somewhat likely
3   Neither likely nor unlikely
4   Somewhat unlikely
5   Very unlikely
9   (DO NOT READ) Don't know/no answer

(ROTATE RESPONSE OPTIONS IN PARENS)
EM-38.   Currently, employers are permitted to campaign for political candidates in the workplace. That is, employers can send messages to workers, post flyers, and hold mandatory meetings to endorse political
candidates for the presidency, Congress, and state government. Do
you think that this kind of campaigning by employers in the workplace (should be limited by law) or (should remain unlimited)?
1   Should remain unlimited
2   Should be limited by law
9   (DO NOT READ) Don't know/no answer

2016 CCES Survey

I added the following questions to the 2016 wave of the Cooperative Congressional Election Study, an online survey intended to be nationally representative of the population of American adults. The survey included 1,000 respondents and 459 respondents who reported being employed by someone else (i.e., non-self-employed workers). More information on the design and methodology of the CCES can be found at https://cces.gov.harvard.edu/. Full text for each of the substantive items used from the 2016 CCES appears below:

COL311

MULTIPLE CHOICE

Employer Contact

Only show if respondent is employed and COL301 does not equal 1. Randomize options except for COL311_F.

Did your top managers and supervisors at your main job do any of the following things in the past two years? Check all that apply.

COL311_A   Reminded you to register to vote or vote

COL311_B   Discussed candidates

COL311_C   Discussed legislation, policy, or other political issues

COL311_D   Held events about politics

COL311_E   Asked you to donate to, or volunteer for, a political campaign

COL311_F   {Fixed} Something else related to politics or political issues (please specify) [Text Box]

COL312

SINGLE CHOICE

Employer Ideology

Only show if respondent is employed and COL301 does not equal 1. Reverse options, except for 6.

Would you say that your top managers and supervisors at your main job are generally liberal, conservative, or what?

1   Very liberal

2   Liberal

3   Moderate

4   Conservative

5   Very conservative

6   {Fixed} Don't know

COL315

SINGLE CHOICE

Employer Monitoring Perceptions

Only show if respondent is employed and COL301 does not equal 1. Reverse options, except for 5.

How likely is it that your main employer can track your political views and actions, such as keeping track of whether you voted or which candidates you support?

1   Very likely
2   Somewhat likely
3   Somewhat unlikely
4   Very unlikely
5   {Fixed} Don't know

COL316

MULTIPLE CHOICE

Employer Political Discovery

Only show if respondent is employed and COL301 does not equal 1.

Has a manager or supervisor at your main job ever discovered whether you voted or which candidates you support? Check all that apply.

COL316_A   Discovered whether I voted
COL316_B   Discovered which candidates I support
COL316_C   Discovered something else about my politics (Please specify)
                 [Text box]

COL317

SINGLE CHOICE

Employer Retaliation Perception—Advancement

Only show if respondent is employed and COL301 does not equal 1. Reverse options, except for 5.

How likely is it that you might miss out on opportunities for advancement or promotion at your main job because of your political views or actions, including which candidates you support?

1   Very likely
2   Somewhat likely

3 Somewhat unlikely
4 Very unlikely
5 {Fixed} Don't know

COL318

MULTIPLE CHOICE

Employer Retaliation Happened

Only show if respondent is employed and COL301 does not equal 1. Randomize options except for COL318_D.

As far as you can remember, have any of the following things happened to someone at your main job in part because of his or her political views or actions? Check all that apply.

COL318_A Someone was fired
COL318_B Someone missed out on a promotion
COL318_C Someone was treated unfairly
COL318_D {Fixed} Other (please specify) [Text Box]

COL405

SINGLE CHOICE

Union Contact

Did a labor union contact you about politics or political issues during the past two years?

1 Yes
2 No

COL407

GRID

Randomize order of rows.

Here are some actions that employers might take. Do you think that these actions should be permitted or prohibited by law?

Columns

1 Should be <u>permitted</u> by law
2 Should be <u>prohibited</u> by law
3 Don't know

ROWS
   COL407_A   Firing rank-and-file workers for supporting a specific politi-
              cal candidate or party
   COL407_B   Asking rank-and-file workers to support a specific political
              candidate or party
   COL407_C   Asking rank-and-file workers to support bills in Congress or
              state governments
   COL407_D   Firing rank-and-file workers for supporting specific
              political issues
   COL407_E   Promoting rank-and-file workers for supporting a specific
              political candidate or party
   COL407_F   Promoting rank-and-file workers for supporting specific
              political issues

COL414

GRID

Only show if respondent is employed and COL301 does not equal 1. Randomize rows.

Please think about the following political proposals. Would you say your <u>top managers and supervisors</u> at your main job support or oppose these proposals?

Columns
   1   Support
   2   Oppose
   3   Don't know
   4   {Not shown: Skipped}

ROWS
   COL414_A   Repeal the Affordable Care Act (also known as Obamacare)
   COL414_B   Raise the federal minimum wage to $12/hr by 2020
   COL414_C   Require a minimum amount of renewable fuels (wind, solar,
              and hydroelectric) in the generation of electricity even if
              electricity prices increase somewhat
   COL414_D   Reduce the budget deficit by cutting spending instead of
              raising taxes

2016 Worker Survey Experiment

The final survey of workers I designed and fielded for this book involved a sample of 1,214 employed individuals provided by SSI, Inc., including 1,014 private-sector workers. While this was not a national probability sample, SSI selected respondents who would broadly match the distribution of employed workers in the United States. Below I compare the distribution of respondents in the SSI sample with the overall distribution of workers on a variety of characteristics. In addition, I provide the substantive survey items from the SSI survey experiment.

	Employed Civilian Adults	*SSI Sample*
Age		
18 to 24	11%	12%
25 to 44	44%	43%
45 to 64	40%	37%
65 to 74	5%	6%
75 to 80+	1%	1%
Hispanic Origin		
Non-Hispanic	84%	86%
Hispanic	16%	14%
Race		
White alone	80%	81%
Black alone	11%	11%
Other	9%	8%
Region		
Northeast	18%	19%
Midwest	22%	23%
South	36%	35%
West	23%	23%
Sex		
Male	53%	52%
Female	47%	48%
Total Size	146,799,000	1,214

Experiment 1: Minimum Wage Policy Preferences

❑ Treatment 1: Employer Message with Threat of Job Loss

Suppose you received the following letter at work from your top managers. Please read the following excerpt from the letter:

Dear valued co-worker,

There are a number of politicians who are currently calling for an increase in the federal minimum wage. Those politicians argue that an increase would help lift workers out of poverty. Unfortunately, the academic evidence paints a very different picture.

According to a recent review by economists at the Federal Reserve Board and the University of California, Irvine, most economic research shows that a higher minimum wage reduces employment for the youngest and least-skilled workers, thus hurting many of the same workers that it is supposed to help. This is supported by research from economists from American and Cornell University who studied the states that raised their minimum wages between 2003 and 2007 and found no associated reduction in poverty.

Your top managers here are also agreed that if the federal government were to raise the federal minimum wage, it would hurt our sales and force us to lay off a number of workers. Your job—and the jobs of your coworkers—might be at risk.

❑ Treatment 2: Generic Arguments against Minimum Wage

There are a number of politicians who are currently calling for an increase in the federal minimum wage. Those politicians argue that an increase would help lift workers out of poverty. Please read the following information about increasing the federal minimum wage:

According to a recent review by economists at the Federal Reserve Board and the University of California, Irvine, most economic research shows that a higher minimum wage reduces employment for the youngest and least-skilled workers, thus hurting many of the same workers that it is supposed to help. This is supported by research from economists from American and Cornell University who studied the states that raised their minimum wages between 2003 and 2007 and found no associated reduction in poverty.

❑   Treatment 3: Baseline

Please click to continue.

❑   Preferences for $15 an hour Federal Minimum Wage

The federal minimum wage is currently $7.25 per hour. Do you favor or oppose raising the federal minimum wage to $15 per hour?

- ○   Strongly favor (1)
- ○   Somewhat favor (2)
- ○   Neither favor nor oppose (3)
- ○   Somewhat oppose (4)
- ○   Strongly oppose (5)
- ○   Don't know (6)

Experiment 2: Contacting Congress about Health Insurance Tax

❑   Treatment 1: Employer Message with Threat of Job Loss

Suppose you received the following letter at work from your top managers. Please read the following excerpt from the letter:

Dear valued co-worker,

As part of the health reform law enacted in 2010, employers will have to pay a new sales tax on health insurance plans offered through the workplace. Congressional budget estimates show that this tax will represent over $101 billion between 2013 and 2022. Research suggests that this tax will raise the costs of health insurance for everyone, and may reduce future private sector employment by 125,000 workers.

Your top managers here are agreed that the health insurance tax will raise our costs of doing business, and make it harder to offer competitive wages and benefits to our workers.

Congress is currently discussing a bill that would cut the health insurance tax, and we urge you to contact your Member of Congress to support the bill. Calling or emailing your Member of Congress will help your management continue to offer competitive wages and benefits.

❏   Treatment 2: Generic Information against Health Insurance Tax

Please read the following information:

As part of the health reform law enacted in 2010, employers will have to pay a new sales tax on health insurance plans offered through the workplace. Congressional budget estimates show that this tax will represent over $101 billion between 2013 and 2022. Research suggests that this tax will raise the costs of health insurance for everyone, and may reduce future private sector employment by 125,000 workers.

❏   Treatment 3: Baseline

Please click to continue.

❏   Willingness to Contact Congress about Health Insurance Tax Repeal

Congress is currently debating legislation that would cut a new sales tax on health insurance plans offered through the workplace. How likely are you to contact your Member of Congress about this issue?

- ◯ Very likely (1)
- ◯ Somewhat likely (2)
- ◯ Neither likely nor unlikely (3)
- ◯ Somewhat unlikely (4)
- ◯ Very unlikely (5)
- ◯ Don't know (6)

YouGov Survey of Employers

Below I summarize the descriptive statistics for the managers surveyed by YouGov as part of the firm survey. Between December 15, 2014, and January 5, 2015, 756 YouGov respondents were targeted to take this survey. The sample included C-suite officers, board members, presidents, senior vice presidents, and managers who were at firms that employed more than one worker. Between August 20 and 31, 2015, 395 YouGov respondents from the first wave of the employer survey were successfully recontacted.

	Share of Firms Responding to Survey (Initial Wave)
Industry	
Agriculture	1.0%
Mining	1.0%
Construction	8.8%
Manufacturing	11.8%
Wholesale trade	2.8%
Retail trade	7.3%
Transportation/utilities	4.0%
Information	6.3%
Financial activities	8.8%
Professional/business services	23.3%
Education/health services	10.5%
Leisure/hospitality	5.8%
Other services	9.0%
Firm Size (in U.S.)	
2 to 4	20.9%
5 to 9	16.2%
10 to 19	11.2%
20 to 49	11.0%
50 to 99	7.8%
100 to 199	7.4%
200 to 249	2.7%
250 to 499	5.5%
500 to 999	4.5%
1,000 or more	12.7%

The exact text from both YouGov firm survey waves appears below.

December 2014–January 2015 Wave

Q1 [check boxes, can select multiple]: Recent polling has found that workers consistently report that employers are the most credible source of information about political issues affecting the workplace, and a number of employers have begun to contact their workers with information about politics and elections in recent years.

   To the best of your knowledge, has your firm ever contacted its workers about the following political issues? Select all options that apply to your firm.

- ❑   Information about registering to vote (1)
- ❑   Information about turning out to vote on Election Day (2)
- ❑   Information endorsing a political candidate (3)
- ❑   Information about a presidential candidate (4)
- ❑   Information about a political candidate for the U.S. House of Representatives (5)
- ❑   Information about a political candidate for the U.S. Senate (6)
- ❑   Information about a political candidate for state government (7)
- ❑   Information about a specific issue or piece of legislation (8)
- ❑   Information about contacting a legislator about an issue (9)
- ❑   Information about donating to a political candidate (10)
- ❑   Other kinds of political information (11)

Q2 [radio buttons]: In general, how difficult is it for your firm to fill job openings for non-management positions?

- ○   Very difficult to fill non-management openings (1)
- ○   Somewhat difficult (2)
- ○   Neither difficult nor easy (3)
- ○   Somewhat easy (4)
- ○   Very easy to fill non-management openings (5)

Q3 [radio buttons]: According to surveys by the American Management Academy, many employers report monitoring workers' emails and other Internet usage. How frequently, if at all, does your company monitor workers' email, social media, and other Internet activities?

- ○   Never monitor email, social media, and Internet usage (1)
- ○   Sometimes monitor email, social media, and Internet usage (2)
- ○   Frequently monitor email, social media, and Internet usage (3)
- ○   Always monitor email, social media, and Internet usage (4)

Q4 [text boxes]: Businesses engage in politics in a variety of ways, including forming political action committees, buying political advertisements, hiring lobbyists, and joining business associations. Thinking about your firm's political activities, which of the following have been most effective at changing public policy? Please rank the following activities in descending order of how effective you think they are in changing government policy, where a "1" indicates your firm's MOST EFFECTIVE activity. Leave blank any options that are irrelevant to your firm.

_____ Contacting workers about voting (1)
_____ Contacting workers about policy issues (2)
_____ Contacting workers about other forms of political participation (3)
_____ Making campaign contributions to political candidates (4)
_____ Buying political issue advertisements during elections (5)
_____ Hiring lobbyists or political consultants (6)
_____ Working with the Business Roundtable (7)
_____ Working with the U.S. Chamber of Commerce (8)
_____ Working with the American Legislative Exchange Council (9)
_____ Working with the National Federation of Independent Business (10)
_____ Working with another business association (11)

August–September Wave
Q1 [check boxes, can select multiple]: Recent polling has found that workers consistently report that employers are the most credible source of information about political issues affecting the workplace, and a number of employers have begun to contact their workers with information about politics and elections in recent years.

To the best of your knowledge, has your firm ever contacted its workers about the following political issues? Select all options that apply to your firm.

- ❑ Information about registering to vote (1)
- ❑ Information about turning out to vote on Election Day (2)
- ❑ Information endorsing a political candidate (3)
- ❑ Information about a presidential candidate (4)
- ❑ Information about a political candidate for the U.S. House of Representatives (5)
- ❑ Information about a political candidate for the U.S. Senate (6)
- ❑ Information about a political candidate for state government (7)
- ❑ Information about a specific issue or piece of legislation (8)
- ❑ Information about contacting a legislator about an issue (9)
- ❑ Information about donating to a political candidate (10)
- ❑ Other kinds of political information (11—If selected, show text box; prompt "What information?")

Q2 [check boxes, can select multiple; show only if response to Q1]: When your firm contacted its workers about politics or political issues, which issues did your firm discuss with workers? Select all options that apply to your firm.

- ❑ The environment (1)
- ❑ Taxes (2)
- ❑ Regulation (3)
- ❑ Trade (4)
- ❑ Health care (5)
- ❑ Education and training (6)
- ❑ Unions (7)
- ❑ Employment and jobs (8)
- ❑ Any other issue (9—If selected, show text box; prompt "Which issue?")

Q3 [check boxes, can select multiple; show only if response to Q1]: When your firm contacted its workers about politics or political issues, what were the goals your firm hoped to achieve? Select all options that apply to your firm.

- ❑ Pass legislation (1—If selected, show check box options A. "At the state or local level"; B. "At the federal level")
- ❑ Stop legislation (2—If selected, show check box options A. "At the state or local level"; B. "At the federal level")
- ❑ Pass state ballot initiative or referendum (3)
- ❑ Stop state ballot initiative or referendum (4)
- ❑ Pass a regulation (5—If selected, show check box options A. "At the state or local level"; B. "At the federal level")
- ❑ Stop a regulation (6—If selected, show check box options A. "At the state or local level"; B. "At the federal level")
- ❑ Support a political candidate (7—If selected, show options A. "Candidate for state or local office"; B. "Candidate for the House"; C. "Candidate for the Senate"; D. "Candidate for the presidency")
- ❑ Oppose a political candidate (8—If selected, show options A. "Candidate for state or local office"; B. "Candidate for the House"; C. "Candidate for the Senate"; D. "Candidate for the presidency")
- ❑ Educate workers (9)
- ❑ Other (10—If selected, show text box; prompt "What goals?")

Q4 [check boxes, can select multiple; show only if response to Q1]: Many firms target the political information they provide to workers. When your firm contacted its workers about politics or political issues, did your firm target the workers who received political information? Select all the options that apply to your firm.

❏ Targeted by workers' past engagement in political activities (1)
❏ Targeted by workers' voter registration or turnout record (2)
❏ Targeted by workers' position, division, or occupation (3)
❏ Targeted by workers' residence (4)
❏ Targeted by location of store, office, plant, or factory (5)
❏ Targeted by workers' demographic characteristics, including age or race (6)
❏ Targeted in another way (7—If selected, show text box; prompt "How did you target workers?")

Q5 [check boxes, can select multiple; show only if response to Q1]: Does your firm use software to contact your workers about politics or political issues? Select all the options that apply to your firm.

❏ Use software from the Business-Industry Political Action Committee (BIPAC) (1)
❏ Use software from another business association or organization (2—If selected, show text box; prompt "Which organization?")
❏ Use software designed in-house (3)

Q6 [radio buttons, can only select one; show only if response to Q1]: Compared to five years ago (2010), would you say that your firm's communications to its workers about politics and political information are more frequent, less frequent, or about the same frequency? Just give your best estimate.

○ More frequent (1)
○ About the same (2)
○ Less frequent (3)

Q7 [radio buttons, can only select one]: Are any of the workers at your firm represented by a union?

○ Yes (1)
○ No (2)

Q8 [radio buttons, can only select one]: Is your firm publicly traded?

- ○ Yes (1)
- ○ No (2)
- ○ Not applicable (3)

YouGov Survey Experiment of Managers (October 2016)

Text in brackets randomized.

Suppose that there was a [Democratic/Republican/{blank}] politician running for [the U.S. House of Representatives in a district where your business operates/the U.S. Senate in a state where your business operates/the legislature in a state where your business operates]. The politician is proposing a policy that would [benefit your business/hurt your business]. Your business has [only a few/some/many] of its workers in the constituency of the politician, who is [an incumbent/a challenger]. The election [is receiving a lot of media attention/is not receiving a lot of media attention]. Other businesses in your sector [have backed the candidate/have not backed the candidate]. You anticipate that [the candidate will likely win/the candidate will likely lose/the election will be very close]. [Your workers generally support the candidate/Your workers generally oppose the candidate/Your workers are mixed in their support for this candidate/You don't know how your workers feel about this candidate]. [You are worried that some of your workers might protest if you communicate about the politicians in this election./{blank}]

Thinking about this election, how likely is your business to . . .

	Very likely	Somewhat likely	Neither likely nor unlikely	Somewhat unlikely	Not at all likely
Donate to candidates in this election?					
Donate to political organizations involved in this election?					
Tell your workers about candidates' positions in this election?					
Hold political events for the candidates in this election?					
Encourage your workers to vote for a particular candidate in this election?					

Randomize whether respondent views option 1 or 2. Should indicate which option respondent viewed with variable. Randomize order of items (i.e., "Encouraged workers . . ."). Question response is single choice.

Option 1

Businesses communicate to their workers about a variety of issues. Please review the following list and indicate **how many** of the things your business has done in the past. We don't want to know which things your business has done, just **how many** things your business has done in the past.

- ☐ Encouraged workers to learn about the costs of labor unions
- ☐ Encouraged workers to engage in environmentally friendly activities
- ☐ Encouraged workers to donate to charities
- ☐ Encouraged workers to learn about financial literacy

- ■ Nothing (0)
- ■ One (1)
- ■ Two (2)
- ■ Three (3)
- ■ Four (4)

Option 2

Businesses communicate to their workers about a variety of issues. Please review the following list and indicate **how many** of the things your business has done in the past. We don't want to know which things your business has done, just **how many** things your business has done in the past.

- ☐ Encouraged workers to learn about the costs of labor unions
- ☐ Encouraged workers to engage in environmentally friendly activities
- ☐ Encouraged workers to donate to charities
- ☐ Encouraged workers to learn about financial literacy
- ☐ Encouraged workers to vote for particular political candidates

- ■ Nothing (0)
- ■ One (1)
- ■ Two (2)
- ■ Three (3)
- ■ Four (4)
- ■ Five (5)

Summary of Corporate Interviews

Below I summarize the interviews I conducted with 32 top corporate managers at large American employers and the 9 interviews I conducted with government affairs representatives at business associations. Both the top corporate managers and trade association representatives were randomly selected from lists of companies and associations. See the main text for more details.

Number	Mobilization	Industry
1	0	Professional, Scientific, and Technical Services
2	1	Manufacturing
3	1	Finance and Insurance
4	0	Manufacturing
5	1	Manufacturing
6	1	Utilities
7	1	Mining, Quarrying, and Oil and Gas Extraction
8	1	Manufacturing
9	1	Telecommunications
10	1	Manufacturing
11	1	Manufacturing
12	1	Manufacturing
13	1	Retail
14	0	Accommodations
15	1	Manufacturing
16	0	Manufacturing
17	0	Diversified Manufacturing
18	1	Finance and Insurance
19	1	Manufacturing
20	1	Mining, Quarrying, and Oil and Gas Extraction

21	1	Manufacturing
22	1	Transportation
23	1	Professional, Scientific, and Technical Services
24	1	Manufacturing
25	1	Information
26	1	Manufacturing
27	1	Mining, Quarrying, and Oil and Gas Extraction
28	1	Finance and Insurance
29	1	Finance and Insurance
30	0	Rental and Leasing
31	1	Telecommunications
32	1	Retail

Summary of Association Interviews

Number	Industry
1	Manufacturing
2	Telecommunications
3	General
4	Mining, quarrying, and oil and gas extraction
5	Other energy
6	Manufacturing
7	Manufacturing
8	Manufacturing
9	Retail

2016 Congressional Staffer Survey

To examine how senior legislative staffers perceive, process, and respond to different interests in the policymaking process, Matto Mildenberger, Leah Stokes, and I designed and fielded a survey instrument with the top policy legislative staffers in each congressional office.

We began the distribution of our survey instrument by using the Leadership Directories database to identify congressional staffers who were either chiefs of staff or legislative directors in every U.S. House and U.S. Senate office as of July 2016. In cases where staffers did not have those exact titles, we identified the individuals who would serve as the top policy staffers in the office. We recorded the email of each staffer, and then sent an initial email invitation for those staffers to participate in our survey on August 18, 2016.

The title of the email message was "Inquiry from a Columbia University Professor," and the body of the email described the survey, emphasized its confidential and academic nature, and provided the contact information for all three of the principal investigators (see below for email invitation text). Two follow-up emails were sent to staffers, on August 24 and August 31. To increase the response rate of the survey, we partnered with the Legislative Branch Capacity Working Group, a project of the New America Foundation and the R Street Institute intended to support the study of Congress and develop reforms that will increase congressional capacity. The Working Group agreed to circulate a short invitation to participate in the survey to its members on its website and email list, which contained a number of legislative staffers. We also partnered with the office of U.S. Representative John P. Sarbanes (D-MD), which agreed to circulate a "Dear Colleague'" letter to all congressional offices encouraging top staffers to participate in the survey. After each email solicitation we removed staffers from our list who requested that we no longer email them. We also replaced the contact information for staffers who were either on leave (for instance, maternity, paternity, or military leave) or were no longer working in the position listed for them with the corresponding replacement staffers. In all, we made 16 such replacements.

Our final sample includes 101 subjects from 91 offices, for a total response rate of 9.6 percent, in line with other studies of congressional staff. For instance, our response rate is similar to the response rates the Congressional Management Foundation obtained (~15%) in its studies of congressional offices.

Below I have reproduced the first and follow-up email text we sent to staffers:

Dear [Staffer First Name],

My name is Alex Hertel-Fernandez and I am a Professor of International and Public Affairs at Columbia University. I am writing to request 5 minutes of your time to participate in a confidential academic research study. The purpose of this project is to better understand the experiences of senior congressional staffers, such as yourself. As part of this study, we want to ask you a series of simple questions about the work you do through a short survey.

The study is part of an academic research project run by myself, along with two other professors at the University of California, Santa Barbara. All of your responses will be kept confidential, which means we will not associate any of your answers with your name, or the name of your Congressperson.

You can take our confidential academic survey **HERE**.

You can also access the survey by copying and pasting the URL link below into your browser:

https://ucsbltsc.qualtrics.com/SE?Q_DL=4T7CLXd11rjPlhb_eg4F-HSH8kpqrVwF_MLRP_2nsydVYZllA0K1v&Q_CHL=gl.

If you have any questions about this research project, please email me at ah3467@columbia.edu, or call me at 765-430-2063.

Thank you for your time and consideration of this request.

We look forward to your participation and learning about your experiences in Congress.

Sincerely,

Alex, Matto, and Leah

Alex Hertel-Fernandez, School of International and Public Affairs, Columbia University

Matto Mildenberger, Department of Political Science, University of California, Santa Barbara

Leah Stokes, Department of Political Science, University of California, Santa Barbara

---

Dear [Staffer First Name],

My name is Alex Hertel-Fernandez and I am a Professor of International and Public Affairs at Columbia University. I am writing to follow up on an email that I sent you about a 5-minute confidential academic research study I am conducting with two other professors at the University of California, Santa Barbara.

We are trying to understand how senior congressional staffers such as yourself gather and review information about policy proposals. Importantly, the survey is completely confidential. No information will be publicly identified back to staff members who participate. Participation in the survey will give academic researchers like us valuable insights into the legislative process.

You can take our confidential academic survey **HERE**.

You can also access the survey by copying and pasting the URL link below into your browser:

https://ucsbltsc.qualtrics.com/SE?Q_DL=4T7CLXd11rjPlhb_eg4F-HSH8kpqrVwF_MLRP_2nsydVYZllA0K1v&Q_CHL=gl.

Thank you in advance for considering our request. We know that staffers are exceptionally busy and so we appreciate your time.

Sincerely,

Alex, Matto, and Leah

Alex Hertel-Fernandez, School of International and Public Affairs, Columbia University

Matto Mildenberger, Department of Political Science, University of California, Santa Barbara

Leah Stokes, Department of Political Science, University of California, Santa Barbara

---

Dear [Staffer First Name],

My name is Alex Hertel-Fernandez and I am a Professor of International and Public Affairs at Columbia University. I wanted to send you a final reminder about a 5-minute confidential academic research study I am conducting with two other professors at the University of California, Santa Barbara. Your participation, which is completely confidential, will help academics like us to better understand how legislative staffers do their jobs.

You can take our confidential academic survey **HERE**.

You can also access the survey by copying and pasting the URL link below into your browser:

https://ucsbltsc.qualtrics.com/SE?Q_DL=4T7CLXd11rjPlhb_eg4F-HSH8kpqrVwF_MLRP_cu14gxeZ0hIWXtP&Q_CHL=gl.

Thank you in advance for considering our request.

We appreciate your patience and your time, especially because we know how busy you are. This is the final reminder email we will send about this survey.

Sincerely,

Alex, Matto, and Leah

Alex Hertel-Fernandez, School of International and Public Affairs, Columbia University

Matto Mildenberger, Department of Political Science, University of California, Santa Barbara

Leah Stokes, Department of Political Science, University of California, Santa Barbara

Below I have reproduced the messages from the Legislative Branch Working Group and the "Dear Colleague" letter from Representative Sarbanes's office to encourage participation in the survey.

August 29, 2016

Congressional Staff: Help Scholars Understand Your Needs

How do legislative staffers gather and review information about policy proposals? What resources could help congressional staff create and evaluate legislative proposals to deal with pressing social and economic issues?

We are a team of three academic political scientists based at Columbia University and the University of California, Santa Barbara who are trying to answer these questions through a short, confidential survey of congressional staffers. The survey is being supported with a Congressional Research Grant awarded by the Dirksen Congressional Center, a non-profit, non-partisan research organization.

Our survey, which we anticipate will take around five to seven minutes to complete, asks Congressional staff about different considerations that they have weighed when evaluating public policy. Importantly, the survey is completely confidential. No information will be publicly identified back to staff members who participate. The Institutional Review Boards at Columbia University and the University of California, Santa Barbara have both approved the survey on the condition of this confidentiality.

We understand that many congressional offices have standing policies against taking surveys, but we hope that staffers might make an exception for this project given its academic and confidential nature. Participation in the survey will give academic researchers valuable insights into the legislative process on Capitol Hill, and may yield new conclusions about how to provide better resources to congressional offices.

Senior legislative staff—including Chiefs of Staff and Legislative Directors—should have already received a link in their email to the survey from me (ah3467@columbia.edu) on Wednesday, August 24th.

Interested respondents can also contact us for more information or questions, including requests to participate.

Thank you in advance for considering our request. We know that staffers are exceptionally busy and so we appreciate your time. We look forward to learning more about your work in Congress!

Alexander Hertel-Fernandez is Assistant Professor of International and Public Affairs at Columbia University's School of International and Public Affairs. Matto Mildenberger and Leah Stokes are assistant professors of political science at the University of California, Santa Barbara.

Participate in Congressional Staff Research Study
From: The Honorable John P. Sarbanes
Sent By: **raymond.omara@mail.house.gov**
Date: 8/30/2016

Dear Colleague:
I am writing to invite your senior legislative staff to participate in a confidential academic research study that is being conducted by professors at Columbia University and the University of California, Santa Barbara. Senior staff in your office should have received an email to the survey earlier this month. The survey is being supported with a Congressional Research

Grant awarded by The Dirksen Congressional Center, a non-profit, non-partisan organization named for the late Senator Everett McKinley Dirksen.

The researchers are hoping to better understand the experiences of U.S. Congressional staff, in particular, how staff members gather information about legislation and policy. The survey is completely confidential; no information will be publicly identified back to staff members who partici-pate. Participation in the survey will give academic researchers valuable insights into the legislative process on Capitol Hill, and may yield new con-clusions about how to provide better resources to Congressional offices to help Members of Congress and their staffs.

Senior legislative staff—including Chiefs of Staff and Legislative Directors—should have received an email to the survey earlier this month. Interested respondents can also contact the research team for more information or questions. The team consists of Professor Alexander Hertel-Fernandez, Columbia University School of International and Public Affairs (ah3467@columbia.edu), Professor Matto Mildenberger, University of California, Santa Barbara (mildenberger@polsci.ucsb.edu), and Professor Leah Stokes, University of California, Santa Barbara (stokes@polsci.ucsb.edu).

Thank you for your consideration of this request.
Sincerely,
John P. Sarbanes
Member of Congress

The next table summarizes the composition of our survey respondents com-pared to the overall population of top legislative staffers in all congressional offices. In general, our sample closely resembles the overall population of both senior staff overall and congressional offices. Our sample was slightly more likely to consist of legislative directors or other staffers as compared to the overall sample of all legislative directors and chiefs of staff and was also slightly more likely to come from the Senate rather than the House. About 1 percent of our sample came from top congressional leadership, as compared to 3 percent of all top staffers.

The largest difference between our survey sample and the overall population of staffers was in partisanship: slightly over half of our sample (54%) came from Democratic offices, while in Congress as a whole only 43 percent of top staffers work in Democratic offices. Nevertheless we still have a sufficient number of

Republican respondents to disaggregate our analyses by partisanship, and within both Democratic and Republican respondents we see that the ideological orientation of staffers' members of Congress is quite similar to the overall distribution of congressional ideology, as measured by standard DW-NOMINATE ideal points for the 113th Congress (McCarty et al. 2006). The average Democratic and Republican ideal points in our sample were nearly identical to the average ideal points for all congressional Democrats and Republicans, as were the 50th, 25th, and 75th percentiles of our sample. Our sample is also very strongly representative of the overall Congress by region and congressional seniority.

Of course we can observe balance only on observed characteristics, and it may be the case that our sample is skewed because of some unobserved characteristic. Nevertheless we have few reasons to believe that is the case based on available evidence. In sum, we are generally confident of the representativeness of our sample on most observable characteristics.

	Survey Sample	*Whole Sample*	*Absolute Difference*
Job Title			
Chief of staff	43%	50%	7
Legislative director/other	57%	50%	3
Chamber			
House	72%	80%	8
Senate	28%	20%	8
Party			
Democrat	54%	43%	11
Republican	46%	57%	11
Region			
Midwest	21%	23%	2
Northeast	20%	17%	3
South	35%	36%	1
West	25%	24%	1
Congressional Leadership			
Leadership	1%	3%	2

Congressional Seniority

Average years in Congress	9	10	1
Median years in Congress	7	7	0

Census Division

East North Central	15%	14%	1
East South Central	3%	6%	3
Mountain	6%	9%	3
Mid-Atlantic	8%	11%	3
Northeast	12%	6%	6
Pacific	19%	15%	4
South Atlantic	23%	19%	4
West North Central	6%	9%	3
West South Central	9%	11%	2

Ideological Measures

Democrats

DW-NOMINATE 1st Mean	−0.40	−0.38	0.02
DW-NOMINATE 1st Median	−0.42	−0.39	0.03
DW-NOMINATE 1st 25th percentile	−0.46	−0.45	0.01
DW-NOMINATE 1st 75th percentile	−0.32	−0.30	0.02

Republicans

DW-NOMINATE 1st Mean	0.69	0.69	0
DW-NOMINATE 1st Median	0.73	0.71	0.02
DW-NOMINATE 1st 25th percentile	0.61	0.55	0.06
DW-NOMINATE 1st 75th percentile	0.83	0.83	0

The following are the substantive questions from the legislative staffer survey used in the book:

☐ Influences on Policy Decisions

Think about the policy proposals you have worked on during your time on the Hill. What shaped your thinking on whether your member should support or oppose these policies?

Indicate how important each of the following considerations was in shaping your advice to your Member on various policy proposals:

	Extremely important (1)	Very important (2)	Moderately important (3)	Slightly important (4)	Not at all important (5)
Information from the Congressional Budget Office (CBO) (1)	○	○	○	○	○
Information from the Government Accountability Office (GAO) (2)	○	○	○	○	○
Information from the Congressional Research Service (CRS) (3)	○	○	○	○	○
Public opinion of your Member's constituents (4)	○	○	○	○	○
Public opinion of the country as a whole (5)	○	○	○	○	○
Party leaders' opinions (6)	○	○	○	○	○
Information from businesses (7)	○	○	○	○	○
Information from unions (8)	○	○	○	○	○
Information from think tanks (9)	○	○	○	○	○
Concerns about primary opponents (10)	○	○	○	○	○
Concerns about re-election (11)	○	○	○	○	○
Communication from your Members' constituents (12)	○	○	○	○	○

☐   Utility of Business Strategies

Businesses often contact Congressional offices to support or oppose policy proposals. Thinking about the ways that businesses have contacted your office about policy proposals in the past year, which strategies have been most useful to your office as you deliberate over legislation?

	Extremely useful (1)	*Very useful (2)*	*Moderately useful (3)*	*Slightly useful (4)*	*Not at all useful (5)*
Having their employees write to your office with their opinions about policy (1)	O	O	O	O	O
Having their employees support your member's electoral campaign (2)	O	O	O	O	O
Offering research and assistance drafting legislation, including model bill language (3)	O	O	O	O	O
Offering political advice, such as talking points and polling data (4)	O	O	O	O	O

☐   Constituent Communications Survey Experiment

Imagine your office is considering a bill that is under debate in Congress. Your office receives [2, 20, 200] letters from constituents [supporting, opposing] this bill. The letters have very [similar, different] wording to one another. The letter writers identify themselves as [employees of a large company based in your constituency, constituents, members of a non-profit citizens group].

	Very (1)	*Somewhat (2)*	*Not Very (3)*	*Not at All (4)*
How LIKELY are you to mention these letters to your Member? (1)	O	O	O	O
How SIGNIFICANT would these letters be in your advice to your Member about their position on the bill? (2)	O	O	O	O
How REPRESENTATIVE do you think these letters are of your constituents' opinions? (3)	O	O	O	O

Chapter 3 Appendix
Reconciling Employer Mobilization Reports
between Managers and Workers

One reason employer reports of mobilization may be higher than employee reports of mobilization is that employers are not sending messages to all of their workers all of the time. This analysis provides some suggestive evidence of the role of targeting in explaining the differential rates of employer mobilization on the firm and worker surveys across different industries. The plot below shows the strong relationship between the proportion of firms reporting targeting political messages to workers (by industry, from the firm survey) and the proportion of workers reporting mobilization by sector. This plot indicates that fewer workers report receiving political messages in industries where more firms target their messages (regression line coefficient = -0.18, standard error = 0.07, R squared = 0.43, N = 11 sectors). Extrapolating from this relationship we would expect that 41 percent of workers would report mobilization if no firms targeted messages—much closer to the 50 percent we would expect based on the firm survey than the 25 percent actually reported in the worker survey.

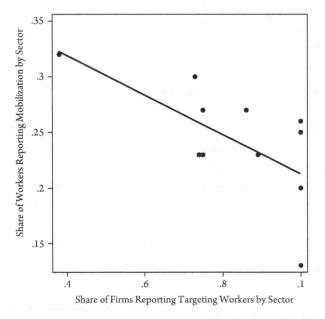

In chapter 3 I note that managers indicated that targeting political messages by workers' past political participation and voter status and history were the most effective means of targeting. This analysis provides the basis for the claim, showing how various forms of targeting are correlated with managers ranking mobilization of workers as their most effective strategy for changing public policy. (The various forms of targeting correspond to dummy variables indicating if a firm targeted its political messages on that basis.) The outcome in this logistic regression is a binary indicator for whether a manager listed mobilization as the firm's most effective political strategy. Note that about 28 percent of managers targeting their political messages (the sample of managers included in the regression) reported that mobilization was their firm's most effective political strategy.

As the next table reveals, targeting by past participation and voter status and history are the means of targeting most strongly correlated with listing mobilization as a firm's most effective political strategy.

	Outcome is listing mobilization as most effective strategy (0/1)
Target by past participation	2.65*
	(1.49)
Target by voter status and history	1.92**
	(0.83)
Target by worker position in firm	−0.18
	(0.83)
Target by worker residence	−2.94*
	(1.70)
Target by firm location	−0.27
	(0.91)
Target by worker demographic	−0.60
	(1.36)
N	76
Pseudo R-Squared	0.10

Logistic regression results. * 0.10, ** 0.05, *** 0.01.
Data from YouGov firm survey.

Vignette Experiment with Corporate Managers

Below I present results from the vignette survey experiment of corporate managers from the October 2016 survey. The outcome in this analysis is a binary indicator, marking whether or not managers said they would be more likely to give traditional donations (either to candidates or organizations) rather than mobilizing their workers into politics to affect the election (by telling employees about a candidate, encouraging workers to vote for a candidate, or holding events with a candidate).

The treatment is a binary indicator for whether or not respondents were shown a prompt warning them about the potential for backlash from their workers with a mobilization campaign ("You are worried that some of your workers might protest if you communicate about the politicians in this election"). The following analysis shows that there is a strong effect of that prompt on managers' decisions to rank traditional strategies as being more likely over mobilization tactics.

	Manager ranks political donations over employee mobilization (0/1)
Manager saw worker backlash text	0.07**
	(0.03)
N	508
R-Squared	0.01

Standard errors clustered by sector.
OLS regression results. * 0.10, ** 0.05, *** 0.01.
Data from YouGov firm survey experiment.

Chapter 4 Appendix
Regression Results, Effect of Union Membership on Receipt of Conservative Union Messages from Employer

In chapter 4 I note that union members are actually more likely to have reported receiving anti-union messages than non-union members. I arrive at this claim by examining the correlation between workers who had reported receiving employer messages about unions that were described as either ideologically "somewhat conservative" or "very conservative" and union membership. The outcome in this logistic regression is thus a binary indicator for whether workers reported receiving a conservative political message about unions from their employer (7% of contacted workers, the sample for this regression, reported receiving such messages). These results show that union members are more likely than non-union members to receive conservative messages against unions, suggesting that employers are not coordinating with unions on mobilization efforts.

	Outcome is receiving conservative message about labor unions from employer (0/1)
Union member	1.73***
	(0.59)
N	272
Pseudo R-Squared	0.07

Logistic regression results. * 0.10, ** 0.05, *** 0.01.
Data from SSRS worker survey.
Survey weights applied.

Chapter 5 Appendix
State Anti-coercion and Speech Laws and Employer Mobilization

In chapter 5 I argue that the presence of state laws protecting worker political speech on or off the job or banning employer political coercion do not seem to affect overall rates of employer mobilization, coercive mobilization, or uncomfortable mobilization. The following states have provisions in place (according to Volokh 2011–12) to protect against some type of political coercion: California, Colorado, Louisiana, Minnesota, Montana, Nebraska, Nevada, New Mexico, New York, South Carolina, and West Virginia. The following states and the District of Columbia have provisions in place protecting employee political speech on or off the job: Arizona, California, Colorado, Connecticut, Georgia, Hawaii, Idaho, Illinois, Iowa, Kentucky, Louisiana, Massachusetts, Minnesota, Missouri, Montana, Nebraska, Nevada, New Mexico, New York, North Dakota, Ohio, Oregon, South Carolina, Tennessee, Washington, West Virginia, and Wyoming. The following logistic regression results show that laws protecting against coercion or protecting employee political speech (binary indicators for state) do not reduce the presence of employer mobilization, uncomfortable employer mobilization, or mobilization that involves threats, using data from the 2015 worker survey. In fact more workers report receiving uncomfortable messages in states with laws against political coercion.

	Outcome is receiving employer political message (0/1)	*Outcome is receiving uncomfortable employer political message (0/1)*	*Outcome is receiving employer political message with threat (0/1)*
State has law against coercion	0.10 (0.17)	0.81** (0.34)	0.40 (0.26)
N	1,001	1,001	1,001
Pseudo R-Squared	0.0003	0.02	0.004

Standard errors clustered by state.
Logistic regression results. * 0.10, ** 0.05, *** 0.01.
Data from SSRS worker survey.
Survey weights applied.

	Outcome is receiving employer political message (0/1)	Outcome is receiving uncomfortable employer political message (0/1)	Outcome is receiving employer political message with threat (0/1)
State has law protecting speech	0.01 (0.15)	0.06 (0.36)	−0.02 (0.31)
N	1,001	1,001	1,001
Pseudo R-Squared	0	0	0

Standard errors clustered by state.
Logistic regression results. * 0.10, ** 0.05, *** 0.01.
Data from SSRS worker survey.
Survey weights applied.

Predicting Increase in Employer Mobilization between 2010 and 2015

In chapter 5 I describe an analysis of whether currently mobilizing firms in 2015 were mobilizing more, less, or about the same as they were in 2010. I describe a very strong correlation between whether a company was participating in BIPAC's Prosperity Project and whether the firm had increased their political mobilization efforts since 2010.

This logistic regression analysis shows the basis for that claim, assessing the correlation between Prosperity Project membership and reporting increasing mobilization from 2010 to 2015 (measured as a binary indicator), after accounting for other firm characteristics, including company size (in nine categories), publicly traded ownership (binary indicator), unionization (binary indicator), and sector fixed effects (ten sectors). Twenty-two percent of mobilizing firms in the regression sample reported increasing their mobilization since 2010, and 10 percent of mobilizing firms in the regression sample reported BIPAC participation.

As the logistic regression results indicate, participation in BIPAC's Prosperity Project was a substantively and statistically significant predictor of whether or not firms reported increasing their mobilization activities over this period.

	Outcome is reporting increase in mobilization from 2010 to 2015 (0/1)
BIPAC Prosperity Project member	1.71**
	(0.83)
Company size	0.13
	(0.11)
Publicly traded	0.45
	(1.03)
Unionized	−0.59
	(0.66)
Firm sector fixed effects (10)	Y
N	165
R-Squared	0.10

Logistic regression results. * 0.10, ** 0.05, *** 0.01. Data from YouGov firm survey.

Chapter 6 Appendix
Minimum Wage SSI Survey Experiment

The following OLS regression shows the causal effect of a private-sector worker reading generic messages arguing against a minimum wage increase or a letter from an employer with that same text and the threat of job loss or wage cuts on preferences for a \$15/hour minimum wage (binary indicator for support/oppose; "strongly favor" or "somewhat favor" coded as 1). The excluded category contains workers who saw no message.

	Outcome is preferring \$15/hour federal minimum wage (0/1)
Employer letter against minimum wage	−0.07*
	(0.04)
Generic message against minimum wage	−0.03
	(0.04)
N	756
R-Squared	0.01

OLS regression results. * 0.10, ** 0.05, *** 0.01.
Data from SSI worker survey experiment.

The second analysis shows that there is a strong interaction effect between the receipt of employer letters and workers' perceptions of their employment prospects (binary indicator), but not generic messages. Employer letters had a much stronger negative effect on workers who felt insecure in their employment prospects.

	Outcome is preferring \$15/hour federal minimum wage (0/1)
Employer letter against minimum wage	−0.20**
	(0.08)
Generic message against minimum wage	−0.13
	(0.08)
Secure employment prospects (0/1)	0.08
	(0.07)

Employer letter X secure	0.19**
	(0.09)
Generic message X secure	0.12
	(0.10)
N	756
R-Squared	0.04

OLS regression results. * 0.10, ** 0.05, *** 0.01.
Data from SSI worker survey experiment.

Contacting Congress Survey Experiment

The following OLS regression assesses the causal effect of employer messages and generic messages criticizing the health insurance tax on the likelihood that workers will contact Congress about repealing the health insurance tax. The outcome is a binary indicator for the likelihood of contacting Congress ("very likely" or "somewhat likely" to contact Congress about repealing the health insurance tax coded as 1). The analysis shows that employer messages, but not generic messages, make workers more likely to contact Congress about repealing the health insurance tax. The excluded category contains workers who saw no message.

	Outcome is contacting Congress about health insurance tax (0/1)
Employer letter against tax	0.15***
	(0.04)
Generic message against tax	0.02
	(0.04)
N	742
R-Squared	0.01

OLS regression results. * 0.10, ** 0.05, *** 0.01.
Data from SSI worker survey experiment.

The second analysis shows that, as with preferences for the minimum wage, there is a strong interaction effect between the receipt of employer letters, but not generic messages, and workers' perceptions of their employment prospects. Employer letters had a much stronger effect on workers who felt insecure in their employment prospects.

	Outcome is contacting Congress about health insurance tax (0/1)
Employer letter against tax	0.28***
	(0.08)
Generic message against tax	0.10
	(0.08)
Secure employment prospects	0.24***
	(0.07)
Employer letter X secure	−0.17*
	(0.10)
Generic message X secure	−0.10
	(0.10)
N	742
R-Squared	0.04

OLS regression results. * 0.10, ** 0.05, *** 0.01.
Data from SSI worker survey experiment.

2016 CCES Analysis of Employer Mobilization and Worker Attitudes on the Environment and the Minimum Wage

The regression shows the effect of managerial support for two policies (renewable energy standards and raising the federal minimum wage) on worker support for those policies, controlling for a range of individual worker characteristics. Managerial support is strongly related to workers' own opinions.

	Outcome is support for renewable energy standards (0/1)	*Outcome is support for raising the minimum wage (0/1)*
Managers support policy (0/1)	0.18*** (0.06)	0.26*** (0.06)
Age	0.04** (0.02)	0.01 (0.02)
Age squared	−0.00** (0.00)	−0.00 (0.00)
Male	−0.03 (0.06)	0.01 (0.05)
White	0.19 (0.13)	0.09 (0.11)
Black	0.04 (0.15)	0.13 (0.14)
Hispanic	0.20*** (0.08)	0.10 (0.07)
Some college	−0.10 (0.09)	−0.07 (0.08)
College or more	0.08 (0.10)	−0.02 (0.09)
Family income 2nd quartile	−0.12 (0.11)	−0.23** (0.10)
Family income 3rd quartile	−0.30*** (0.10)	−0.27*** (0.09)
Family income 4th quartile	−0.31*** (0.10)	−0.37*** (0.09)
Political ideology (conservative)	−0.06* (0.03)	−0.08*** (0.03)
Employer ideology (conservative)	−0.01 (0.03)	0.00 (0.03)

Democrat	0.09	0.31***
	(0.08)	(0.07)
Republican	−0.33***	−0.13*
	(0.08)	(0.07)
Industry fixed effects	Y	Y
N	201	202
R-Squared	0.48	0.58

OLS regression results. * 0.10, ** 0.05, *** 0.01.
Data from 2016 CCES.
Survey weights applied.

The next table shows the effect of employer mobilization on respondents' scores on a 0–8 political knowledge scale, which asked respondents to identify the partisan affiliation of their governor, representative, and two senators, and also to name the party holding the majority in the House, Senate, and their state's upper and lower legislative chambers. (Each item is scored 0/1, with 1 indicating a correct response, and then summed together.) The average respondent in the regression sample got five of these items correct. Employer mobilization is not related to greater political knowledge scores.

	Outcome is political knowledge score (0–8 items)
Reported employer mobilization during election (0/1)	0.10
	(0.29)
Age	0.11
	(0.08)
Age squared	−0.00
	(0.00)
Male	1.64***
	(0.30)
White	0.39
	(0.60)
Black	0.97
	(0.71)

Hispanic	−0.40
	(0.36)
Some college	0.84**
	(0.40)
College or more	1.30***
	(0.42)
Family income 2nd quartile	−0.35
	(0.51)
Family income 3rd quartile	0.08
	(0.47)
Family income 4th quartile	−0.04
	(0.48)
Political ideology (conservative)	-0.26*
	(0.14)
Employer ideology (conservative)	0.10
	(0.14)
Democrat	−0.58
	(0.36)
Republican	0.07
	(0.41)
Industry fixed effects	Y
N	257
R-Squared	0.37

OLS regression results. * 0.10, ** 0.05, *** 0.01.
Data from 2016 CCES.
Survey weights applied.

2016 CCES Analysis of Employer Mobilization and Worker Political Participation

The next table summarizes the OLS regressions from the CCES data, which show the effects of employer, union, and party contact on participation (on the 0–5 scale), with varying controls. Employer mobilization is nearly as effective as union and party mobilization. Standard errors clustered by House district in Model 3 and by state in Model 4.

	Outcome is political participation index (0–5 acts)			
Employer mobilization	0.15* (0.09)	0.22** (0.09)	0.22** (0.11)	0.24*** (0.07)
Union mobilization	0.52*** (0.13)	0.38*** (0.13)	0.38** (0.16)	0.31 (0.22)
Campaign mobilization	0.70*** (0.07)	0.37*** (0.07)	0.37*** (0.08)	0.36*** (0.08)
Age		0.01 (0.01)	0.01 (0.01)	0.01 (0.01)
Age squared		−0.00 (0.00)	−0.00 (0.00)	−0.00 (0.00)
Male		0.19*** (0.07)	0.19** (0.09)	0.10 (0.07)
White		−0.06 (0.13)	−0.06 (0.19)	−0.09 (0.18)
Black		−0.11 (0.17)	−0.11 (0.20)	−0.07 (0.20)
Hispanic		−0.15* (0.08)	−0.15 (0.10)	−0.12 (0.08)
Some college		0.04 (0.08)	0.04 (0.08)	0.04 (0.08)

College or more		0.12 (0.09)	0.12 (0.10)	0.18 (0.11)
Family income 2nd quartile		0.39*** (0.10)	0.39*** (0.12)	0.40*** (0.12)
Family income 3rd quartile		0.19** (0.09)	0.20* (0.11)	0.27*** (0.09)
Family income 4th quartile		0.50*** (0.10)	0.50*** (0.11)	0.57*** (0.09)
Political interest (1–4)		0.19*** (0.04)	0.19*** (0.04)	0.21*** (0.03)
Strong partisan (0/1)		0.17** (0.07)	0.17** (0.08)	0.18** (0.08)
Union member		−0.12 (0.15)	−0.12 (0.18)	−0.03 (0.19)
Church attendance (1–6)		−0.00 (0.02)	−0.00 (0.02)	0.01 (0.02)
Voted in 2012		0.45*** (0.09)	0.45*** (0.13)	0.44*** (0.09)
Absolute Partisan Voting Index			0.00 (0.00)	0.01 (0.01)
State effects	N	N	N	Y
N	823	720	720	720
R-Squared	0.13	0.3	0.30	0.39

OLS regression results. * 0.10, ** 0.05, *** 0.01.
Data from 2016 CCES. All adults.
Survey weights applied.

The next table summarizes OLS regressions from the CCES data, which show the effects of employer, union, and party contact on participation (on the 0–5 scale), with varying controls. Employer mobilization is nearly as effective as union and party mobilization. Standard errors clustered by House district in Model 3 and by state in Model 4. These models include only non-self-employed workers, and results are nearly the same as the previous model for employer mobilization. (Union mobilization is no longer significant.)

	Outcome is political participation index (0–5 acts)			
Employer mobilization	0.20** (0.10)	0.31*** (0.10)	0.30** (0.13)	0.33*** (0.11)
Union mobilization	0.37** (0.16)	−0.02 (0.20)	−0.00 (0.21)	−0.26 (0.21)
Campaign mobilization	0.61*** (0.10)	0.51*** (0.10)	0.51*** (0.11)	0.48*** (0.13)
Age		0.04 (0.03)	0.04 (0.03)	0.06* (0.03)
Age squared		−0.00* (0.00)	−0.00* (0.00)	−0.00** (0.00)
Male		0.16 (0.10)	0.16 (0.12)	0.08 (0.08)
White		−0.01 (0.22)	−0.01 (0.20)	−0.04 (0.19)
Black		0.02 (0.27)	0.03 (0.25)	0.01 (0.26)
Hispanic		0.02 (0.13)	0.04 (0.12)	−0.01 (0.08)
Some college		−0.10 (0.14)	−0.11 (0.14)	−0.08 (0.14)
College or more		0.00 (0.15)	0.01 (0.13)	0.13 (0.13)
Family income 2nd quartile		0.08 (0.17)	0.05 (0.23)	0.17 (0.15)

Family income 3rd quartile		−0.03 (0.16)	−0.06 (0.22)	0.09 (0.14)
Family income 4th quartile		0.37** (0.17)	0.35* (0.21)	0.51*** (0.16)
Political interest (1–4)		0.27*** (0.07)	0.27*** (0.07)	0.30*** (0.06)
Strong partisan (0/1)		0.13 (0.11)	0.13 (0.12)	0.12 (0.13)
Union member		0.22 (0.18)	0.21 (0.21)	0.42** (0.18)
Church attendance (1–6)		−0.01 (0.03)	−0.01 (0.03)	0.01 (0.02)
Voted in 2012		0.45*** (0.15)	0.46** (0.20)	0.31** (0.13)
Absolute Partisan Voting Index			−0.01 (0.01)	−0.00 (0.01)
State effects	N	N	N	Y
N	370	338	338	338
R-Squared	0.11	0.32	0.32	0.47

OLS regression results. * 0.10, ** 0.05, *** 0.01.
Data from 2016 CCES.
Only non-self-employed workers included.
Survey weights applied.

The next table summarizes OLS regressions from the CCES data, which show the interactive effect of perceptions of employer monitoring, perceptions of employer retaliation, and employer political contact on political participation in 2015–16. Perceptions of employer monitoring and retaliation increase the effects of employer mobilization.

	Outcome is political participation index (0–5 acts)	
Employer mobilization (0/1)	0.45***	0.56***
	(0.11)	(0.11)
Perceives possibility of employer monitoring (0/1)	−0.18 (0.12)	
Employer mobilization X monitoring	0.72*** (0.20)	
Perceives possibility of employer retaliation (0/1)		−0.22* (0.12)
Employer mobilization X retaliation		0.48** (0.21)
Age	0.03	0.03
	(0.02)	(0.02)
Age squared	−0.00	−0.00
	(0.00)	(0.00)
Male	−0.10	−0.12
	(0.09)	(0.10)
White	0.00	0.07
	(0.20)	(0.20)
Black	−0.14	−0.14
	(0.23)	(0.24)
Hispanic	−0.01	0.06
	(0.12)	(0.12)
Some college	0.12	0.12
	(0.12)	(0.12)
College or more	0.19	0.22
	(0.13)	(0.13)
Family income 2nd quartile	−0.11	−0.15
	(0.14)	(0.14)
Family income 3rd quartile	−0.13	−0.15
	(0.14)	(0.14)

Family income 4th quartile	0.36** (0.15)	0.31** (0.15)
Political interest (1–4)	0.31*** (0.06)	0.32*** (0.06)
Strong partisan (0/1)	0.06 (0.10)	0.03 (0.10)
Union member	0.10 (0.14)	0.18 (0.14)
Church attendance (1–6)	−0.04 (0.03)	−0.04 (0.03)
Voted in 2012	0.47*** (0.12)	0.47*** (0.12)
N	417	418
R-Squared	0.38	0.37

OLS regression results. * 0.10, ** 0.05, *** 0.01.
Data from 2016 CCES.
Only non-self-employed workers included.
Survey weights applied.

Chapter 7 Appendix
Top Legislative Staffer Survey Experiment
on Constituent Communications

I used the 2016 survey of top legislative aides to test whether communications that were purportedly from employees of a large business were taken more seriously than communications from ordinary constituents and representatives of non-profit citizens groups. Using the survey experiment, the following regression results show that hypothetical messages from employees were more likely to be perceived as being "significant" and "representative" of constituent opinions than letters from ordinary constituents or representatives of non-profit citizens' groups (these are the two excluded categories). The questions are "How LIKELY are you to mention these letters to your Member?"; "How SIGNIFICANT would these letters be in your advice to your Member about their position on the bill?"; and "How REPRESENTATIVE do you think these letters are of your constituents' opinions?" The outcomes are one through four measures of each question, scaled so that higher values indicate greater likelihood, significance, or representativeness. The results show that employee letters were considered to be more significant and representative by legislative staffers.

	How likely to mention letters? (1–4)	How significant are letters? (1–4)	How representative are letters? (1–4)
Employee letters	0.21	0.32*	0.49***
	(0.25)	(0.18)	(0.16)
N	82	82	81
R-Squared	0.01	0.04	0.10

OLS regression results. * 0.10, ** 0.05, *** 0.01; standard errors clustered by office.
Data from legislative staffer survey experiment.

The next table shows the interactive effect between a binary indicator for staffers reporting that business interests are an "extremely important or very important" influence on their decisions in their office (versus "moderately important," "somewhat important," or "not at all") and employee letters for the "how likely to mention letters" outcome. The results show that staffers who are less reliant on business interests are actually more likely to report employee letters to their bosses.

	How likely to mention letters? (1–4)
Employee letters	0.57*
	(0.33)
Business very important (0/1)	0.32
	(0.29)
Employee letter X business very important	−0.93*
	(0.48)
N	82
R-Squared	0.06

OLS regression results. * 0.10, ** 0.05, *** 0.01; standard errors clustered by office
Data from legislative staffer survey experiment.

The next table shows the interactive effect between 2011–15 district or state unemployment and employee letters for all outcomes (from American Community Survey data). The results show that staffers from districts and states with higher unemployment are more likely to say that employee letters are significant and representative (last two columns). Unemployment ranged from 0.04 to 0.14 across all districts and states.

	How likely to mention letters? (1–4)	*How significant are letters? (1–4)*	*How representative are letters? (1–4)*
Employee letters	−0.92	−0.68	−1.17
	(1.03)	(0.73)	(0.79)
Unemployment rate	−8.00	−10.98**	−11.24**
	(6.54)	(4.85)	(5.13)

Letters X unemployment	14.23 (11.33)	13.08* (7.77)	20.76** (8.96)
N	82	82	81
R-Squared	0.03	0.08	0.17

OLS regression results. * 0.10, ** 0.05, *** 0.01; standard errors clustered by office.
Data from legislative staffer survey experiment.

Alaskan Ballot Measure Analysis

The regressions below summarize the relationship between the share of workers in each Alaskan lower legislative district employed in the extractive resources sector and the share of voters supporting repealing the tax cuts for oil producers, with and without Obama's vote share in the 2012 election. Districts with greater employment in the extractive resources sector were less likely to vote for the repeal of the oil production tax cuts.

	Outcome is share of voters supporting oil production tax cut repeal	
Extractive resources employment share	−1.93*** (0.59)	−1.51* (0.76)
Obama vote share 2012		0.13 (0.14)
N	39	39
R-Squared	0.23	0.24

OLS regression results. * 0.10, ** 0.05, *** 0.01.

The next regression summarizes the relationship between the share of workers in each Alaskan lower legislative district employed in the extractive resources sector and the difference in support for the ballot measure between regular voters and absentee/early voters. The regression results show that districts with greater employment in the extractive resources sector saw a bigger gap in support for the oil tax cuts between regular and absentee/early voters, with absentee/early voters more likely than regular voters to vote against the repeal of the cuts.

	Outcome is difference in support for oil production tax credits between regular and absentee/early voters
Extractive resources employment share	0.73*** (0.21)
N	39
R-Squared	0.24
OLS regression results. * 0.10, ** 0.05, *** 0.01.	

The next regression summarizes the relationship between the share of workers in each Alaskan lower legislative district employed in the extractive resources sector and the difference in absentee/early voters from 2010 to 2014. The regression results show that districts with greater employment in the extractive resources sector saw a bigger increase in absentee/early voting from 2010 to 2014.

	Outcome is change in absentee/early voting from 2010 to 2014
Extractive resources employment share	0.39* (0.21)
N	39
R-Squared	0.08
OLS regression results. * 0.10, ** 0.05, *** 0.01.	

Employer Information and Perceptions of the ACA in 2011

The data for this analysis come from the Kaiser Family Foundation's Health Tracking Poll from December 2011; more information is available from http://kff.org/tag/tracking-poll/.

I include the following variables in the analysis:

You and your family better off under ACA: Binary indicator for whether or not respondents perceive themselves and their family to be better off under the ACA; see text for details. This is one of the three outcomes I examine.

Whole country better off under ACA: Binary indicator for whether or not respondent perceives the whole country to be better off under the ACA; see text for details. This is the second of the three outcomes I examine.

Switched stance from unfavorable to favorable after learning more about employer mandate: Binary indicator for whether individuals switched from an unfavorable to a favorable stance on the individual mandate after they were given information saying "Under the reform law, most Americans would still get coverage through their employer and so would automatically satisfy the requirement without having to buy any new insurance," "Without such a requirement, insurance companies would still be allowed to deny coverage to people who are sick," "Without such a requirement, people may wait until they are seriously ill to buy health insurance, which will drive up health insurance costs for everyone," or "People would not be held to this requirement if the cost of new coverage would consume too large a share of their income."

Knowledge of the ACA: One through four scale of individuals' self-reported knowledge of the health reform law and how it will affect them and their family personally, ranging from "A lot" to "Not at all."

Education: Coded as three categories: high school or less, some college, or college or more.

Race and ethnicity: Binary indicators for white, non-Hispanic; black, non-Hispanic; and Hispanic.

Partisanship: Binary indicators for Democrats and Republicans.

Political ideology: Coded as three categories: liberal, moderate, or conservative.

Health condition: Coded as five categories: excellent, very good, good, only fair, or poor.

Household income: Coded in seven categories: <$20,000; $20,000 to $39,999; $40,000 to $49,999; $50,000 to $74,999, $75,000 to $89,999; $90,000 to $99,999; and $100,000 or more.

Gender: Binary indicator.

Age: Coded in six categories: 18–24; 25–34; 35–44; 45–54; 55–64; and 65 and above.

Health insurance status: Binary indicators for public insurance, individually purchased insurance, employer-provided health insurance, and other insurance.

Below I present logistic regression results showing the effect of receiving information from an employer about the ACA on perceptions of the ACA's effect on respondents' self and family (left column) and on the whole country (right column), after controlling for the receipt of other kinds of information and for other individual demographic characteristics.

	Outcome is believe self/family better off under ACA (0/1)	*Outcome is believe whole country better off under ACA (0/1)*
Rely on employers	−0.70**	−0.48*
	(0.28)	(0.25)
Rely on state agencies	0.27	0.60*
	(0.24)	(0.32)
Rely on Republican politicians	−0.18	0.17
	(0.30)	(0.35)
Rely on Democratic politicians	0.15	0.07
	(0.29)	(0.22)
Rely on newspapers	0.60**	0.91***
	(0.24)	(0.28)
Rely on national TV	−0.40	0.08
	(0.26)	(0.22)
Rely on local TV	0.26	−0.29
	(0.28)	(0.25)
Rely on health insurers	0.35	−0.01
	(0.24)	(0.30)
Rely on friends or family	0.23	−0.04
	(0.28)	(0.27)
Rely on federal agencies	−0.18	−0.07
	(0.28)	(0.25)
Rely on doctors	−0.02	−0.33
	(0.21)	(0.31)
Rely on cable TV	0.06	0.02
	(0.23)	(0.21)
Knowledge about ACA (1–4)	0.31***	0.07
	(0.11)	(0.11)
Some college	0.13	0.17
	(0.28)	(0.31)
College or more	0.42*	0.79**
	(0.24)	(0.33)

White	−0.94**	−0.38
	(0.43)	(0.41)
Black	−0.58	0.15
	(0.53)	(0.53)
Hispanic	0.57	1.11**
	(0.47)	(0.52)
Moderate	−0.58**	−0.36
	(0.28)	(0.26)
Conservative	−0.93***	−1.33***
	(0.34)	(0.39)
Democrat	0.70**	1.34***
	(0.36)	(0.31)
Republican	−1.24**	−1.36***
	(0.49)	(0.40)
Only fair health	1.21**	1.02*
	(0.54)	(0.59)
Good health	0.40	0.24
	(0.51)	(0.52)
Very good health	0.23	0.40
	(0.54)	(0.59)
Excellent health	0.83*	1.05*
	(0.49)	(0.55)
Household income	−0.08	0.12**
	(0.06)	(0.06)
Female	−0.58***	−0.40*
	(0.21)	(0.23)
25–34	−0.87**	−1.37**
	(0.43)	(0.57)
35–44	−0.36	−0.82
	(0.40)	(0.52)
45–54	−0.26	−0.53
	(0.43)	(0.52)

55–64	−0.43	−0.40
	(0.32)	(0.53)
65+	−0.64	−0.73
	(0.46)	(0.69)
Public insurance	0.81	0.01
	(0.73)	(0.83)
Individual insurance	1.02	0.30
	(0.74)	(0.72)
Employer insurance	0.61	−0.05
	(0.66)	(0.68)
Other insurance source	−0.58	−0.16
	(1.09)	(0.93)
N	739	726
Pseudo R-Squared	0.23	0.34

Standard errors clustered by state.
Logistic regression results. * 0.10, ** 0.05, *** 0.01.
Data from Kaiser Family Foundation Tracking Poll.
Survey weights applied.

Next I examine whether individuals reporting having employer-provided health insurance were more likely to indicate that they relied on employer information about the ACA. The regression results indicate that individuals with employer-provided health insurance were no more or less likely to report relying on employer information about the ACA.

	Outcome is relying on employer information (0/1)
Employer insurance	−0.36
	(0.85)
Knowledge about ACA (1–4)	0.39***
	(0.12)
Some college	−0.23
	(0.35)

College or more	0.14
	(0.28)
White	1.48*
	(0.80)
Black	1.00
	(0.92)
Hispanic	1.70**
	(0.74)
Moderate	−0.06
	(0.28)
Conservative	−0.53
	(0.41)
Democrat	−0.64
	(0.43)
Republican	0.42
	(0.37)
Only fair health	1.33
	(1.14)
Good health	1.27
	(1.18)
Very good health	1.13
	(1.11)
Excellent health	1.23
	(1.11)
Household income	0.00
	(0.06)
Female	0.02
	(0.23)
25–34	1.42**
	(0.69)
35–44	0.44
	(0.65)

45–54	1.24*
	(0.65)
55–64	0.52
	(0.65)
65+	−0.50
	(0.71)
Public insurance	−1.79**
	(0.90)
Individual insurance	−0.99
	(1.04)
Other insurance source	−0.25
	(1.20)
N	782
Pseudo R-Squared	0.17

Standard errors clustered by state.
Logistic regression results. * 0.10, ** 0.05, *** 0.01.
Data from Kaiser Family Foundation Tracking Poll.
Survey weights applied.

In a similar vein, I combine data on the receipt of employer-provided information with data on employer-provided health insurance to see if employer information was more meaningful for individuals who relied on their employers for health insurance coverage. I find no evidence for such an effect.

	Outcome is believe self/family better off under ACA (0/1)	*Outcome is believe whole country better off under ACA (0/1)*
Rely on employer	−0.70	−0.60
	(0.62)	(0.65)
Employer insurance	0.61	−0.09
	(0.64)	(0.73)

Rely on employer X employer insurance	0.01 (0.65)	0.16 (0.75)
Rely on state agencies	0.27 (0.24)	0.59* (0.32)
Rely on Republican politicians	−0.18 (0.30)	0.18 (0.35)
Rely on Democratic politicians	0.15 (0.29)	0.07 (0.22)
Rely on newspapers	0.60** (0.24)	0.91*** (0.28)
Rely on national TV	−0.40 (0.26)	0.09 (0.22)
Rely on local TV	0.26 (0.28)	−0.29 (0.25)
Rely on health insurers	0.35 (0.24)	−0.01 (0.30)
Rely on friends or family	0.23 (0.28)	−0.04 (0.27)
Rely on federal agencies	−0.18 (0.28)	−0.06 (0.25)
Rely on doctors	−0.02 (0.22)	−0.33 (0.32)
Rely on cable TV	0.06 (0.23)	0.02 (0.21)
Knowledge about ACA (1–4)	0.31*** (0.11)	0.07 (0.12)
Some college	0.13 (0.28)	0.17 (0.31)
College or more	0.42* (0.24)	0.79** (0.33)
White	−0.94** (0.43)	−0.38 (0.42)

Black	−0.58	0.15
	(0.54)	(0.54)
Hispanic	0.57	1.12**
	(0.47)	(0.52)
Moderate	−0.58**	−0.36
	(0.28)	(0.26)
Conservative	−0.93***	−1.33***
	(0.34)	(0.39)
Democrat	0.70**	1.34***
	(0.36)	(0.32)
Republican	−1.24**	−1.37***
	(0.51)	(0.41)
Only fair health	1.21**	1.02*
	(0.54)	(0.59)
Good health	0.40	0.24
	(0.52)	(0.52)
Very good health	0.23	0.40
	(0.54)	(0.59)
Excellent health	0.83*	1.04*
	(0.49)	(0.55)
Household income	−0.08	0.12**
	(0.06)	(0.06)
Female	−0.58***	−0.41*
	(0.21)	(0.22)
25–34	−0.87**	−1.35**
	(0.43)	(0.57)
35–44	−0.36	−0.80
	(0.39)	(0.53)
45–54	−0.26	−0.51
	(0.42)	(0.52)
55–64	−0.43	−0.39
	(0.32)	(0.52)
65+	−0.64	−0.72
	(0.47)	(0.69)

Public insurance	0.81	−0.01
	(0.72)	(0.85)
Individual insurance	1.02	0.29
	(0.74)	(0.73)
Other insurance source	−0.58	−0.17
	(1.09)	(0.93)
N	739	726
Pseudo R-Squared	0.23	0.34

Standard errors clustered by state.
Logistic regression results. * 0.10, ** 0.05, *** 0.01.
Data from Kaiser Family Foundation Tracking Poll.
Survey weights applied.

Next I present logistic regression results showing the effect of receiving information from an employer about the ACA on the likelihood that respondents will change their mind about the individual mandate after hearing arguments in favor of the mandate. (Note that this analysis only includes respondents who indicated that they were initially unfavorable to the individual mandate.)

	Outcome is changing stance on individual mandate after hearing pro-mandate arguments (0/1)
Rely on employers	−0.70*
	(0.37)
Rely on state agencies	0.77*
	(0.41)
Rely on Republican politicians	0.02
	(0.35)
Rely on Democratic politicians	−0.38
	(0.29)
Rely on newspapers	0.75***
	(0.25)
Rely on national TV	−0.10
	(0.22)

Rely on local TV	−0.14
	(0.31)
Rely on health insurers	−0.23
	(0.24)
Rely on friends or family	−0.39
	(0.24)
Rely on federal agencies	−0.02
	(0.31)
Rely on doctors	−0.54*
	(0.28)
Rely on cable TV	−0.19
	(0.31)
Knowledge about ACA (1–4)	−0.24*
	(0.14)
Some college	−0.37
	(0.32)
College or more	−0.13
	(0.31)
White	0.65
	(0.57)
Black	1.12*
	(0.65)
Hispanic	1.07**
	(0.53)
Moderate	−0.13
	(0.28)
Conservative	−0.50
	(0.38)
Democrat	−0.14
	(0.35)
Republican	−0.52
	(0.37)
Only fair health	−0.17
	(0.56)

Good health	−0.32
	(0.63)
Very good health	−0.29
	(0.60)
Excellent health	−0.76
	(0.62)
Household income	−0.03
	(0.07)
Female	0.49*
	(0.28)
25–34	−0.04
	(0.55)
35–44	−0.60
	(0.60)
45–54	0.13
	(0.65)
55–64	−0.02
	(0.59)
65+	0.13
	(0.67)
Public insurance	−1.90**
	(0.76)
Individual insurance	−1.26*
	(0.70)
Employer insurance	−1.25*
	(0.66)
Other insurance source	0.72
	(1.23)
N	465
Pseudo R-Squared	0.14

Standard errors clustered by state.
Logistic regression results. * 0.10, ** 0.05, *** 0.01.
Data from Kaiser Family Foundation Tracking Poll.
Survey weights applied.

Chapter 8 Appendix

2014 CCES Analysis and BIPAC Employer Mobilization

I use data from the 2014 CCES (more information available at http://projects .iq.harvard.edu/cces/home) to assess the effect of BIPAC mobilization on voter choices in the 2014 senatorial and gubernatorial elections.

I use the following variables from the Common Content, public release of the 2014 CCES:

Vote for a Democratic Senatorial Candidate: Binary indicator for whether a voter in the 2014 senatorial elections reported voting for a Democratic candidate. This is the first of two outcomes I assess. Only respondents who reported voting in these elections are included in the analysis.

Vote for a Democratic Gubernatorial Candidate: Binary indicator for whether a voter in the 2014 gubernatorial elections reported voting for a Democratic candidate. This is the second of the two outcomes. Only respondents who reported voting in these elections are included in the analysis.

BIPAC Employer Mobilization Intensity: The number of GOTV messages sent through BIPAC's Prosperity Project platform in each state standardized by the number of employees in a state. Employees by state from the Bureau of Labor Statistics; GOTV messages from internal BIPAC data. I use quartiles of this measure.

Union Membership: Binary indicator for whether respondent is in a union.

Education: Coded as three categories: high school or less, some college, or college or more.

Gender: Binary indicator.

Family Income: Continuous variable indicating self-reported family income: <$10,000; $10,000 to $19,999; $20,000 to $29,999; $30,000 to $39,999; $40,000 to $49,999; $50,000 to $59,999; $60,000 to $69,999; $70,000 to $79,999; $80,000 to $99,999; $100,000 to $119,999; $120,000 to $149,999; $150,000 to $199,999; $200,000 to $249,999; or $250,000 or more.

Race and Ethnicity: Binary indicators for white, Non-Hispanic; black, Non-Hispanic; Hispanic; and Asian. Excluded category is other, Non-Hispanic.

Partisan Affiliation: Indicator for Democrat, Republican, or independent.

Ideological Orientation: One through five scale of self-reported ideological orientation.

Lagged Democratic Candidate Performance: Democratic vote share in the previous senatorial or gubernatorial election.

Note that I restrict my analysis to only those respondents in the labor force (employed, unemployed, or temporarily unemployed) who could have plausibly received employer messages from BIPAC.

Below I present logistic regression results showing the relationship between BIPAC mobilization intensity and individual vote choices in the 2014 elections for U.S. gubernatorial candidates. Greater BIPAC mobilization decreases the likelihood of a vote for a Democratic governor.

	Outcome is voted for Democratic governor (0/1)
BIPAC mobilization 2nd quartile	−0.50** (0.21)
BIPAC mobilization 3rd quartile	−0.35 (0.23)
BIPAC mobilization 4th quartile	−0.95*** (0.27)
Union member	0.43*** (0.16)
Some college	0.03 (0.14)
College or more	0.24* (0.14)
Male	−0.19* (0.10)
Family income	−0.05*** (0.01)
White	0.24 (0.18)
Black	1.32*** (0.24)
Hispanic	0.60*** (0.21)

Asian	−0.38
	(0.53)
Republican	−3.52***
	(0.17)
Independent	−1.93***
	(0.13)
Political ideology (conservative)	−0.87***
	(0.06)
Lagged Democratic vote share	0.01
	(0.01)
N	10,879
Pseudo R-Squared	0.45

Standard errors clustered by state.
OLS regression results. * 0.10, ** 0.05, *** 0.01.
Only workers in the labor force included.
Survey weights applied.

Contributions to BIPAC-Endorsed Candidates from Employees at BIPAC-Affiliated Companies

In the final analysis I examine the contributions from employees at BIPAC-affiliated companies to BIPAC-endorsed candidates. (I used FEC data from Adam Bonica's Database on Ideology, Money in Politics, and Elections: https://data.stanford.edu/dime.) The analysis shows that employees at BIPAC-affiliated companies (on BIPAC's board of directors or steering committee for the Prosperity Project) were more likely to donate to BIPAC-endorsed candidates.

	Donations from employees at BIPAC-affiliated companies ($)
BIPAC-endorsed candidate	675.41***
	(141.83)
N	52,733
R-Squared	0.001

Standard errors clustered by contributor.
2014 election cycle data.
OLS regression results. * 0.10, ** 0.05, *** 0.01.

I also show that employees at BIPAC-affiliated companies were more likely to donate to BIPAC-endorsed candidates after BIPAC made an endorsement (drawing on endorsement announcements on BIPAC's website). This is true even if I add fixed effects for the company at which employees worked and fixed effects for the month-year of the contribution.

	Donations from employees at BIPAC-affiliated companies to BIPAC-endorsed candidates ($)	
Contribution made after BIPAC endorsement	414.61*	1233.59**
	(246.32)	(466.93)
Company fixed effects	N	Y
Month fixed effects	N	Y
N	82	82
R-Squared	0.01	0.78

Standard errors clustered by contributor.
2014 election cycle data.
OLS regression results. * 0.10, ** 0.05, *** 0.01.

NOTES

Preface

1. This account draws from "Independence Institute's Freedom Alliance Lunch with Linda J. Hansen" 2014; Truth Tour 2012; Stan 2011b.
2. Nolan 2016. See "Course 3: American Job Security," 27, 17.
3. Hansen 2011, 20.
4. Nolan 2016. See "Course 3: American Job Security," 36.
5. The "Independence Institute" 2014.
6. Stan 2011b, Truth Tour 2012.

Introduction

1. Eaton 2012.
2. Ravel and Weintraub 2015.
3. Greenhouse 2012.
4. Elk 2012b.
5. Starbucks 2015.
6. Keyes 2012.
7. Job Creators Network 2014a. See also Gruss 2014.
8. Crum 2010.
9. CNN/Opinion Research Corporation Poll, April 2009.
10. This is likely only a conservative measure of true lobbying spending; see, e.g., Drutman 2015.
11. Schlozman et al. 2012, 442.
12. Hertel-Fernandez 2014.
13. Gilens and Page 2014.
14. Gilens and Page 2014, 575.
15. Hacker and Pierson 2016; Skocpol and Hertel-Fernandez 2016a.
16. For a libertarian case against "regressive rent-seeking," see, e.g., Teles 2014.

Chapter 1

1. Starbucks 2016. One could argue that given socioeconomic disparities in voter registration and turnout, even seemingly nonpartisan efforts to get out the vote could have partisan and ideological implications. For instance, Sean McElwee (2015) has shown that nonvoters tend to prefer a more expansive government than voters, so one could argue that efforts to expand turnout will have a liberal effect. For the purposes of my analysis, however, I focus on the more direct intentions of companies in engaging their workers in politics. Because Starbucks

has made a concerted effort to keep partisan and ideological content out of their voting drive, I consider this an instance of nonpartisan mobilization.

2. See http://turbo.vote/.
3. Of course socially responsible behavior can also contribute to financial performance under some circumstances. See Flammer 2015.
4. On reviews of other corporate political tactics, see especially Schlozman et al. 2012; Drutman 2015; Baumgartner et al. 2009; Vogel 1989; Hacker and Pierson 2010.
5. Hindman and Wilkie 2012.
6. Hindman and Wilkie 2012.
7. Job Creators Network 2014c.
8. Hall and Deardorff 2006; see also Clawson et al. (1992) on campaign contributions. On interest group reputations for electoral advantage and access to legislative agendas, see Hansen 1991; Baumgartner et al. 2009, 127.
9. National Association of Manufacturers 2014.
10. Kollman 1998. Employer mobilization thus encompasses some forms of outside lobbying— such as when employers recruit workers to contact Congress—but goes beyond it as employers incorporate electoral appeals to their workers or try to change how their workers think about politics.
11. Kollman 1998, 8.
12. DuPont n.d.
13. Walker 2014.
14. Kramer 2000, 72–73.
15. Stan 2012. See also leaked course materials in Nolan 2016.
16. Schlozman et al. 2012, 401.
17. Kramer 2000, 112.
18. Kramer 2000, 112.
19. Baumgartner et al. 2009, especially chapter 8; Schlozman et al. 2012, especially chapter 14.
20. Baumgartner et al. 2009, 157.
21. Kramer 2000, 116.
22. See also Schlozman et al. 2012, 395.
23. See, e.g., Panagopoulos et al. 2016.
24. Verba et al. 1995.
25. Mutz and Mondak 2006.
26. Abrams et al. 2010.
27. Lichtenstein 2002.
28. Leighley and Nagler 2007.
29. Ahlquist et al. 2014; Ahlquist and Levi 2013; Kim and Margalit 2017.
30. Han 2014, 14. See also Han 2016.
31. Han 2014, 16.
32. E.g., Swenson 2002; Estevez-Abe et al. 2001.
33. *National Labor Relations Board v. Gissel Packing Co., Inc.* 395 U.S. 575, 617 (1969).
34. Frymer 2007, 110–11.
35. Ravel and Weintraub 2015, 1.
36. Brady et al. 1999.
37. For major interventions, see Dahl 1957, 1958; Crenson 1971; Mills (1956) 2000; Block 1977; Polsby 1962; Bachrach and Baratz 1962.
38. Gaventa 1982.
39. Lindblom 1977; 1982.
40. Lindblom 1982, 327.
41. Lindblom 1982, 328.

Chapter 2

1. See, e.g., Glynn 2013.
2. I followed best practices in designing this list experiment (Glynn 2013), reducing the likelihood that respondents would select either no or all responses (which would reveal that they

had selected the sensitive item or not) while minimizing variance. Following Blair and Imai (2012), I used the *List* R package to test for the presence for design effects and was unable to detect any.

3. On the importance of legislative staff, see Salisbury and Shepsle 1981. More recently see Montgomery and Nyhan 2017.

Chapter 3

1. Heyman 2015; Ward 2014a.
2. One reason I identify a much greater prevalence of mobilization among private-sector firms than Schlozman et al. (2012, 403)'s review of corporate websites is that much of the mobilization content may not be accessible to the public or housed on their main websites. I will describe these custom portals in more detail in this and the following chapter.
3. The 2004, 2006, and 2008 estimates are in SHRM 2008. The 2016 estimates are from personal communication with SHRM.
4. Difference in means statistically significant at $p < 0.05$. The 95 percent confidence intervals were 6 percent to 50 percent of managers.
5. Importantly, there was not differential reporting of mobilization by the job rank of respondents. Higher ranked respondents were not, for instance, more likely to describe mobilization than were lower ranked managers.
6. See, e.g., Drutman (2015) on the tendency of government affairs officers to overstate their effectiveness to companies.
7. These other forms of participation included hiring lobbyists, giving political contributions to candidates, buying electoral ads, and participating in various business associations.
8. Hersh 2015. Matching to these records is not always straightforward, however (see, e.g., Berent et al. 2016).
9. Kramer 2000, 20.
10. Conlin and Lozada 2015.
11. Dudley 2013.
12. Kramer 2000, 84.
13. Kramer 2000, 84.
14. Kramer 2000, 98.
15. Kramer 2000, 98.
16. Kramer 2000, 98–99.
17. Kramer 2000, 98–99.
18. Crum 2010.
19. Crum 2010.
20. See Lockheed Martin 2012.
21. Berfield 2015.
22. Berfield 2015.
23. Lohr 2014.
24. Kramer 2000, 20.
25. See Dayton Area Chamber of Commerce 2008.
26. Wehrman 2015.
27. Kang 2009.
28. Snyder and Brush 2009.
29. Yackee and Yackee 2006, 137.
30. Culpepper 2010; Hertel-Fernandez 2016.
31. The difference was statistically significant at $p < 0.05$.

Chapter 4

1. Eaton 2012.
2. Eaton 2012.
3. Banerjee 2012.
4. Banerjee 2012.

5. Mufson 2012.
6. Mufson 2012.
7. Mufson 2012.
8. Banerjee 2012.
9. MacGillis 2012.
10. MacGillis 2012.
11. MacGillis 2012.
12. Cochenour 2014.
13. Quoted in Ward 2014b.
14. MacGillis 2012.
15. Drabold 2016.
16. MacGillis 2012.
17. Allstate/*National Journal* Heartland Monitor Poll XXI 2014.
18. See the appendix to this chapter for a more detailed analysis that shows how targeting can help to explain the differences in reported mobilization between the firm and worker surveys by industry.
19. See the results reported in Hertel-Fernandez 2017.
20. Lafer 2012.
21. Good 2012.
22. See Job Creators Network 2014b.
23. 2009 Innovation Award submission from Meaghan Killion Joyce (International Paper). Available from author.
24. Zornick 2012.
25. Kramer 2000, 83.
26. Zornick 2012.
27. Greenhouse 2012.
28. Snyder and Brush 2009.
29. On businesses' incentives to strategically oppose legislation, see Broockman 2012; Hacker and Pierson 2002.
30. Abelson 2016.
31. Keyes 2015.
32. Bronfenbrenner 1997.
33. DuPont n.d.
34. AGC n.d.-a, n.d.-b.
35. AGC n.d.-a, 6.
36. In general my findings of the effects of union messages on worker behavior are consistent with past research that shows how unions can increase turnout and change workers' political preferences (Ahlquist et al. 2014; Leighley and Nagler 2007; Flavin and Hartney 2015; Kim and Margalit 2017).
37. Ames and Elk 2011.
38. Gerber et al. 2012, 84.
39. Schlozman et al. 2012.
40. For one summary, see McElwee 2015.
41. Lukes 2005; Gaventa 1982.
42. Bartels 2003; Converse 1964; Zaller 1992.

Chapter 5

1. Phillips-Fein 2009, chapter 5.
2. Phillips-Fein 2009, 108.
3. Stan 2011a. For an overview of Americans for Prosperity and the Koch political network, see Skocpol and Hertel-Fernandez 2016b.
4. "Independence Institute's Freedom Alliance Lunch with Linda J. Hansen" 2014.
5. Windsor 2014.
6. Brandeis 1914.
7. Bensel 2004; Keyssar 2001.

8. *The Public* 1908, 704.
9. *The Public* 1908, 703.
10. Hill 2005, 122.
11. Hill 2005, 122.
12. Keyssar 2001, 129.
13. Kollman 1998, 145.
14. Hamburger 2004.
15. Clawson et al. 1992, 14–15.
16. *Time* 1962.
17. Weidenbaum 1980, 52-3.
18. Birnbaum 2004. For earlier statistics, see Heath et al. 1995, 275.
19. BIPAC 2014c, 2016.
20. Hindman and Wilkie 2012.
21. Quoted in Reclaim Democracy n.d.
22. Waterhouse 2013, 55.
23. Waterhouse 2013, 58.
24. Waterhouse 2013, 81.
25. Waterhouse 2013, 57–58.
26. Silk and Vogel 1976, 65.
27. Walker 2014.
28. Lichtenstein 2002.
29. Weil 2014; Lambert et al. 2014.
30. Weil 2014; Mishel et al. 2012; Lichtenstein 2002.
31. Quoted in Reich 2004.
32. 2009 Innovation Award submission from Meaghan Killion Joyce (International Paper). Available from author.
33. American Management Association 2014.
34. Rosen 2014.
35. Liptak 2010.
36. Hansen et al. 2015.
37. Coates 2012.
38. *Harvard Law Review* 2014.
39. Hindman and Wilkie 2012.
40. Hindman and Wilkie 2012.
41. Volokh 2011–12.
42. I find these effects looking at a range of different outcomes. Workers in states with laws against workplace political coercion and protecting political speech at work were no less likely to report receiving any employer political messages, report receiving messages with threats of job loss or wage cuts, or report receiving messages that made them uncomfortable compared to workers in states without such laws.
43. Ames and Elk 2011.
44. Rose 1962.
45. PL103-94 Section 4 §610.
46. Though see Clawson et al. (1992, 14) on corporate pressure on white-collar executives to donate to corporate PACs in earlier time periods.
47. See U.S. Energy Information Administration 2015.
48. Walther et al. 2016.
49. Lenhard 2016.
50. McGregor 2016.
51. McGregor 2016.
52. Secunda 2008, 2010; Bronfenbrenner 2009.
53. Secunda 2010, 20.
54. This account draws from Cottin 1972.
55. Cottin 1972, 124.
56. Cottin 1972, 129.
57. Waterhouse 2013, 28.

58. The relevant FEC decision was *Sun Oil* (1975).
59. Waterhouse 2013, 28.
60. The *New York Times* article is quoted in Phillips-Fein 2009, 188. For a more general account of corporate political activities during this period, see Drutman 2015; Vogel 1989; Hacker and Pierson 2010.
61. See also Hamburger 2006.
62. Tierney 2004.
63. BIPAC 2001.
64. Quoted in BIPAC 2001.
65. Quoted in BIPAC 2001.
66. Berke 1997.
67. Quoted in BIPAC 2001.
68. Boatright et al. 2006, 133.
69. BIPAC 2014c, 3.
70. BIPAC 2014c, 3.
71. See estimate reported in BIPAC 2014a.
72. BIPAC 2009, 2.
73. BIPAC 2009, 2.
74. Hamburger 2006.
75. Hamburger 2004.
76. Hoover 2015.
77. Hoover 2015.
78. Hamburger 2004.
79. Skinner 2006, 83.
80. BIPAC 2012, 1.
81. Hoover 2015.
82. Birnbaum 2004.
83. Birnbaum 2004.
84. Birnbaum 2004.
85. Birnbaum 2004. Baumgartner et al. (2009) give an example of the importance of the Business Roundtable's newly developed mobilization capacities around trade with China (112–13).
86. Kramer 2000.
87. Sharn 2014.
88. Cain 2013.
89. See Job Creators Network n.d.
90. Ortiz 2015, 23.
91. Windsor 2014.
92. Birnbaum 2004.
93. BIPAC 2010.
94. BIPAC 2010.
95. Wilson 2010.
96. Elk 2012a.
97. Zornick 2012.
98. Ames and Elk 2011.
99. Schulman 2014; Mayer 2016, chapter 9.
100. Difference statistically significant at $p < 0.01$.
101. Walker 2014. See also Kollman 1998.
102. Keim 1985; Weidenbaum 1980.
103. Heath et al. 1995, 275.
104. Heath et al. 1995, 275.
105. Ames and Elk 2011.
106. Hamburger 2004.
107. Heath et al. 1995, 275.
108. See especially Vogel 1989; Waterhouse 2013; Hacker and Pierson 2010.
109. See, for instance, Waterhouse 2013, chapter 3.

110. Martin 1995; see also Martin and Swank 2012.
111. See especially Mizruchi 1992; Schifeling 2013; Spillman 2012.

Chapter 6

1. Quoted in BIPAC 2016.
2. NELP 2015.
3. See Ortiz 2016.
4. Addady 2016.
5. Lipton 2014.
6. Difference between letter and control condition significant at $p < 0.05$; difference between generic and control condition significant at $p = 0.14$; difference between generic and letter condition significant at $p = 0.18$ (one-tailed tests).
7. On the issues with conditioning on posttreatment variables in an experimental context, see, e.g., Montgomery et al. 2016.
8. The difference between the letter and control condition is significant for employees who were worried about finding new employment ($p < 0.01$) and nonsignificant for employees who were not worried about their employment prospects ($p = 0.38$; both one-tailed). The difference in differences is statistically significant at $p < 0.05$ (one-tailed).
9. Kelly 2016.
10. CBO 2016, 12–13.
11. Ferris 2015.
12. The differences between the employer message group and the control and generic message groups are both significant at $p < 0.05$ (one-tailed tests).
13. The difference between the letter and control condition is significant for employees who were worried about finding new employment ($p < 0.01$) and nonsignificant for employees who were not worried about their employment prospects ($p = 0.12$; both one-tailed). The difference in differences is statistically significant at $p < 0.05$ (one-tailed).
14. Indeed Brady et al. (1999) find that political recruiters are often "rational prospectors," which would mean that employers might be strategically targeting workers who would be most likely to respond to managerial appeals.
15. These differences are all significant at $p < 0.05$.
16. Achen and Bartels 2016; Carpini and Keeter 1996.
17. The difference was a change of 0.15 units on the 0–8 scale, significant at $p = 0.72$.
18. To measure competitiveness, I use the absolute value of the Cook Partisan Voting Index. I apply state fixed effects to account for state variation.
19. Neither the difference between employer mobilization and union mobilization nor employer mobilization and party mobilization is significant at conventional levels.
20. Difference statistically significant at $p < 0.01$.
21. Difference significant at $p < 0.05$.

Chapter 7

1. For background on the Export-Import battle, see Weisman 2015; Gold and Hamburger 2015.
2. Dillow 2015.
3. See BIPAC n.d.-a.
4. CMF 2011.
5. Fitch et al. 2017, 14.
6. Fitch et al. 2017, 13.
7. Drutman 2015; Hall and Deardorff 2006; Hertel-Fernandez 2014.
8. This is consistent with Hansen 1991.
9. See CMF n.d.
10. The difference between employee letters and constituent letters and non-profit citizens group letters is statistically significant at $p < 0.10$.
11. The difference between employee letters and constituent letters and non-profit citizens group letters is statistically significant at $p < 0.05$.

12. The difference in the effect of the employee letters and constituent letters and non-profit citizens group letters is 2.19 units on the 1–4 scale for staffers who said that business information was "not at all" important in their decisions ($p < 0.05$) and –0.38 units for staffers who said that business information was "extremely important" ($p = 0.22$). The difference in estimates is significant at $p < 0.05$.

13. The difference in the effect of the employee letters and constituent letters and non-profit citizens group letters is 0.10 units on the 1–4 scale for staffers in below-average unemployment districts and states ($p = 0.77$) and 0.72 for staffers in above-average unemployment districts and states ($p < 0.01$). The difference in estimates is significant at $p = 0.12$.

14. The difference in the effect of the employee letters and constituent letters and non-profit citizens group letters is 0.10 units on the 1–4 scale for staffers in below-average unemployment districts and states ($p = 0.73$) and 0.89 for staffers in above-average unemployment districts and states ($p < 0.01$). The difference in estimates is significant at $p < 0.05$.

15. See also Hansen 1991; Kollman 1998.

16. See also Butler 2014 for similar findings but with an alternative mechanism.

17. Lane 2008.

18. Rosen 2007.

19. Hatch 2014.

20. Hatch 2014.

21. Johnson 2014.

22. BIPAC 2013.

23. BIPAC 2013.

24. BIPAC 2013.

25. Ballotpedia 2014.

26. Troll 2014.

27. Ballotpedia 2014.

28. Ballotpedia 2014.

29. Ballotpedia 2014.

30. Ballotpedia 2014.

31. PPP 2014.

32. Prosperity Alaska n.d.

33. See Prosperity Alaska n.d.

34. See Prosperity Alaska n.d.

35. This account from Woodman 2014.

36. Difference statistically significant at $p < 0.01$.

37. Difference statistically significant at $p < 0.10$.

38. See National Association of Manufacturers n.d. for BIPAC's early voting campaign generally, and Prosperity Alaska n.d. for Alaska specifically.

39. Difference between high and low quartile significant at $p < 0.05$.

40. Difference statistically significant at $p < 0.10$.

41. Jamieson 2012.

42. Jamieson 2012.

43. Jamieson 2012.

44. Lipscomb 2012.

45. Lipscomb 2012.

46. Ungar 2012.

47. Strasser 2012.

48. "Independence Institute's Freedom Alliance Lunch with Linda J. Hansen" 2014.

49. Though see Jacobs and Mettler (2016) for evidence of recent shifts in public support for the ACA, especially for those who have experienced the benefits of the policy.

50. Collins et al. 2012.

51. Difference statistically significant at $p < 0.01$.

52. Difference statistically significant at $p < 0.10$.

53. These pro-ACA arguments included the following: "Under the reform law, most Americans would still get coverage through their employers and so would automatically satisfy the requirement without having to buy any new insurance"; "Without such a requirement, insurance

companies would still be allowed to deny coverage to people who are sick"; "Without such a requirement, people may wait until they are seriously ill to buy health insurance, which will drive up health insurance costs for everyone"; and "People would not be held to this requirement if the cost of new coverage would consume too large a share of their income."

54. The question text: "Next, I'm going to read you several elements of the health reform law. As I read each one, please tell me whether you feel very favorable, somewhat favorable, somewhat unfavorable, or very unfavorable about it. The law will require nearly all Americans to have health insurance by 2014 or else pay a fine. Would you say you feel very favorable, somewhat favorable, somewhat unfavorable or very unfavorable about that?"

55. The question text: "What if you heard that . . . ? Would you still have an unfavorable view of requiring nearly all Americans to have health insurance, or would you now have a favorable view of that requirement?"

56. Difference statistically significant at $p < 0.10$.

57. Long et al. 2016.

58. Cited in BIPAC 2016.

Chapter 8

1. Levis 2012.
2. Boslet and Leusner 2009.
3. Berfield 2012.
4. Nolan 2012.
5. BIPAC 2014c, 4, 5.
6. BIPAC 2014c.
7. BIPAC 2014b.
8. Difference statistically significant at $p < 0.01$.
9. Babenko et al. 2016.
10. I extracted contribution data from Adam Bonica's (2013) "Database on Ideology, Money in Politics, and Elections."

Chapter 9

1. Weber 2014.
2. Schrage 2016.
3. Han 2014.
4. Panagopoulos et al. 2016.
5. For examples, see Mares and Young 2016; Frye et al. 2014.
6. Landale 2016.

Conclusion

1. Mutz and Mondak 2006. See also Estlund 2003.
2. Mondak and Mutz 2001, 36.
3. Bishop 2008. See also Estlund (2003) for a similar qualitative argument.
4. Bartels 2005; Gilens 2001; Carpini and Keeter 1996.
5. Pintor et al. 2002, 78–79.
6. Fisk and Poueymirou 2015.
7. Based on 2014 Qualtrics survey of 1,000 adult Americans, including 559 respondents in the labor force. The survey sample was designed to match the overall national population along several important dimensions (including education and gender), and I estimated raked weights to ensure that the sample matched the 2013 labor force on age, gender, education, unemployment, race, and Hispanic ethnicity. Although not a national probability sample, the Qualtrics respondents thus closely resembled the national labor force across a range of relevant demographic characteristics.
8. Bartels 2008; Winters and Page 2009; Gilens and Page 2014; Gilens 2012; Hacker and Pierson 2010.

9. Lynn and Longman 2010; Teles 2015.
10. Glastris 2016.
11. Bronfenbrenner 2009, 1. See also Logan 2006.
12. Bronfenbrenner 2009, 13.
13. Meyerson 2010.
14. Freeman 2007.
15. Survey by Public Welfare Foundation 2010.
16. Shaiken 2007.
17. Crain and Matheny 2014.
18. Freeman and Medoff 1985, 9.
19. Freeman and Medoff 1985, 9.
20. 2 U.S.C. §441b(b)(2).
21. Ravel and Weintraub 2015.
22. *Harvard Law Review* 2014.
23. Secunda 2010.
24. Hertel-Fernandez and Secunda 2016.
25. Hertel-Fernandez and Secunda 2016.
26. Senate Committee on Governmental Affairs 1993, 10.
27. Senate Committee on Governmental Affairs 1993, 93.
28. Senate Committee on Governmental Affairs 1993, 117.
29. See Bebchuk and Jackson (2010) on this problem with corporate political speech more generally.
30. See especially *Harvard Law Review* 2014; Secunda 2010.
31. *First National Bank of Boston v. Bellotti* (435 U.S. 765 [1978]).
32. Coates 2015.
33. Balkin 1999, 14.
34. Pokempner 1965.
35. Totenberg 2016. *Abood v. Detroit Board of Education* (1977) created this precedent for public-sector workers. In the private-sector context, the law varies by whether a state has passed "right to work" legislation. In these states, workers in union-represented employment have the right to refuse to pay the union for the services the union provides workers. In states that have not passed "right to work" legislation, federal law enables unions to charge nonmembers who benefit from the union's representation dues and fees that cover the costs of collective bargaining and contract administration. The Supreme Court ruled in *Communications Workers of America v. Beck* (1988) that unions in such states cannot charge workers for political activities. The *Friedrichs v. California Teachers Association* Supreme Court case in 2016 would have made it illegal for public-sector unions in any state to collect any dues from nonmembers. With the unexpected death of Justice Antonin Scalia, the Court deadlocked over the case, essentially upholding the decision of the lower federal court that had sided with the unions.
36. Zingales 2012; Curry 2015.
37. Teles 2014.
38. Beckel 2010; Carney 2015.
39. Baker 2015.
40. See Edwards and Filion (2009) for one estimate of the federal contract workforce.
41. Volokh 2014.
42. This is increasingly the story of worker rights legislation, including union laws.
43. See Bipartisan Policy Center 2016.
44. Locke et al. 2007; but see McDonnell et al. (2015) on the power of social activism, and boycotts in particular, to change corporate behavior.
45. See section 7 of the National Labor Relations Act of 1935.
46. NLRB Case Number 04-CA-147314.
47. See Copland 2015.
48. Finseth 2010.
49. Dahl 1977, 8. I thank Paul Frymer for reminding me of this argument by Dahl.
50. See also Alex Gourevitch's (2013) conception of labor republicanism, which emphasizes the importance of freedom from domination. I thank Suresh Naidu for raising this point. See also Elizabeth Anderson's (2017) description of employers as "private governments."

WORKS CITED

Abelson, Reed. 2016. "Despite Fears, Affordable Care Act Has Not Uprooted Employer Coverage." *New York Times*, April 4, 2016.

Abrams, Samuel, Torben Iversen, and David Soskice. 2010. "Informal Social Networks and Rational Voting." *British Journal of Political Science* 41:229–57.

Achen, Christopher, and Larry Bartels. 2016. *Democracy for Realists: Why Elections Do Not Produce Responsive Government*. Princeton, NJ: Princeton University Press.

Addady, Michal. 2016. "This Fast Food CEO Wants to Replace Workers with Robots." *Fortune*, March 17, 2016.

AGC. n.d.-a. "Engaging Your Members about Politics and Public Policy." Washington, DC. https://www.agc.org/sites/default/files/Files/Advocacy/AGC%20Grassroots%20-%20Chapter%20Guide%20to%20Employer%20Employee%20Engagement.pdf

———. n.d.-b. "Guide to Hosting a Meet and Greet for Candidates and Members of Congress." Washington, DC. http://advocacy.agc.org/wp-content/uploads/2017/01/AGC-Grassroots-Meet-and-Greet-Guide.pdf

Ahlquist, John, Amanda B. Clayton, and Margaret Levi. 2014. "Provoking Preferences: Unionization, Trade Policy, and the ILWU Puzzle." *International Organization* 68 (1):33–75.

Ahlquist, John, and Margaret Levi. 2013. *In the Interest of Others: Organizations and Social Activism*. Princeton, NJ: Princeton University Press.

Allstate/*National Journal* Heartland Monitor Poll XXI. 2014. "Work/Life Balance." Crosstabs provided by Allstate and on file with author.

American Management Association. 2014. "The Latest on Workplace Monitoring and Surveillance." http://www.amanet.org/training/articles/the-latest-on-workplace-monitoring-and-surveillance.aspx

Ames, Mark, and Mike Elk. 2011. "Big Brothers: Thought Control at Koch." *The Nation*, April 20, 2011.

Anderson, Elizabeth. 2017. *Private Government: How Employers Rule Our Lives (and Why We Don't Talk about It)*. Princeton, NJ: Princeton University Press.

Babenko, Ilona, Viktar Fedaseyeu, and Song Zhang. 2016. "Do CEOs Affect Employee Political Choices?" Unpublished manuscript. https://papers.ssrn.com/sol3/papers.cfm?abstract_id=2954449

Bachrach, Peter, and Morton S. Baratz. 1962. "Two Faces of Power." *American Political Science Review* 56 (4):947–52.

Baker, Peter. 2015. "Obama Orders Federal Contractors to Provide Workers Paid Sick Leave." *New York Times*, September 7, 2015.

Balkin, Jack M. 1999. "Free Speech and Hostile Environments." *Columbia Law Review* 99 (8):2295–2320.

Ballotpedia. 2014. "Alaska Oil Tax Cuts Veto Referendum, Ballot Measure 1 (August 2014)." Accessed June 3, 2015. http://ballotpedia.org/Alaska_Oil_Tax_Cuts_Veto_Referendum,_ Ballot_Measure_1_(August_2014).

Banerjee, Neela. 2012. "Ohio Miners Say They Were Forced to Attend Romney Rally." *Los Angeles Times*, August 29, 2012.

Bartels, Larry. 2003. "Democracy with Attitudes." In *Electoral Democracy*, ed. M. B. MacKuen and G. Rabinowitz. Ann Arbor: University of Michigan Press.

———. 2005. "Homer Gets a Tax Cut: Inequality and Public Policy in the American Mind." *Perspectives on Politics* 3 (1):15–31.

———. 2008. *Unequal Democracy: The Political Economy of the New Gilded Age.* Princeton, NJ: Princeton University Press.

Baumgartner, Frank R., Jeffrey M. Berry, Marie Hojnacki, David C. Kimball, and Beth L. Leech. 2009. *Lobbying and Policy Change: Who Wins, Who Loses, and Why.* Chicago: University of Chicago Press.

Bebchuk, Lucian A., and Robert J. Jackson. 2010. "Corporate Political Speech: Who Decides?" *Harvard Law Review* 124 (1):83–117.

Beckel, Michael. 2010. "Senate Republicans Again Block DISCLOSE Act, Designed to Reveal Special Interest Spending." *Open Secrets Blog.* Washington, DC: Center for Responsive Politics.

Bensel, Richard Franklin. 2004. *The American Ballot Box in the Mid-Nineteenth Century.* New York: Cambridge University Press.

Berent, Matthew K., Jon A. Krosnick, and Arthur Lupia. 2016. "Measuring Voter Registration and Turnout in Surveys: Do Official Government Records Yield More Accurate Assessments?" *Public Opinion Quarterly* 80 (3):597–621.

Berfield, Susan. 2012. "Why Time-Share King David Siegel Thinks He Got Bush Elected." *Bloomberg Business Week*, August 3, 2012.

———. 2015. "How Walmart Keeps an Eye on Its Massive Workforce." *Bloomberg Business Week*, November 24, 2015.

Berke, Richard L. 1997. " 'Issue Ads' by Labor Fell Short in Elections, Business Group Says." *New York Times*, August 7, 1997.

BIPAC. 2001. "Outline for Prosperity: Prosperity Project Overview and Business and the American Electorate." Washington, DC: Business-Industry Political Action Committee.

———. 2009. "Biennial Report: Building on the Strength of Our Success." Washington, DC: Business-Industry Political Action Committee.

———. 2010. "Court Ruling Reaffirms Role of Corporate Issue Messaging in Elections." Washington, DC: Business-Industry Political Action Committee.

———. 2012. "Charting the Course for Business Political Involvement since 1963." Washington, DC: Business-Industry Political Action Committee.

———. 2013. "BIPAC Case Statement." Washington, DC: Business-Industry Political Action Committee.

———. 2014a. "BIPAC/P2 State Deployment Partner Conference Shares Best Practices in Grassroots Issue and Political Advocacy." San Diego, CA: Business-Industry Political Action Committee.

———. 2014b. "Largest U.S. Grassroots Business Network Announces Key Endorsements for 2014 Elections." Washington, DC: Business-Industry Political Action Committee.

———. 2014c. "ROI Report." Washington, DC: Business-Industry Political Action Committee.

———. 2016. "2016 Employer to Employee Engagement Study." Washington, DC: Business-Industry Political Action Committee.

———. n.d.-a. "Successful Telephone Calls to Legislators." http://bipac.net/page.asp?g=ip_ test&content=toolkit_telephone_calls&parent=BIPAC.

Bipartisan Policy Center. 2016. "BPC Leading National Effort with Corporate, Nonprofit Organizations to Improve the Electoral Process." February 16. http://bipartisanpolicy.org/press-release/national-initiative-electoral-process/.

Birnbaum, Jeffrey H. 2004. "Businesses Point Workers toward Ballot Boxes." *Washington Post*, March 21, 2004.

Bishop, Bill. 2008. *The Big Sort: Why the Clustering of Like-Minded America Is Tearing Us Apart.* New York: Houghton Mifflin.

Blair, Graeme, and Kosuke Imai. 2012. "Statistical Analysis of List Experiments." *Political Analysis* 20 (1):47–77.

Block, Fred. 1977. "The Ruling Class Does Not Rule." *Socialist Revolution* 33:6–28.

Boatright, Robert G., Michael J. Malbin, Mark J. Rozell, and Clyde Wilcox. 2006. "Interest Groups and Advocacy Organizations after BCRA." In *The Election after Reform: Money, Politics, and the Bipartisan Campaign Reform Act*, ed. M. J. Malbin. New York: Rowman & Littlefield.

Bonica, Adam. 2013. "Database on Ideology, Money in Politics, and Elections: Public Version 1.0." Computer file. Palo Alto, CA: Stanford University Libraries.

Boslet, Mike, and Jim Leusner. 2009. "Mr. Big." *Orlando*, June.

Brady, Henry E., Kay Lehman Schlozman, and Sidney Verba. 1999. "Prospecting for Participants: Rational Expectations and the Recruitment of Political Activists." *American Political Science Review* 93 (1):153–68.

Brandeis, Louis D. 1914. "Other People's Money and How the Bankers Use It." University of Louisville, Louis D. Brandeis School of Law, Library. https://louisville.edu/law/library/special-collections/the-louis-d.-brandeis-collection/other-peoples-money-by-louis-d.-brandeis.

Bronfenbrenner, Kate. 1997. "We'll Close! Plant Closings, Plant-Closing Threats, Union Organizing and NAFTA." *Multinational Monitor* 18 (3):8–14.

———. 2009. "No Holds Barred: The Intensification of Employer Opposition to Organizing." Washington, DC: Economic Policy Institute.

Broockman, David. 2012. "The 'Problem of Preferences': Medicare and Business Support for the Welfare State." *Studies in American Political Development* 26 (2):83–106.

Butler, Daniel. 2014. *Representing the Advantaged: How Politicians Reinforce Inequality.* New York: Cambridge University Press.

Cain, Herman. 2013. "Job Creators Oppose DC Propaganda." *Newsmax*, April 15, 2013.

Carney, Jordain. 2015. "GOP Blocks Minimum Wage, Sick Leave Proposals." *The Hill*, August 5, 2015.

Carpini, Michael X. Delli, and Scott Keeter. 1996. *What Americans Know about Politics and Why It Matters.* New Haven, CT: Yale University Press.

CBO. 2016. "Private Health Insurance Premiums and Federal Policy." Washington, DC: Congressional Budget Office.

Center for Responsive Politics. "Lobbying Spending Database." Washington, DC: Center for Responsive Politics. https://www.opensecrets.org/lobby/top.php?indexType=c&showYear=2017.

Clawson, Dan, Alan Neustadtl, and Denise Scott. 1992. *Money Talks: Corporate PACs and Political Influence.* New York: Basic Books.

CMF. 2011. "Communicating with Congress: How Citizen Advocacy Is Changing Mail Operations on Capitol Hill." Washington, DC: Congressional Management Foundation.

———. n.d. "Dealing with Backlogged Mail." http://www.congressfoundation.org/component/content/article/85-resources/82-dealing-with-backlogged-mail-in-congressional-offices.

CNN/Opinion Research Corporation Poll. 2009. Retrieved from the Roper Center for Public Opinion Research, iPoll. April 23–26, 2009.

Coates, John C. 2012. "Corporate Politics, Governance, and Value before and after *Citizens United." Journal of Empirical Legal Studies* 9 (4):657–96.

———. 2015. "Corporate Speech and the First Amendment: History, Data, and Implications." *Constitutional Commentary* 30 (2):223–76.

Cochenour, Jean F. 2014. "Complaint against Robert E. Murray, Murray Energy Corporation, and Consolidation Coal Company." In *14-C-681*, ed. Circuit Court for Monongalia County, West Virginia.

Collins, Sara R., Stuart Guterman, Rachel Nuzum, Mark A. Zezza, Tracy Garber, and Jennie Smith. 2012. "Health Care in the 2012 Presidential Election: How the Obama and Romney Plans Stack Up." Washington, DC: Commonwealth Fund.

Conlin, Michelle, and Lucas Iberico Lozada. 2015. "The New US Office Politics: Funding Your Boss's Political Causes." Reuters, May 11, 2015.

Converse, Philip. 1964. "The Nature of Belief Systems in Mass Publics." In *Ideology and Discontent*, ed. D. Apter. New York: Free Press.

Copland, James R. 2015. "Special Report: Public Pension Funds' Shareholder-Proposal Activism." *Proxy Monitor*. http://www.proxymonitor.org/Forms/2015Finding3.aspx.

Cottin, Jonathan. 1972. "Business-Industry Political Action Committee, BIPAC." In *Political Brokers*, ed. J. G. Smith. Washington, DC: Liveright/National Journal.

Crain, Marion, and Ken Matheny. 2014. "Beyond Unions, Notwithstanding Labor Law." *University of California, Irvine Law Review* 4:561–608.

Crenson, Matthew A. 1971. *The Un-Politics of Air Pollution: A Study of Non-Decision-Making in the Cities.* Baltimore: Johns Hopkins University Press.

Crum, Elizabeth. 2010. "Harrah's Bosses Put Squeeze on Employees to Vote in Pro-Reid Effort." *National Review*, November 2, 2010.

Culpepper, Pepper D. 2010. *Quiet Politics and Business Power: Corporate Control in Europe and Japan.* New York: Cambridge University Press.

Curry, Bill. 2015. "Here's How Bernie Sanders Could Win: The One Issue Where Hillary's Vulnerable, and Where the Tea Party Might Be Right." *Salon*, June 14, 2015.

Dahl, Robert A. 1957. "The Concept of Power." *Behavioral Science* 2 (3):201–15.

———. 1958. "A Critique of the Ruling Elite Model." *American Political Science Review* 52 (2):463–69.

———. 1977. "On Removing Certain Impediments to Democracy in the United States." *Political Science Quarterly* 92 (1):1–20.

Dayton Area Chamber of Commerce 2008. *Focus.* Fall. http://www.daytonchamber.org/default/assets/File/Focus_2008fall.pdf.

Dillow, Clay. 2015. "Boeing, GE Beat Tea Party as Congress Revives Export-Import Bank." *Fortune*, December 4, 2015.

Drabold, Will. 2016. "Donald Trump Heads for Coal Industry Fundraiser in West Virginia." *Time*, June 27, 2016.

Drutman, Lee. 2015. *The Business of America Is Lobbying.* New York: Oxford University Press.

Dudley, Renee. 2013. "Wal-Mart to HP Reap Worker Political Donations through Charities." *Bloomberg BusinessWeek*, December 23, 2013.

DuPont. N.d. "Frequently Asked Questions." *EmployeeVoice.* http://www.bipac.net/dupont/dupont_faqs.pdf.

Eaton, Sabrina. 2012. "Coal Miners Lost Pay When Mitt Romney Visited Their Mine to Promote Coal Jobs." *Cleveland Plain Dealer*, August 28, 2012.

Edwards, Kathryn, and Kai Filion. 2009. "Outsourcing Poverty: Federal Contracting Pushes Down Wages and Benefits." Washington, DC: Economic Policy Institute.

Elk, Mike. 2012a. "In Conference Call, Romney Urged Businesses to Tell Their Employees How to Vote." *In These Times*, October 17, 2012.

———. 2012b. "Koch Sends Pro-Romney Mailing to 45,000 Employees While Stifling Workplace Political Speech." *In These Times*, October 14, 2012.

Estevez-Abe, Margarita, Torben Iversen, and David Soskice. 2001. "Social Protection and the Formation of Skills: A Reinterpretation of the Welfare State." In *Varieties of Capitalism: The Institutional Foundations of Comparative Advantage*, ed. P. Hall and D. Soskice. New York: Oxford University Press.

Estlund, Cynthia. 2003. *Working Together: How Workplace Bonds Strengthen a Diverse Democracy.* New York: Oxford University Press.

Ferris, Sarah. 2015. "How Democrats Prevailed over Obama on the 'Cadillac Tax.'" *The Hill*, December 21, 2015.

Finseth, Eric John. 2010. "Shareholder Activism by Public Pension Funds and the Rights of Dissenting Employees under the First Amendment." *Harvard Journal of Law and Public Policy* 34 (1):289–366.

Fisk, Catherine, and Margaux Poueymirou. 2015. "Harris v. Quinn and the Contradictions of Compelled Speech." *Loyola of Los Angeles Law Review* 48 (2):439–92.

Fitch, Bradford, Kathy Goldschmidt, and Nicole Folk Cooper. 2017. "Citizen-Centric Advocacy: The Untapped Power of Constituent Engagement." Washington, DC: Congressional Management Foundation.

Flammer, Caroline. 2015. "Does Corporate Social Responsibility Lead to Superior Financial Performance? A Regression Discontinuity Approach." *Management Science* 61 (11):2549–68.

Flavin, Patrick, and Michael T. Hartney. 2015. "When Government Subsidizes Its Own: Collective Bargaining Laws as Agents of Political Mobilization." *American Journal of Political Science* 59 (4):896–911.

Freeman, Richard. 2007. "Do Workers Still Want Unions? More Than Ever." Washington, DC: Economic Policy Institute.

Freeman, Richard B., and James L. Medoff. 1985. *What Do Unions Do?* New York: Basic Books.

Frye, Timothy, Ora John Reuter, and David Szakonyi. 2014. "Political Machines at Work: Voter Mobilization and Electoral Subversion in the Workplace." *World Politics* 66 (2):195–228.

Frymer, Paul. 2007. *Black and Blue: African Americans, the Labor Movement, and the Decline of the Democratic Party.* Princeton, NJ: Princeton University Press.

Gaventa, John. 1982. *Power and Powerlessness: Quiescence and Rebellion in an Appalachian Valley.* Urbana: University of Illinois Press.

Gerber, Alan S., Gregory A. Huber, David Doherty, and Conor M. Dowling. 2012. "Is There a Secret Ballot? Ballot Secrecy Perceptions and Their Implications for Voting Behaviour." *British Journal of Political Science* 43 (1):77–102.

Gilens, Martin. 2001. "Political Ignorance and Collective Policy Preferences." *American Political Science Review* 95 (2):379–96.

———. 2012. *Affluence and Influence: Economic Inequality and Political Power in America.* Princeton, NJ: Princeton University Press.

Gilens, Martin, and Benjamin I. Page. 2014. "Testing Theories of American Politics: Elites, Interest Groups, and Average Citizens." *Perspectives on Politics* 12 (3):564–81.

Glastris, Paul. 2016. "Elizabeth Warren's Consolidation Speech Could Change the Election." *Washington Monthly*, June 30, 2016.

Glynn, Adam N. 2013. "What Can We Learn with Statistical Truth Serum: Design and Analysis of the List Experiment." *Public Opinion Quarterly* 77 (S1):159–72.

Gold, Matea, and Tom Hamburger. 2015. "Inside the Big GOP Fight over the Influential Export-Import Bank." *Washington Post*, March 27, 2015.

Good, Chris. 2012. "U.S. Chamber of Commerce Calls Elizabeth Warren 'Catastrophically Antibusiness.'" *ABC News*, October 18, 2012.

Gourevitch, Alex. 2013. "Labor Republicanism and the Transformation of Work." *Political Theory* 41 (4):591–617.

Greenhouse, Steven. 2012. "Here's a Memo from the Boss: Vote This Way." *New York Times*, October 26, 2012.

Gruss, Jean. 2014. "Call the Roll." *Job Creators Network*, June 17. https://www.jobcreatorsnetwork.com/call-the-roll/.

Hacker, Jacob S., and Paul Pierson. 2002. "Business Power and Social Policy: Employers and the Formation of the American Welfare State." *Politics and Society* 30 (2):277–325.

———. 2010. *Winner-Take-All Politics: How Washington Made the Rich Richer—and Turned Its Back on the Middle Class*. New York: Simon and Schuster.

———. 2016. *American Amnesia: How the War on Government Led Us to Forget What Made America Prosper*. New York: Simon and Schuster.

Hall, Richard L., and Alan V. Deardorff. 2006. "Lobbying as Legislative Subsidy." *American Political Science Review* 100 (1):69–84.

Hamburger, Tom. 2004. "Workplace Now Terrain of Politics." *Los Angeles Times*, October 29, 2004.

———. 2006. "Corporations Curtail Political Involvement This Year." *Los Angeles Times*, November 5, 2006.

Han, Hahrie. 2014. *How Organizations Develop Activists: Civic Associations and Leadership in the 21st Century*. New York: Oxford University Press.

———. 2016. "The Organizational Roots of Political Activism: Field Experiments on Creating a Relational Context." *American Political Science Review* 110 (2):296–307.

Hansen, John Mark. 1991. *Gaining Access: Congress and the Farm Lobby, 1919–1981*. Chicago: University of Chicago Press.

Hansen, Linda J. 2011. *Prosperity 101: Job Security through Business Prosperity*. New Berlin, WI: Prosperity 101.

Hansen, Wendy L., Michael S. Rocca, and Brittany Leigh Ortiz. 2015. "The Effects of *Citizens United* on Corporate Spending in the 2012 Presidential Election." *Journal of Politics* 77 (2):535–45.

Harvard Law Review. 2014. "*Citizens United* at Work: How the Landmark Decision Legalized Political Coercion in the Workplace." 128:669–90.

Hatch, Caslon. 2014. "Anchorage SB21 Debate Draws Standing-Room-Only Crowd." *KTUU*, July 23, 2014.

Heath, Robert L., William Douglas, and Michael Russell. 1995. "Constituency Building: Determining Employees' Willingness to Participate in Corporate Political Activities." *Journal of Public Relations Research* 7 (4):273–88.

Hersh, Eitan D. 2015. *Hacking the Electorate*. New York: Cambridge University Press.

Hertel-Fernandez, Alexander. 2014. "Who Passes Business's 'Model Bills'? Policy Capacity and Corporate Influence in U.S. State Politics." *Perspectives on Politics* 12 (3):582–602.

———. 2016. "Corporate Interests and Conservative Mobilization across the U.S. States." PhD dissertation, Harvard University.

———. 2017. "American Employers as Political Machines." *Journal of Politics* 79 (1): 105–17.

Hertel-Fernandez, Alexander, and Paul M. Secunda. 2016. "Citizens Coerced: A Legislative Fix for Workplace Political Intimidation Post–*Citizens United*." *UCLA Law Review* 64 (2).

Heyman, Daniel. 2015. "Ex-Executive Pleads Guilty in Toxic Spill in West Virginia." *New York Times*, August 19, 2015.

Hill, Jeffrey J. 2005. "Lives of the Workforce in the Industrial Revolution." In *The Industrial Revolution in America: Iron and Steel, Railroads, Steam Shipping*, ed. K. Hillstrom and L. C. Hillstrom. Santa Barbara, CA: ABC-CLIO.

Hindman, Nate C., and Christina Wilkie. 2012. "Wynn Employee Voter Guide Pressures Workers to Vote Right." *Huffington Post*, October 26, 2012.

Hoover, Kent. 2015. "How Employers Can Get Workers to Vote for Pro-Business Candidates." *Business Journals: Washington Bureau*, September 16, 2015.

"Independence Institute's Freedom Alliance Lunch with Linda J. Hansen." 2014. February 13, 2014, accessed March 19, 2016. *YouTube*. https://www.youtube.com/watch?v=-k_5elCprnw.

International Paper in North America. N.d. "Meaghan Killion Joyce: Political Affairs Manager. Issues: PAC, Grassroots." http://www.internationalpaper.com/company/regions/north-america/government-relations/contacts/meaghan-killion-joyce.

Jacobs, Lawrence R., and Suzanne Mettler. 2016. "Liking Health Reform but Turned Off by Toxic Politics." *Health Affairs* 35 (5):1-8.

Jamieson, Dave. 2012. "Cintas CEO Scott Farmer Assails Obamacare in Election Email to Employees." *Huffington Post*, October 26, 2012.

Job Creators Network. 2014a. "E2E in Action: College Hunks Hauling Junk." Accessed March 19, 2016. *YouTube.* https://www.youtube.com/watch?v=0Ypn6s7I7Mg.

———. 2014b. "E2E Training Introduction." *YouTube*, July 31. https://www.youtube.com/watch?time_continue=46&v=FwX8ZH9QajY.

———. 2014c. "JCN Hispanic Business Leaders Summit: Miami FL." Accessed March 19, 2016. *YouTube.* https://www.youtube.com/watch?v=6Vox_MQgJ14.

———. n.d. "Membership Tiers." https://www.jobcreatorsnetwork.com/membership/.

Johnson, Kirk. 2014. "Alaska Referendum Upholds Tax System for Oil Companies." *New York Times*, August 27, 2014.

Kang, Cecilia. 2009. "FCC Chief to Propose New Rules for How Firms Control Internet Traffic." *Washington Post*, September 19, 2009.

Keim, Gerald D. 1985. "Corporate Grassroots Programs in the 1980s." *California Management Review* 28 (1):110–23.

Kelly, Nora. 2016. "How Many Workers Will the Cadillac Tax Hit?" *The Atlantic*, January 28, 2016.

Keyes, Scott. 2012. "Billionaire CEO Threatens to Fire Employees If Obama Wins." *ThinkProgress*, October 9, 2012.

———. 2015. "CEO Who Said He'd Probably Have to Fire Employees If Obama Won Is Now Giving Them Raises." *ThinkProgress*, January 5, 2015.

Keyssar, Alexander. 2001. *The Right to Vote: The Contested History of Democracy in the United States.* New York: Basic Books.

Kim, Sung Eun, and Yotam Margalit. 2017. "Informed Preferences? The Impact of Unions on Workers' Policy Views." *American Journal of Political Science* 61(3): 728–43.

Kollman, Ken. 1998. *Outside Lobbying: Public Opinion and Interest Group Strategies.* Princeton, NJ: Princeton University Press.

Kramer, Tony. 2000. *Winning at the Grassroots: A Comprehensive Manual for Corporations and Associations.* Washington, DC: Public Affairs Council.

Lafer, Gordon. 2012. "Very Unwise for Employers to Tell Employees How to Vote." Washington, DC: Economic Policy Institute.

Lambert, Susan J., Peter J. Fugiel, and Julia R. Henly. 2014. "Precarious Work Schedules among Early-Career Employees in the US: A National Snapshot." Chicago: University of Chicago School of Social Service Administration.

Landale, James. 2016. "EU Referendum: Airbus Warns Out Vote May Hit Investment." *BBC News*, April 4, 2016.

Lane, Alexander. 2008. "Palin Sought More Taxes and More Development from Oil Companies." *Politifact*, September 1, 2008.

Leighley, Jan E., and Jonathan Nagler. 2007. "Unions, Voter Turnout, and Class Bias in the U.S. Electorate, 1964–2004." *Journal of Politics* 69 (2):430–41.

Lenhard, Robert. 2016. "Coercing Contributions at Work: The FEC's Latest Decision." *Inside Political Law* (Covington & Burling LLP), June 9, 2016.

Levis, Laura. 2012. "The Queen of Versailles." *Harvard Magazine*, November–December.

Lichtenstein, Nelson. 2002. *State of the Union: A Century of American Labor.* Princeton, NJ: Princeton University Press.

Lindblom, Charles. 1977. *Politics and Markets: The World's Political Economic Systems.* New York: Basic Books.

———. 1982. "The Market as Prison." *Journal of Politics* 44 (2):324–36.

Lipscomb, Jessica. 2012. "Papa John's CEO: Obamacare Likely to Raise Costs, Result in Employee's Hours Being Cut." *Naples Daily News*, November 7, 2012.

Liptak, Adam. 2010. "Justices, 5–4, Reject Corporate Spending Limit." *New York Times*, January 21, 2010.

Lipton, Eric. 2014. "Fight over Minimum Wage Illustrates Web of Industry Ties." *New York Times*, February 9, 2014.

Locke, Richard, Thomas Kochan, Monica Romis, and Fei Qin. 2007. "Beyond Corporate Codes of Conduct: Work Organization and Labour Standards at Nike's Suppliers." *International Labour Review* 146 (1–2):21–40.

Lockheed Martin. 2012. "LM Wisdom." Brochure. http://www.lockheedmartin.com/content/dam/lockheed/data/isgs/documents/ISGS-LMWISDOM-Brochure.pdf.

Logan, John. 2006. "The Union Avoidance Industry in the United States." *British Journal of Industrial Relations* 44 (4):651–75.

Lohr, Steve. 2014. "Unblinking Eyes Track Employees." *New York Times*, June 21, 2014.

Long, Michelle, Matthew Rae, Gary Claxton, and Anthony Damico. 2016. "Trends in Employer-Sponsored Insurance Offer and Coverage Rates, 1999–2014." Washington, DC: Kaiser Family Foundation.

Lukes, Steven. 2005. *Power: A Radical View*. 2nd edition. London: Palgrave Macmillan.

Lynn, Barry C., and Phillip Longman. 2010. "Who Broke America's Jobs Machine?" *Washington Monthly*, March–April 2010.

MacGillis, Alec. 2012. "Coal Miner's Donor." *New Republic*, October 4, 2012.

Mares, Isabela, and Lauren Young. 2016. "Buying, Expropriating, and Stealing Votes." *Annual Review of Political Science* 19:267–88.

Martin, Cathie Jo. 1995. "Nature or Nurture? Sources of Firm Preference for National Health Reform." *American Political Science Review* 89 (4):898–913.

Martin, Cathie Jo, and Duane Swank. 2012. *The Political Construction of Business Interests: Coordination, Growth, and Equality*. New York: Cambridge University Press.

Mayer, Jane. 2016. *Dark Money: The Hidden History of the Billionaires behind the Rise of the Radical Right*. New York: Doubleday Press.

McCarty, Nolan, Keith T. Poole, and Howard Rosenthal. 2006. *Polarized America: The Dance of Ideology and Unequal Riches*. Cambridge, MA: MIT Press.

McDonnell, Mary-Hunter, Brayden G. King, and Sarah A. Soule. 2015. "A Dynamic Process Model of Private Politics: Activist Targeting and Corporate Receptivity to Social Challenges." *American Sociological Review* 80 (3):654–78.

McElwee, Sean. 2015. "Why Voting Matters: Large Disparities in Turnout Benefit the Donor Class." Washington, DC: Demos.

McGregor, Jena. 2016. "What Your Boss Can and Can't Do When It Comes to Politics at Work." *Washington Post*, October 21, 2016.

Meyerson, Harold. 2010. "Under Obama, Labor Should Have Made More Progress." *Washington Post*, February 10, 2010.

Mills, C. Wright. (1956) 2000. *The Power Elite*. New York: Oxford University Press.

Mishel, Lawrence, Josh Bivens, Elise Gould, and Heidi Shierholz. 2012. *The State of Working America*. Washington, DC: Economic Policy Institute, Cornell University Press.

Mizruchi, Mark S. 1992. *The Structure of Corporate Political Action*. Cambridge, MA: Harvard University Press.

Mondak, Jeffery J., and Diana C. Mutz. 2001. "Involuntary Association: How the Workplace Contributes to American Civic Life." Paper presented at the Midwest Political Science Association annual meetings, Chicago.

Montgomery, Jacob M., and Brendan Nyhan. 2017. "The Effects of Congressional Staff Networks in the U.S. House of Representatives." *Journal of Politics* 79(3): 745–61.

Montgomery, Jacob M., Brendan Nyhan, and Michelle Torres. 2016. "How Conditioning on Post-Treatment Variables Can Ruin Your Experiment and What to Do about It." Unpublished working paper. http://www.dartmouth.edu/~nyhan/post-treatment-bias.pdf

Mufson, Steven. 2012. "After Obama Reelection, Murray Energy CEO Reads Prayer, Announces Layoffs." *Washington Post*, November 9, 2012.

Mutz, Diana C., and Jeffery J. Mondak. 2006. "The Workplace as a Context for Cross-Cutting Political Discourse." *Journal of Politics* 68 (1):140–55.

National Association of Manufacturers. 2014. "Public Policy." July 25, 2014. Accessed March 19, 2016. http://nahad.org/aws/NAHAD/pt/sd/news_article/92118/blank/blank/true.

———. N.d. "Conducting Get Out the Vote Activities." http://www.themanufacturinginstitute. org/~/media/2F518AFDCC84483F9DE10C9B1BF9BCFD/Conducting_GOTV_ Activities.pdf.

NELP. 2015. "New Poll Shows Overwhelming Support for Major Minimum Wage Increase: Advocates Back Federal Legislation for $12.50 Wage." Washington, DC: National Employment Law Project.

Nolan, Hamilton. 2012. "The CEO Who Built Himself America's Largest House Just Threatened to Fire his Employees if Obama's Elected." *Gawker*, October 9, 2012. Accessed September 29, 2015. http://gawker.com/5950189/the-ceo-who-built-himself-americas-largest-house-just-threatened-to-fire-his-employees-if-obamas-elected.

———. 2016. "Documents: How a Major Company Bombards Employees with Right-Wing Propaganda." *Gawker*, October 9, 2016. Accessed June 13, 2013. http://gawker.com/ documents-how-a-major-company-bombards-employees-with-1781111355.

Ortiz, Alfredo. 2015. "The War on Small Business: Fighting Back through Education." Job Creators Network. https://s3.amazonaws.com/storage.citizensforethics.org/wp-content/uploads/ 2016/12/08182735/2015CFADayForum_Ortiz.pdf

———. 2016. "Minimum Wage, Minimum Opportunity." Job Creators Network. https://www .jobcreatorsnetwork.com/opeds/minimum-wage-minimum-opportunity/.

Panagopoulos, Costas, Donald P. Green, Jonathan Krasno, Michael Schwam-Baird, Eric Moore, and Kyle Endres. 2016. "Risky Business: Does Corporate Political Giving Affect Consumer Behavior?" Unpublished manuscript. http://rubenson.org/wp-content/uploads/2016/10/ Panagopoulos-etal.pdf

Phillips-Fein, Kim. 2009. *Invisible Hands: The Making of the Conservative Movement from the New Deal to Reagan*. New York: Norton.

Pintor, Rafael López, Maria Gratschew, and Kate Sullivan. 2002. "Voter Turnout Rates from a Comparative Perspective." In *Voter Turnout since 1945: A Global Report*, ed. R. L. Pintor and M. Gratschew. Stockholm: International Institute for Democracy and Electoral Assistance.

Pokempner, Joseph K. 1965. "Employer Free Speech under the National Labor Relations Act." *Maryland Law Review* 25 (2):111–47.

Polsby, Nelson W. 1962. "Community Power: Some Reflections on the Recent Literature." *American Sociological Review* 27 (6):838–41.

PPP. 2014. "Begich Leads Challengers in Re-Election Bid." Raleigh, NC: Public Policy Polling.

Prosperity Alaska. N.d. "About Us." http://prosperityalaska.org.

The Public. 1908. "Corrupt Coercion of the Labor Vote by Republican Managers." 2 (11).

Public Welfare Foundation. 2010. "Paid Sick Days: Attitudes and Experiences Survey." Retrieved from the Roper Center for Public Opinion Research, iPoll. March 18–May 6, 2009.

Ravel, Ann M., and Ellen L. Weintraub. 2015. "Statement of Reasons, MUR 6651." Washington, DC: Federal Election Commission.

Reclaim Democracy. N.d. "The Powell Memo (Also Known as the Powell Manifesto)." http:// reclaimdemocracy.org/powell_memo_lewis.

Reich, Brian. 2004. "The Prosperity Project: Corporate Voter Outreach on the Sly." *Personal Democracy Media*, December 10, 2004. https://personaldemocracy.com/content/ prosperity-project-corporate-voter-outreach-sly.

Rose, Henry. 1962. "A Critical Look at the Hatch Act." *Harvard Law Review* 75 (3):510–26.

Rosen, Jeffrey. 2014. "Ruth Bader Ginsburg Is an American Hero." *New Republic*, September 28, 2014.

Rosen, Yereth. 2007. "UPDATE 2: Legislators Approve Higher Alaska Oil Tax." Reuters, November 16, 2007.

Salisbury, Robert H., and Kenneth A. Shepsle. 1981. "U.S. Congressman as Enterprise." *Legislative Studies Quarterly* 6 (4):559–76.

Schifeling, Todd. 2013. "Defense against Recession: U.S. Business Mobilization, 1950–1970." *American Journal of Sociology* 119 (1):1–34.

Schlozman, Kay Lehman, Sidney Verba, and Henry E. Brady. 2012. *The Unheavenly Chorus: Unequal Political Voice and the Broken Promise of American Democracy*. Princeton, NJ: Princeton University Press.

Schrage, Michael. 2016. "Sentiment Analysis Can Do More Than Prevent Fraud and Turnover." *Harvard Business Review*, January 5, 2016.

Schulman, Daniel. 2014. *Sons of Wichita: How the Koch Brothers Became America's Most Powerful and Private Dynasty*. New York: Grand Central.

Secunda, Paul M. 2008. "Toward the Viability of State-Based Legislation to Address Workplace Captive Audience Meetings in the United States." *Comparative Labor Law and Policy Journal* 29 (2):209–46.

———. 2010. "Addressing Political Captive Audience Workplace Meetings in the Post–*Citizens United* Environment." *Yale Law Journal Online* 120:17–26.

Senate Committee on Governmental Affairs. 1993. "Hatch Act Reform Amendments of 1993: Hearings before the Committee on Governmental Affairs, United States Senate, 103rd Congress." Washington, DC: U.S. Government Printing Office.

Shaiken, Harley. 2007. "Unions, the Economy, and Employee Free Choice." Washington, DC: Economic Policy Institute, Agenda for Shared Prosperity.

Sharn, Lori. 2014. "For Associations, Voter Registration Drives Go High-Tech." *CEO Update*, October 17, 2014.

SHRM. 2008. "What Does Your Organization Do to Encourage Employees to Vote in Elections?" Alexandria, VA: Society for Human Resource Management.

Silk, Leonard, and David Vogel. 1976. *Ethics and Profits: The Crisis of Confidence in American Business*. New York: Simon and Schuster.

Skinner, Richard M. 2006. *More Than Money: Interest Group Action in Congressional Elections*. New York: Rowman & Littlefield.

Skocpol, Theda, and Alexander Hertel-Fernandez. 2016a. "The Koch Effect: The Impact of a Cadre-Led Network on American Politics." Paper presented at the annual Southwest Political Science Association meetings, San Juan, Puerto Rico, January 8.

———. 2016b. "The Koch Network and Republican Party Extremism." *Perspectives on Politics* 14 (3):681–99.

Snyder, Jim, and Sillia Brush. 2009. "Some Firms Push Employees to Lobby." *The Hill*, October 28, 2009.

Spillman, Lyn. 2012. *Solidarity in Strategy: Making Business Meaningful in American Trade Associations*. Chicago: University of Chicago Press.

Stan, Adele M. 2011a. "How Workers Learned to Fear Unions in Wisconsin." *AlterNet/The Investigative Fund at The Nation*, June 2, 2011.

———. 2011b. "*Wall Street Journal* Honcho Shills for Secret Worker 'Education' Program Linked to Koch Group." *AlterNet/The Investigative Fund at The Nation*, June 3, 2011.

———. 2012. "Major Retailer Urges Workers to Take 'Civics Course' with Anti-Obama Content." *Alternet*, October 31, 2012.

Starbucks. 2015. "What 'Race Together' Means for Starbucks Partners and Customers." Accessed March 19, 2016. https://news.starbucks.com/news/what-race-together-means-for-starbucks-partners-and-customers

———. 2016. "Re: Message from Howard: Encouraging Civic Engagement." March 7, 2016. Accessed March 19, 2016. http://www.politico.com/f/?id=00000153-5def-d206-af7b-dfffa99c0000.

Strasser, Annie-Rose. 2012. "Applebee's CEO Threatens to Fire Employees and Freeze Hiring Because of Obamacare." *ThinkProgress*, November 9, 2012.

Swenson, Peter. 2002. *Capitalists against Markets: The Making of Labor Markets and Welfare States in the United States and Sweden*. New York: Oxford University Press.

Teles, Steven. 2014. "Restrain Regressive Rent-Seeking." Washington, DC: Cato Institute.

——. 2015. "The Scourge of Upward Redistribution." *National Affairs*, Fall 2015.

Tierney, John. 2004. "Political Points." *New York Times*, July 18, 2004.

Time. 1962. "Business in Politics." August 10, 1962.

Totenberg, Nina. 2016. "Is It Fair to Have to Pay Fees to a Union You Don't Agree With?" *NPR Morning Edition*, January 11, 2016.

Troll, Kate. 2014. "Palin Gets This One Right: Repeal SB 21." *Alaska Dispatch News*, July 10, 2014.

Truth Tour. 2012. "Interview with Herman Cain of Job Creators Solutions." November 5, 2012. Accessed March 19, 2016. *YouTube*. https://www.youtube.com/watch?v=TTJ-wHJSEUQ.

Ungar, Rick. 2012. "Papa John's, Applebee's and Others Pay Huge Price for Anti-Obamacare Politicking." *Forbes*, December 4, 2012.

U.S Election Atlas. "Election Data Spreadsheets." http://uselectionatlas.org/BOTTOM/store_data.php.

U.S. Energy Information Administration. 2015. "Table 10: Major U.S. Coal Producers, 2015." https://www.eia.gov/coal/annual/pdf/table10.pdf.

Verba, Sidney, Kay Lehman Schlozman, and Henry E. Brady. 1995. *Voice and Equality: Civic Voluntarism in American Politics*. Cambridge, MA: Harvard University Press.

Vogel, David. 1989. *Fluctuating Fortunes: The Political Power of Business in America*. New York: Basic Books.

Volokh, Eugene. 2011–12. "Private Employees' Speech and Political Activity: Statutory Protection against Employer Retaliation." *Texas Review of Law and Politics* 16:295–336.

——. 2014. "Does California Law Protect Employee Speech Hostile to Homosexuality, as well as Employee Speech That 'Defend[s]' Homosexuality'?" *Washington Post*, May 5, 2014.

Walker, Edward. 2014. *Grassroots for Hire: Public Affairs Consultants in American Democracy*. New York: Cambridge University Press.

Walther, Steven T., Ann M. Ravel, and Ellen L. Weintraub. 2016. "Statement of Reasons, MUR 6661." Washington, DC: Federal Election Commission.

Ward, Ken. 2014a. "ER Symptoms 'Consistent' with MCHM Exposure." *Charleston (WV) Gazette-Mail*, April 23, 2014.

——. 2014b. "Former Foreman Sues Murray Energy over Firing." *Charleston (WV) Gazette-Mail*, September 9, 2014.

Waterhouse, Benjamin C. 2013. *Lobbying America: The Politics of Business from Nixon to NAFTA*. Princeton, NJ: Princeton University Press.

Weber, Lauren. 2014. "Better to Be Artistic or Responsible? Decoding Workplace Personality Tests." *Wall Street Journal*, September 29, 2014.

Wehrman, Jessica. 2015. "Sick-Leave Fight in Ohio Shows What President Obama Faces." *Columbus (OH) Dispatch*, January 24, 2015.

Weidenbaum, Murray L. 1980. "Public Policy: No Longer a Spectator Sport for Business." *Journal of Business Strategy* 1 (1):46–53.

Weil, David. 2014. *The Fissured Workplace*. Cambridge, MA: Harvard University Press.

Weisman, Jonathan. 2015. "Tea Party Divided by Export-Import Bank." *New York Times*, March 9, 2015.

Wilson, Michael J. 2010. "Businesses Can Now Legally Pressure Workers on Political Issues?" *Huffington Post*, May 1, 2010.

Windsor, Lauren. 2014. "Exclusive: Inside the Koch Brothers' Secret Billionaire Summit." *The Nation*, June 17, 2014.

Winters, Jeffrey, and Benjamin Page. 2009. "Oligarchy in the United States?" *Perspectives on Politics* 7 (4):731–51.

Woodman, Spencer. 2014. "Office Politics: Inside the PAC Teaching Corporate America How to Make Its Employees Vote for the Right Candidates and Causes." *Slate*, October 15, 2014.

World Wealth and Income Database. "Data." http://wid.world/data/

Yackee, Jason Webb, and Susan Webb Yackee. 2006. "A Bias towards Business? Assessing Interest Group Influence on the U.S. Bureaucracy." *Journal of Politics* 68 (1):128–39.

Zaller, John. 1992. *The Nature and Origins of Mass Opinion.* New York: Cambridge University Press.

Zingales, Luigi. 2012. *A Capitalism for the People: Recapturing the Lost Genius of American Prosperity.* New York: Basic Books.

Zornick, George. 2012. "Herman Cain's Nationwide Worker Intimidation Tour." *The Nation,* October 19, 2012.

INDEX